CONTENTS

WHERE TO RETIRE OVERSEAS

The World's 23 Best Places To Live Rich On Any Budget

BY KATHLEEN PEDDICORD AND LAURA SHERIDAN

Published by Lahardan Books

Published by Lahardan Books

ISBN 978-1-958583-14-2

Book and Cover Design by Cristian Landero

ALSO BY THE AUTHOR

Kathleen Peddicord

Buying Real Estate Overseas For Cashflow (And A Better Life)

- How your overseas property can pay for itself—and your visits
- How to build monthly income to fund a dream retirement
- Where to take advantage of big currency discounts

At Home In Ireland

At Home At Los Islotes

Retire Big On Little

How To Retire Overseas

Your New Life Overseas: Portugal (The Algarve)

Your New Life Overseas: Belize

Interested in more of Kathleen's insights and adventures? Scan the QR code to explore her other books and purchase your next read.

ABOUT THE AUTHOR

Kathleen Peddicord has reported on opportunities for Americans to live, retire, and do business overseas for more than 40 years. She has lived in four countries, traveled to more than 80, invested in real estate in 24, established businesses in seven, renovated and built properties in six, and educated her children in five.

Kathleen has moved children, staff, enterprises, household goods, and pets from the east coast of the United States to Waterford, Ireland, then to Paris, France, and finally to Panama City, Panama, where she has based her Live And Invest Overseas business. Peddicord and her husband, Lief Simon, now divide their time between Panama and Paris.

Peddicord was a partner with the Agora Publishing group for 23 years. She opened, staffed, and operated their publishing and real estate offices in Waterford, Ireland; Panama City, Panama; Granada, Nicaragua; Roatan, Honduras; San Miguel de Allende, Mexico; Quito, Ecuador; and Paris, France.

Peddicord launched Live And Invest Overseas in 2008 and has built it into a successful multimillion-dollar business. Today, she shares her firsthand experience of expat life with more than 500,000 readers of her publications, including *Overseas Opportunity Letter* and *Overseas Living Letter.*

Kathleen has been featured often in The New York Times, MSNBC, AARP, CNN, Bloomberg, CNBC, Newsweek, Realtor.com, and more and writes regularly about expat matters, international real estate, and offshore diversification for Forbes and U.S. News & World Report.

Kathleen has written several books including the memoirs "At Home In Ireland" and "At Home At Los Islotes" and her latest title "At Home Abroad," all published by Lahardan Books. Her best-selling "How To Retire Overseas: Everything You Need To Know To Live Well (For Less) Abroad" was published by Penguin Random House in 2018 and her "Buying Real Estate Overseas For Cash Flow (And A Better Life)" was published by Wiley in August 2020.

ACKNOWLEDGEMENTS

If you've been following Live And Invest Overseas for a while, you know that we've long championed the idea that the best opportunities to live better for less are found beyond the borders of the U.S. and Canada.

In fact, everything we do is founded on that principle. Providing information for people considering moving overseas is our identity, and we've been doing this for a long time.

Now this idea has gone mainstream, and it's gratifying to see so many people embracing it.

Our editorial team is made up of real-life expats, so we have first-hand experience with this whole moving abroad thing. We've all been lucky enough to explore the world and immerse ourselves in different cultures...

We've packed up our homes, said goodbye to neighbors and friends, and hopped on planes...

We've experienced culture shock and made fools of ourselves while navigating new languages...

We've applied for residency, filed taxes, and had health care needs taken care of abroad.

The point is that we've been where you are right now as you consider the realities of launching a new life in a new country.

We've asked ourselves the same questions you're asking yourself and sought answers the same way: by consulting trusted sources and then going out and doing the thing in question... often figuring it out as we go but learning a lot along the way.

We determined many factors through decades of advising folks about how to move abroad and making many international relocations ourselves.

We try to strike a balance between subjectivity and objectivity, but ultimately, we believe that word-of-mouth recommendations, personal insights, and hard-won experience are the most valuable things we can offer you.

This book presents our selection of the world's best places to retire overseas. These are beautiful, welcoming, and safe havens that offer compelling lifestyle opportunities.

Our editorial team is constantly scouting new locations throughout the year... assessing each place's livability, speaking with locals and expats, analyzing property markets, experiencing local culture, and so on, to cultivate a well-rounded perspective.

We also have a global network of editors and contributors, including expats, experts, lawyers, real estate agents, and tax advisors, who are on the ground in the places we recommend and can give first-hand perspectives.

I'd like to thank my many roving editors and writers in all the countries we feature in this book for their contributions. They are the eyes, ears, and judgement that allow us to determine which destinations deserve to be included on the list of the top retirement havens in the world.

Special thanks goes to Mónica Linares, Sophia Titley, Victoria Harmer, Kat Kalashian, Lee Harrison, Sharon Lord, Jeff and Joch Woodruff, Lucy Culpepper, Lynn Mulvihill, Bart Walters, Con Murphy, Siri Lise Doub, and Sasha Savinov.

INTRODUCTION

The "Where" Is Everything

"Where do you live?"

For me, the answer to that benign getting-acquainted question is not straightforward.

I spend my time between the Old World and the New, back and forth between Paris and Panama, slipping in and out of life in these very different places.

In Panama City, I live in a high-rise tower with a view of the Pacific Ocean. From our balcony I watch the never-ending line of ships awaiting their turn for passage through the Panama Canal.

My Paris digs are 320 years old, my view a small cobblestoned courtyard. It affords me a front-row seat to day-to-day life in this neighborhood that appears on the earliest maps of Paris.

"*Bonjour*! *Comment ca va*?" my neighbors call to each other cheerfully in passing. The French are nothing if not polite.

In Panama, I drive a Jeep. That means investments in insurance, maintenance, parking spaces, and tanks of gas.

In Paris, I rely on my own two feet to get me most everywhere I go day-to-day. When they give out, I hop on the Metro. A bundle of 10 tickets to load onto your Navigo Easy Pass costs 17.35 euros.

In Panama I shop for groceries at Riba Smith, filling my cart with many things I'd buy if I were doing my weekly shop in the States. Sometimes the import surcharge means I pay more than I would Stateside for the same item. I'm OK with that... and, when I'm not, I abstain.

In Paris, grocery shopping isn't a chore but an anticipated part of my daily routine. Each afternoon I make time for a leisurely walk down rue de Verneuil then rue de l'Université, past the Solferino Metro stop to the Square Samuel-Rousseau and the Basilica of Sainte-Clotilde. My destination is the Franprix opposite the church, but I delay going in. The courtyard in front is a gathering spot for local children. They run and jump and kick a soccer ball back and forth. Their joy holds me.

Finally inside Franprix, I choose fresh produce, meats cut by the butcher, cheese, and wine, because those are the things on offer. You'll find few pre-prepared foods on grocers' shelves in Paris. This forces me to continue to work to improve my kitchen skills.

My Paris wardrobe includes clothes for four seasons. Storing it all within the 112 square meters of our apartment is a challenge.

In Panama the most important wardrobe question is whether or not to grab an umbrella on the way out the door. April through November, the answer is always yes.

In Panama we run our air conditioning whenever we're at home. That makes for a sometimes significant monthly electric bill. Neither my husband Lief nor I like the big expense, but we like the high humidity less.

It might be possible to fit out our centuries-old Paris apartment with air conditioning, but we've avoided that engineering challenge. Instead, come July and August, we close the shutters against the midday sun.

All things considered, I prefer day-to-day life in Paris over that in Panama City, but I didn't become a resident of Panama for the lifestyle. I chose it because it's the best place in the world to base the kind of business I run.

Lief and I arrived in Panama as investors then a funny thing happened. We got to know a hidden corner of this country that's a world apart from boomtown Panama City.

At Los Islotes, on Panama's unsung Veraguas coast, we embrace yet a third lifestyle, one that is a sharp contrast to both our life in Paris and our day-to-day in Panama's capital and that we've grown to treasure.

At Los Islotes, we luxuriate in Nature and extraordinary privacy.

Dramatic Pacific Ocean views tempt from every window. Approaching dawn is heralded by monkey calls and birdsong. I'm up before the sun and happy to be. I can't wait to get outside to see what the new day holds in store.

Our gardens deliver tomatoes, cucumbers, and peppers, watermelons, avocados, and mangoes in abundance. We fish from rocky outcroppings and catch crabs in the estuary. With not much more effort, we could be self-sufficient.

We ride horseback on the beach. We hike and swim, kayak and paddle. We go days without leaving the property.

At Los Islotes we exist in a bubble, isolated from the worries and troubles of our age. We appreciate this more every day.

Lief and I didn't set out to live in three places at once, and this lifestyle is not without challenges. Surely, this would not be for everyone, but we wouldn't trade it. Which piece would we eliminate—the romance of Paris… the business upside of Panama City… the serenity of Veraguas?

Nah.

The good news is that we don't have to choose. In today's world, ever-improving tech makes it easier all the time to stay in touch with both our Live And Invest Overseas team and family and friends all across the globe even as we move among our three home bases.

Before Panama and before Paris, Lief and I lived in Ireland.

We bought a 200-year-old stone house then renovated those 5,000 classic Irish Georgian square feet with care. Our Waterford country home was charming but never warm. Lief put in a standing order with the local fuel supplier who arrived the first of the month every month to refill our oil tank. Even in "summertime," our furnace worked overtime.

The view from every window of our Lahardan House was of rolling farmland, a patchwork quilt in every shade of green. It comes to mind often, and I miss it more with every passing year.

In Ireland I drove a beat-up old sedan. Well, it wasn't beat-up when we bought it, but driving on the left along narrow and winding Irish roads proved a challenge I never was able to rise to. I side-swiped so many stone walls and hedgerows that Lief gave up asking about the source of new dents and scrapes when I pulled into our driveway at the end of each day.

The Irish own summer clothes and sometimes they wear them. I was never tempted. In Ireland I wore a coat and scarf year-round.

My point is that your new life overseas—at whatever stage of your life you choose to launch it—will be different in every way depending on *where* you choose to launch it.

Everything follows from the where. The weather and the view from your bedroom window, the cost of groceries and your annual tax bill, the language your neighbors speak and the ways they fill their Friday nights and Sunday afternoons... all these things and all other things will depend on where you're living.

This world of ours includes about 200 countries. Not all of them are places you'd want to call home, and some stand out as alluring beyond all the rest.

Don't worry. You don't have to consider all aspects of life everywhere. We've done that for you.

In the pages to follow, we direct your attention to the world's 23 best places to live or retire overseas.

How do you choose among this curated list?

Start by considering the world map.

That is, turn the page and keep reading. This is where the fun starts.

Kathleen Peddicord
Los Islotes, Panama, May 2026

The Best Places To Live Rich In
THE AMERICAS

❶ Mexico

- Easy transition to expat life
- Spanish-colonial history
- Undervalued property

❷ Panama

- Incredible nature
- First-world infrastructure
- Large expat communities

❸ Belize

- English-speaking
- Relaxed, Caribbean living
- Stunning nature

❹ Argentina

- Buzzing capital
- Mountains and vineyards
- Friendly locals

❺ Colombia

- Culturally vibrant
- Great health care
- High-quality infrastructure

❻ Uruguay

- European-style living
- Strongest democrazy
- Excellent health care

❼ The Dominican Republic

- Low-cost Caribbean living
- Multicultural community
- Ecotourism and adventure

❽ The Cayman Islands

- Excellent snorkeling and diving
- Relaxed lifestyle
- Tax-free living

FIND IT ON THE MAP:

To help you locate each country, the numbers listed alongside the country name match the numbered locations on the map on the adjacent page.

THE BEST PLACES TO LIVE RICH IN THE AMERICAS

The Best Places To Live Rich In EUROPE

1 France

- Excellent infrastructure
- Picturesque villages
- Great food and wine

2 Malta and Gozo

- Ancient, fascinating history
- Beautiful, rugged coastline
- English-speaking

3 Greece

- Great climate
- Healthy, delicious food
- Dramatic Mediterranean scenery

4 Portugal

- Excellent beaches
- Large expat communities
- Easy residency

5 Ireland

- English-speaking with friendly locals
- Breathtaking scenery
- Rich heritage

6 Spain

- Established expat havens
- Fantastic beaches
- Safe and affordable

7 Italy

- Centuries-old architecture
- Dynamic restaurants and cafés
- Culturally vibrant

8 Montenegro

- Dramatic, fjord-like scenery
- Inexpensive real estate
- Up-and-coming. Soon to join the EU

9 Croatia

- Steeped in history
- A vision for its future
- Striking coastline and islands

10 Northern Cyprus

- Mediterranean climate
- Historical richness
- Affordable cost of living

11 Albania

- Welcomes Americans
- Pioneer territory
- Impressive beaches and mountains

FIND IT ON THE MAP:

To help you locate each country, the numbers listed alongside the country name match the numbered locations on the map on the adjacent page.

THE BEST PLACES TO LIVE RICH IN EUROPE

The Best Places To Live Rich In ASIA

1 Thailand

- Beautiful beaches
- Great for golfers
- Lively night markets for shopping and food

2 The Philippines

- English-speaking
- Abundant natural beauty
- Friendly locals

3 Malaysia

- A foodie-haven
- Top-notch health care
- Tropical climate

4 Vietnam

- Low cost, high standard of living
- Healthy cuisine
- Spectacular scenery

FIND IT ON THE MAP:

To help you locate each country, the numbers listed alongside the country name match the numbered locations on the map on the adjacent page.

THE BEST PLACES TO LIVE RICH IN ASIA

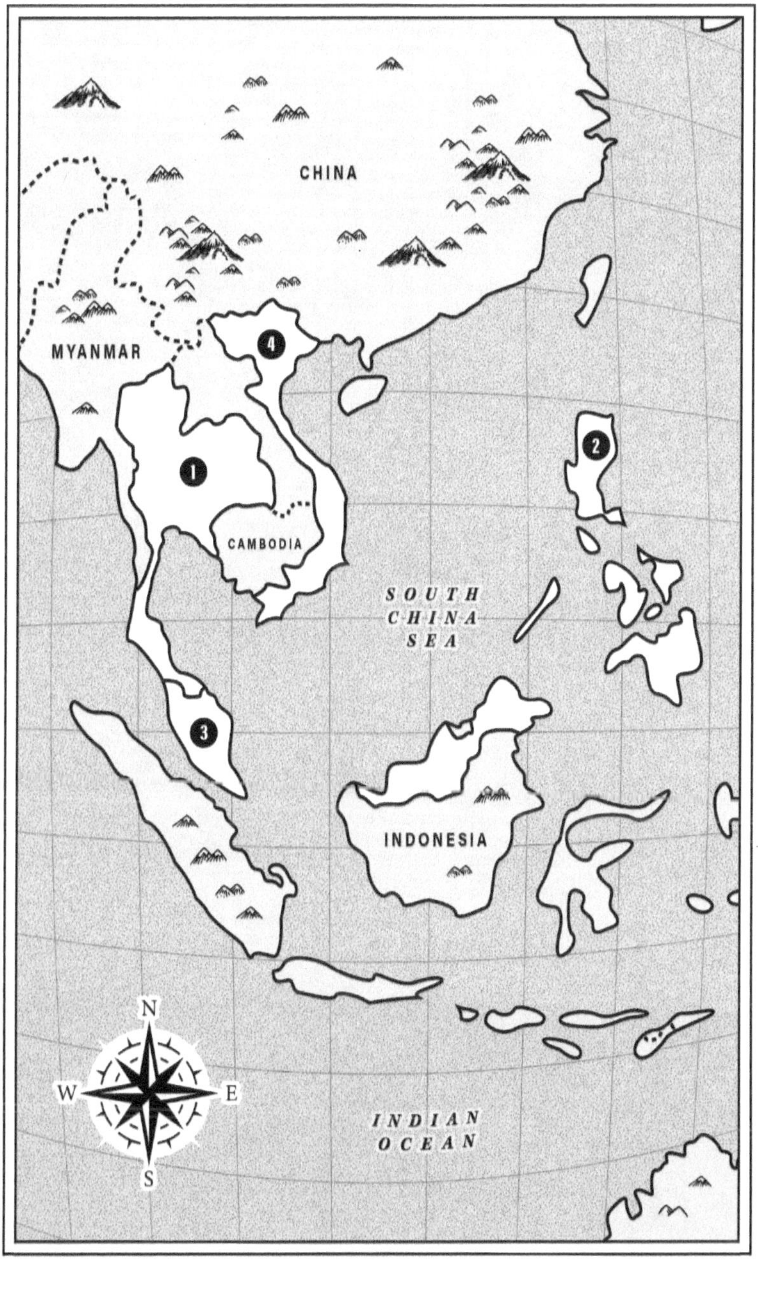

I

START WITH THE WORLD MAP

Our world is alive with opportunity.

I make the getting-started point as I understand that, sometimes, in our current world, we can doubt it.

Specifically, in the context of these pages, our world is alive with opportunity for a rich, rewarding, adventure-filled, and sometimes very affordable life in a place that is welcoming, beautiful, friendly, and safe.

The challenge is not improving your circumstances by moving to a new country. That's the given.

The challenge is choosing the country, because every aspect of your new life will follow from that choice.

Start by taking a look at the world map, focusing on the regions—Europe, Asia, and the Americas.

In the pages to follow, you'll read a lot about your top options in Latin America. That's because it's nearby to North America, where most readers of this book are likely to currently reside, and because it can be cheap and sunny, two things most would-be expats and retirees abroad prioritize.

But there's a world beyond these Americas that can also offer good weather and a low cost of living, as well as, in some cases, some things you won't find here. You'll read more about these places in this book, too.

Ultimately, you're not retiring to a region or even a country. Your new life will be based in a certain neighborhood of a particular city or town. We'll get to that thin-slicing in a moment. First, let's get our broad bearings. You might want to take whole sections of the world map off your list after just brief consideration. And when it comes to making what will be one of the biggest decisions of your life, the process of elimination can be your friend.

Asia

Asia boasts a number of the most cost-friendly places anywhere to call home right now. Pockets of Thailand, Vietnam, Malaysia, and the Philippines can be absurdly cheap.

Living on this side of the planet, you'd also have access to some of the world's most beautiful beaches. Your life would be full of the exotic, the unexpected, and the adventuresome.

That is to say, the culture shock would be significant. For some, this reality is thrilling and invigorating. For others, it's intimidating, even terrifying.

Used to be that many foreign retirees in Asia didn't legalize their status. Historically—in some cases because it seemed easier and in others because formal residency programs weren't an option—expats in this part of the world lived lives built around the border run. They'd leave the country where they were living but not legally resident briefly then return with a renewed tourist visa.

I've never recommended the approach. It's fundamentally insecure and risky. It can also be costly paying for all the associated traveling back and forth across a border—sometimes even more costly than the process of establishing legal residency. Definitely, border running comes with a greater hassle factor than I'm up for.

Today the strategy is also not really possible. More and more countries, including across Asia, are cracking down on the practice. Meantime, more countries in Asia now offer formal legal residency options.

The biggest practical downside to choosing Asia is geography. Thailand, Malaysia, Vietnam, etc., are literally on the other side of the world. You're not hopping back and forth between your new home in Asia and your old one in North America for your grandkids' birthdays.

It can make sense to approach Asia not as a full-time choice but as part of a retire-overseas plan that allows you to enjoy the benefits of Asia (super cheap and super exotic) part-time.

How about a couple of months in Da Lat, Vietnam, or Chiang Mai, Thailand, where your retirement budget would stretch far indeed, followed by a few months in France, say, or Italy?

Europe

Which brings us to Europe. Many would-be expats and retirees abroad dismiss Europe as too expensive. This is not necessarily the case.

Sure, a retiree on a modest budget probably can't afford Paris or Florence, but have you considered southwestern France, where life is quintessentially French but, as well, surprisingly affordable, or Pisa, about an hour from Michelangelo's hometown and dramatically less costly?

One of the big advantages of Europe, compared with other regional new-life-overseas options, is the opportunity it affords for what might be referred to as "high culture." Every country in the world has culture, no question, but not everywhere has world-class museums, opera, and live theater. If you're interested in a life that includes cultural offerings of that variety, you should be looking to the Continent.

Which is not to say it's impossible to enjoy an old-world Continental lifestyle anywhere else.

The Americas

Some cities in South America offer a fair imitation—Buenos Aires, and Medellín, Colombia, to name two. Both are cities of open-air cafés, museums, theaters, art galleries, and antique shops.

And both, you'll note, are in South America, not Central America. The differences between these two regions, even between Panama and Colombia, next-door neighbors, can be striking.

I'm speaking generally and could name exceptions to every point, but, again, generally speaking, South America offers what I'd call more polished options and can be a good place to look if what you want is culture on the cheap.

Central America, by contrast, is, most everywhere, rough around the edges. These are small, developing countries with non-existent budgets for things like art museums. The standout exception is Panama, which increasingly competes at a more international level in all regards, including when it comes to things like cultural entertainment.

Romantics like me in Central America focus on the potential for what could be rather than the reality of what sometimes is.

Others find Central America frustrating, disappointing, even appalling. Garbage and poverty can be facts of everyday life.

On the other hand, this sun-blessed region can be but a quick plane hop away and an affordable and user-friendly place to establish foreign residency.

Pluses and minuses, give and take.

Here's how I'd shorthand the pros and cons of your big-picture options for where to think about reinventing your life and chasing adventure overseas...

The Americas

PROS	CONS
▪ Accessible ▪ Affordable ▪ Great weather ▪ Lack of regulation	▪ Unreliable infrastructure ▪ Manana mentality ▪ Lack of regulation

Europe

PROS	CONS
▪ Developed infrastructure ▪ Culture ▪ World's best health care ▪ Overall quality of life	▪ Language ▪ Cost of living ▪ Weather and length of day ▪ Bureaucracy

Asia

PROS	CONS
▪ Cost of living ▪ Beautiful beaches ▪ Exotic lifestyle	▪ Distance from North America ▪ Language ▪ Unfamiliar

One important question to ask yourself as you consider the world biggest picture is how different do you want your new life to be from your current life. How outside your comfort zone are you up for?

A second critical starting-point question is to do with the size of your budget. Is it big enough to support Europe? I mentioned that life in the Old World can be more affordable than you might imagine, but if your budget is super small and fixed, you might want to cross Europe off your list.

Third, ask yourself what you want your new life to look like. Imagine your ideal lifestyle. Again, to start, think big picture. Coastal or highland? Caribbean Sea or Pacific Ocean? Big city or small town? Focus on the view. What would you most like yours to be every morning when you wake up?

Launching a new life overseas requires time and effort. The point is a better life maybe on a reduced budget. You don't want to undertake this investment only to find yourself living a life you like less than the one you had before. Guarantee that won't happen by staying true to your personal priorities. What do you definitely want your new life to include and what do you by all means want to leave behind? Be clear in your own mind of the answers to those questions then don't compromise as you filter your options.

Back to the map. Now that you have some regional perspective, begin to drill down. You aren't retiring to Portugal or Panama anymore than you're retiring to the United States. You aren't retiring to the Algarve or Lisbon either. Well, you are, but, again, that's only the starting point for your search. Ultimately you must choose an address.

When Lief and I repositioned from Paris to Panama, I wanted to settle in Panama City's old town, Casco Viejo. I'm infatuated by its Spanish-, French-, and American-colonial past and a fan of the architectural legacy that history created. We couldn't find a suitable rental and wanted to be settled in our new digs before our 8-year-old son started his school year, so we opted for convenient and moved into a new-built high-rise. We had an ocean view, but the tower lifestyle wasn't for us. The apartment felt soulless.

As soon as we were able, a year later, we moved across town to Casco Viejo. Turned out, that historic neighborhood was more charming in my imagination than in real life. Traffic, tourists, and lack of parking made day-to-day living painful. We moved out before the end of our lease.

Next stop was a house in the city-center neighborhood of Marbella. We'd tried high-rise living and thought a house would give us more privacy and feel more like home. We found life in Marbella as challenging as it'd been in Casco. Panama City at ground level everywhere is congested, dirty, and loud.

A year later, we were moving again, this time back into an apartment. At last, though, we'd found a building we liked in an ideal location. Lief, young Jackson, and I called Miramar our home for five happy years.

We thought about asking the owners of that rental if they were interested in selling but held off and were glad we did. When Jackson headed off to college, the oversized three-bedroom apartment was more than we needed.

Thanks to our Goldilocks experience across this city, we realized that we already owned the place that suited us best. We took our one-bedroom waterfront rental that we'd bought as an investment a decade earlier off the market and moved into it ourselves. It took us a while to find our way to them, but we've enjoyed those Avenida Balboa digs ever since. They're the perfect base for Lief and me now as we come and go from the Hub of the Americas as empty-nesters.

One more time, from region to country to neighborhood, the where is everything. Your new life overseas can play out dramatically differently if you choose to base yourself just a few miles or even a few blocks one direction or another.

We've got you. In the pages to follow we'll walk you through your best options for reinventing your life overseas big-picture and thin-sliced. Let's go find your just-right fit.

II

MEXICO & CENTRAL AMERICA

Offering a wealth of lifestyle opportunities in an array of sun-drenched havens where the cost of living can be less than half of the average in the United States and Canada, it's clear why so many North Americans have chosen to call Mexico and Central America home.

Close to the U.S. and Canada, this part of the world offers a low cost of living, great weather, top-notch health care, and familiarity. Whether you decide to live full or part-time, these countries give you easy residency options and access to lots of other expats who have already decided to make the move abroad. Plus, because of the proximity, it's easier to travel home—whether it's to see the grandkids or extended family, check on a property or a family business... Whatever the reason, you have the flexibility to come and go whenever you please.

So where are some of the best spots to consider here for those looking to live large for less?

Does living an authentic, local lifestyle and learning Spanish sound appealing to you, or would you feel more at home with a large, English-speaking expat community? Would you rather spend your evenings and weekends at upscale restaurants or visiting museums, or do you prefer outdoor activities like fishing, hiking, water sports, baseball, and adrenaline-filled adventures? Maybe you'd like to have a bit of both?

Your perfect place in the sun will depend on many personal factors... but to get you started in your search, this section covers the expat havens south of the border, where you can likely upgrade your lifestyle and slash your cost of living.

CHAPTER 1

MEXICO

Over the past four decades, Americans have voted Mexico the world's #1 place to live or retire in the way that really counts... they've packed up and moved there. This country is home to more American expats and retirees than any other—at least 1 million and as many as 2 million, depending on the survey.

The highly Americanized culture is only one of the attractions. Mexico's proximity to the United States and Canada is another big plus for the many retirees living there who want to make trips back home to see grandkids every now and then. Plus, the excellent infrastructure makes living easy, residency is straightforward, the country's got many great lifestyle and climate choices, and property is affordable, as is the cost of living.

If you're weak in Spanish, then you'll appreciate Mexico's wealth of English-speakers. In Mazatlán, for example, English is spoken almost everywhere... including the immigration office.

As a new resident, you can import your household effects duty-free. Plus, you can return easily to use Medicare in the U.S. You'll appreciate this one if you are nearing (or over) age 65. You can get good medical care in Mexico... but if you'd rather have a more familiar setting (and let Medicare pay for it), then you're only a drive or a quick flight away from the U.S.

The Mexican government is a stable democracy, with executive, legislative, and judicial branches functioning in a similar way to those in the U.S.

It's a civil law country, so you can forget the threats (and expense) of protecting yourself from frivolous lawsuits or personal injury lawyers.

Mexico is large, broad, and diverse, with hundreds of good living options. There's literally something for everyone. Whatever your preference for climate, you'll find it in Mexico. Throughout the mountains, you'll discover beautiful colonial cities like San Miguel de Allende, Ajijic, Guanajuato, and Oaxaca... places that enjoy mild climates without extreme heat or cold.

But Mexico also offers thousands of miles of beautiful beaches, from temperate to tropical, on both its Atlantic and Pacific coasts. Places like Tulum and Playa del Carmen... Mazatlán and Puerto Vallarta... and Los Cabos and Ensenada, all continue to be popular with expats.

Top Picks For A New Life In Mexico

Mazatlán

Located about midway along Mexico's Pacific coast, and often called "The Pearl of the Pacific," Mazatlán's top selling point is its 13 miles of golden beaches with clean, swimmable waters.

The beaches are lined by a vibrant boardwalk known as the Malecón, one of the longest seaside promenades in the world. It's always abuzz with people walking, exercising, and socializing.

Mazatlán is warm year-round, and beyond the beaches, residents can explore offshore islands, hike in nearby mountains, or visit nature reserves to spot wildlife.

People are friendly, and there's a thriving expat community that is welcoming and supportive, making it easy for newcomers to feel at home quickly.

But what makes Mazatlán different from any other resort town on

Mexico's Pacific Coast?

First, it boasts a sizeable historic district known as the Centro Histórico that is full of charming Spanish-colonial architecture, cobblestone streets, and lively plazas.

This is the place to go for a great meal out, drinks and live music, or a theater performance. From museums to festivals to the art scene, there's always something going on in the Centro Histórico.

Second, Mazatlán is affordable. It's less expensive than its resort-town counterparts like Cancún, Tulum, Playa del Carmen, and Puerto Vallarta. This applies not only to the day-to-day cost of living but also the cost of well-appointed seaside real estate as well.

Third, Mazatlán is more than just a resort town; it's also a real Mexican city of about half a million people. There's a sizeable expat community, but it doesn't overwhelm the local culture.

This is still a Mexican city, which means that you have the opportunity to immerse yourself and have a culturally authentic experience, if you wish to.

On top of this, Mazatlán has many English speakers, and it offers all the familiarity and convenience that make Mexico the most popular international destination for Americans and Canadians. You'll find familiar shops like Home Depot, Sam's Club, Walmart, and AutoZone here, as well as local chains.

If you find the prospect of launching a new life in a new country daunting, Mazatlán could be your soft landing. It also comes with great weather, sandy beaches, a sprawling historic center, and a friendly expat community.

The place to head for great dining, drinks, live music, or other forms of entertainment is the Centro Histórico, the historic center. This sprawling neighborhood of colorful Spanish-colonial architecture contains restored buildings, lively plazas, and cobblestone streets.

You'll find an array of outdoor cafés and international restaurants, as well as theaters, art galleries, shops, and more. There's an active live music scene in Mazatlán, as well as classical music and art.

Mazatlán also has lively traditional events and festivals. It hosts carnival celebrations every February, including parades, live music, and costumes. Art Walk Mazatlán showcases the city's artistic prowess when artists open their studios and galleries, and art-focused events take place.

Mazatlán is famous for beautiful beaches, and right in town, you find miles of well-maintained sandy beaches with warm, swimmable waters. There are different styles of beaches here, with options to suit those who like calm and low-key as well as those who like something a little more active.

You can rent kayaks, jet skis, and wave runners; go on banana boat rides; wakeboard; paddleboard; parasail; surf; scuba dive; or snorkel. You can go on island excursions for more secluded beaches and wildlife sightings. For fishing enthusiasts, there's world-class deep-sea fishing.

Along Mazatlán's waterfront is a boardwalk (the Malecón) that's a hive of activity. It's busy with people strolling, jogging, walking their dogs, and biking pretty much all day. There are facilities for sports like golf and tennis in Mazatlán. El Cid Golf & Country Club and Marina Mazatlán are top local courses.

Beyond the city, there are hiking, biking, and horse-riding opportunities in the foothills of the Sierra Madre mountains. Nearby nature preserves attract birdwatchers and nature lovers.

Costs have risen over time, but Mazatlán continues to provide U.S. and Canadian retirees the chance to enjoy a better quality of life at a lower cost.

Rent costs vary, but you can expect to spend anywhere from $800 to $2,000 per month. Real estate is a great investment in Mazatlán. You can buy a nice, ocean-view condo for around $200,000.

Everything from food and entertainment to housing and utilities costs less here than in the States or Canada... but it also costs less than comparable Mexican resort cities, like Puerto Vallarta. The average cost of living for two is $2,500.

Mazatlán's climate is so dry and hot that it borders on a semi-arid classification. This is a great place for fans of hot, sunny weather and those who don't like the rain.

During summer, temperatures are in the low 90s (30s Celsius); during winter, they're in the low 60s (around 15 Celsius). You'll need air conditioning in your home to live comfortably here. There's not much seasonal variation throughout the year aside from the subtle shift to wetter weather from July to September.

Mazatlán has a mix of public and private medical facilities, including hospitals for insured and uninsured residents.

Expats tend to pay for private insurance to be able to use private hospitals, like Sharp Hospital and Marina Mazatlán Hospital, both of which provide high-quality care at affordable prices. Many doctors are fluent in English and trained abroad.

If you're looking for a big, welcoming, English-speaking community to settle into, Mazatlán provides it. It's home to big numbers of expats, many of whom are from Western Canada and the States.

That said, Mazatlán remains a Mexican national destination. In other words, the expat community isn't overbearing and doesn't dominate the local vibe. It's made up of good folks who are respectful of the local people and culture.

To meet other expats in Mazatlán, join Facebook groups, join in on activities, or head to the Malecón and start chatting with people. Two excellent sources of community intel are the *Pacific Pearl* and *Mazatlán Life* publications.

Public transportation options are diverse, affordable, and widely used. They include buses, taxis, and open-air taxis called *pulmonías*. Still, many expats prefer to have their own car and drive themselves around.

Crime is a risk to foreigners in Mexico, and the country has a reputation for being dangerous (although its GPI ranking is not far behind that of the United States).

Bad news tends to make news headlines, but the reality is that more U.S. and Canadian expats live in Mexico than any other country. Serious crime tends to be localized to certain areas that expats know to avoid.

It's unlikely that you'll experience annoyances like crime or pickpocketing here, let alone serious crime. The government makes extra effort to make things safe because of the big tourist and expat presence.

If you're looking for an easy transition to life overseas to a place that's close and familiar, then take another look at Mazatlán. Here you'll get to enjoy a waterfront Spanish-colonial historic center with vast entertainment and dining options and an affordable beachside life.

Oaxaca

Most people who move to Mexico make a beeline for places like Playa del Carmen and Puerto Vallarta. Both are great places to spend time, but they're expat bubbles.

If you're looking for a place without a Señor Frog's in sight, you'll need to head inland...

Those looking for charming colonial architecture with a vibrant culture that's more Mexico than spring break should turn their gaze towards Oaxaca City.

It checks a lot of boxes: a moderate climate, reasonable prices, flight connections to the States, and high-quality health care.

Also, it isn't super touristy or flooded with gringos. It's becoming more of a popular destination, sure, but the city does not rely on tourism as much as other expat favorites do.

Beyond the obvious draws of nice weather and a low cost of living, this is a fascinating city with a lot to offer...

Oaxaca is the capital of the southwestern Mexican state of the same name. It's famous for its cuisine (such as the versatile *mole* sauce) and its potent libation, mezcal. Your taste buds are in for a treat if you relocate here.

Compared to places like Mexico City or Guadalajara, Oaxaca feels like a small town. It's easy enough to get around on foot, and local buses are cheap and easy to figure out if you need them.

The pastel-colored buildings of Centro with the rolling mountains in the background... The air in the local markets is filled with a variety of intriguing aromas... That smoky taste of a good glass of mezcal... This is life in Oaxaca.

You've got all the conveniences of a big city without many of the annoyances, and it's got more to offer in terms of culture than places like PV or San Miguel.

While not as well connected as other Mexican destinations, Oaxaca does have an international airport. At the moment, there aren't many options for direct flights to the States or Canada... but with its increasing popularity, more flight options will be available soon.

There's plenty to do in Oaxaca. Simply wandering around the Zócalo provides endless entertainment. There are plenty of squares, museums, churches, markets, galleries, and more...

One of the most famous sights in the Zócalo is the stunning Santo Domingo church. Here you'll also find the Museum of Cultures and a lovely botanical garden.

If you're an art-lover, you'll feel right at home in Oaxaca. There are several museums and galleries in Centro, and there's eye-catching street art around every corner.

Eating and drinking are two of the main attractions in Oaxaca. This city is famous for its mole and mezcal. Pronounced "mo-lay," this is a sauce typically made from chili peppers, fruits, nuts, and other spices. There are many different varieties of mole, and you can try most of them in Oaxaca's central markets, such as Mercado 20 de Noviembre.

In its bustling Centro, you'll find colorful colonial buildings and even more colorful clothing and wares from the various indigenous groups that call the area home. The state of Oaxaca is home to about a third of Mexico's indigenous population.

Traditional festivals are a big deal here, including the month-long Guelaguetza that's focused on the dancing and clothing of the indigenous population. The city comes alive in celebration for the entire month of July.

Oaxaca is one of the best places to experience the Day of the Dead, with people coming from all over the world to view the elaborate *ofrendas* (altars) for this important holiday. (Day of the Dead is celebrated annually at the end of October 31/start of November.)

Surrounded by mountains, it should come as no surprise that Oaxaca provides some good hiking opportunities. It doesn't take long to reach the ancient ruins at Monte Albán or the jaw-dropping petrified waterfalls at Hierve el Agua.

The former is an archaeological site built by the Zapotecs around 500 BC. It's one of Mesoamerica's earliest cities. The latter, Hierve el Agua, is a massive waterfall made of two rock shelves that stand almost 300 feet (90 meters) above the ground below.

If beaches are more your vibe, you can jet to the coast for the weekend to places like Puerto Escondido or Huatulco. The journey to the Oaxaca coast across curvy mountain roads is hair-raising, but a quick flight is also an option...

If you're up for living like a local, your money will go a long way, especially if you're earning dollars and spending pesos. Those who find a simple apartment, stick to walking or public transportation, and shop in local markets can live comfortably for a fraction of what it costs up north.

Rentals are available for $500 to $800 per month. You can walk almost everywhere or take the occasional bus or get a taxi for $3. That means a super-low transportation budget—more dinero for you to spend on nice dinners out and some drinks at the fun bars around town.

A couple with modest tastes can easily live off of less than $2,000 here, and that includes rent. Add another $500 to that, and you can enjoy a few nights out on the town and occasional weekend trips to the coast or other nearby towns.

Oaxaca is a regional retreat from hot and humid weather conditions in Mexico's coastal and lowland areas.

It sits at 5,100 feet (1,555 meters) above sea level, which keeps is temperatures cool. Here the average high is 85°F (29°C) and the average low is 56°F (13°C), with an average humidity of 64%.

Oaxaca gets two seasons: rainy, from May to September, and dry, from October to April. It gets about 99 days of precipitation per year for an annual total of 30 inches of rainfall.

On the most basic level, you can see a doctor in the small offices that are attached to most pharmacies. This costs $2 or so and is great if you're feeling under the weather and need a quick diagnosis.

They can give you a quick consultation and write a prescription to be filled next door. Don't expect these doctors to speak English, so come with a friend or a translator if your medical Spanish isn't up to par.

Plastic surgery and dental work are so affordable that some people travel here specifically for operations. Generally, it costs a third (or even less) than it does up north.

There are plenty of qualified dentists and surgeons here, many of whom studied in the States and speak English. Prescription drugs are also way cheaper here than they are in the States.

For more serious matters, Oaxaca is home to plenty of excellent clinics and hospitals, many of which have English-speaking doctors and specialists. Some recommended private hospitals include Hospital del Valle, Clínica Hospital Carmen, and Hospital Reforma.

Oaxaca is home to a sizable expat community of over 20,000, with most hailing from the States and Canada. All sorts of events are going on all the time, so it's easy to get out and meet people. Whether you're into yoga, books, or hiking, there's a club or class for you here.

While a lot of the expats in Oaxaca are retired, there's a growing number of younger digital nomads relocating to the city for months at a time, lured by the vibrancy of this city and supported by the improving infrastructure.

A great resource for prospective and current expats is the Oaxaca Lending Library. They offer a weekly "Welcome to Oaxaca" program, language exchanges, community programs, day trips, and more. You'll want to be a part of this group if relocating here.

Oaxaca is mostly a walkable place. It's a relatively small city that's laid out in a grid plan, at least in the Centro and Reforma neighborhoods. Those who live in these areas can get by without a car.

If you don't feel like hoofing it, there are always local taxis ready and willing to give you a lift.

It's worth it to try to figure out the local bus system. Most locals get around on public buses and *colectivos* (carpool-type mini-vans). Trips typically cost 60 cents around town and a bit more for destinations outside of the center.

To use the local public transportation system, you'll need a basic grasp of Spanish. You also need to familiarize yourself with the routes so you know where to get on and when to call for a stop, either by pushing a button or just hollering "*Bajar*!"

Once you get a grasp on the local bus system, the world is your oyster.

Oaxaca state is one of the safest states in Mexico, and Oaxaca city has a reputation as a safe place to visit. Rates of drug-related violence are low compared to other parts of Mexico.

That said, Oaxaca is one of the poorest states in the country. There's a notable disparity between the rich and poor here. With its recent surge in popularity, some opportunists are taking advantage of the waves of unsuspecting tourists that are arriving here.

Muggings can happen, but they usually occur late at night. Spending time here as an expat, you'll soon learn which areas to avoid and the proper conduct to avoid becoming a victim of crime.

If you're looking for city amenities with a small-town feel, a moderate climate, and a low cost of living, and if you love Mexican culture—the art, the food, the festivals—then you're going to love Oaxaca.

Puerto Vallarta

Puerto Vallarta is located on Mexico's Pacific Coast in the scenic Banderas Bay, surrounded by the Sierra Madre mountains. PV (as it's known) is one of the most visited places in Mexico, but it retains its traditional charm.

While more and more high-rise condos are sprouting up, you can still walk its cobblestone streets and see men on horseback and women pressing fresh corn tortillas.

A long-time favorite destination of retirees and spring-breakers, Puerto Vallarta now attracts expats and digital nomads as well. There's just something about this place that draws people in...

Strolling the oceanfront Malecón is a quintessential PV activity. This promenade is lined with 20+ sculptures along with plenty of shops, restaurants, and bars. It really comes alive at night, especially on the weekends.

PV is an artsy city, with dozens of galleries and artisan shops to peruse. Events like the Southside Shuffle and ArtWalk are great ways to get involved in the local artistic community.

The city is home to several markets. Some of them are open daily while others happen on a weekly basis only in high season. Show your support for local businesses and artisans by coming out to shop and dine in these great local markets.

Perhaps you're more of a wine and dine type. In that case, you will feel like you've died and gone to heaven in Puerto Vallarta. This city is a foodie's paradise with a mind-blowing array of options. From streetside taco vendors to fine-dining on the beach, there's something for every palette and budget.

Puerto Vallarta also has a bit of a reputation as a party town, especially in the Romantic Zone. You'll find no shortage of places to wet your whistle. From trendy cocktail joints to local craft breweries and posh rooftop lounges to dive bars, a night out on the town can be whatever you make of it.

Getting bored isn't an issue here. There's enough to see and do here to keep you busy for years on end... For most, the biggest draw to Puerto Vallarta is the beach.

The main beach in town is Playa Los Muertos (the Beach of the Dead), which is home to the city's iconic sail-shaped pier. Some of the many activities on offer here include: snorkeling, diving, parasailing, jet-skiing, and beach volleyball. Many expats and retirees own their own boats and park them in one of the marinas in the bay.

While it's primarily known as a beach destination, there's lots more to do here than sit in the sand. Puerto Vallarta is also surrounded by mountains. That means hiking, ATV adventures, horseback riding, mountain biking, and other outdoor activities are also at your fingertips.

If you're a fitness buff, you've got plenty of options. Agustin Flores Contreras Municipal Sports Stadium features a track, basketball courts, soccer and baseball fields, and even a skate park.

There are a few golf courses in the area as well as tennis courts you can rent by the hour. You can find gyms of all shapes and sizes here as well as group classes in yoga, CrossFit, pilates, and zumba.

Locals are a proud, resilient, and fun-loving bunch. There's always a fiesta of some sort going on here, regardless of what night of the week it is...

While the high season (November to March) is busy with snowbirds and international vacationers, Puerto Vallarta also attracts a large crowd of national tourists during Semana Santa (Holy Week) and in July when Mexican school children are on vacation.

The town has different vibes depending on the month of the year...

Puerto Vallarta is also proud to be a LGBTQ-friendly destination. Often called the "San Francisco of Mexico," the city hosts a huge Pride Week celebration every year in May. It's more liberal and laid-back than most places in Mexico.

For a popular tourist beach destination, Puerto Vallarta remains an affordable place to live. For a couple, a monthly budget of $3,305 is a good guide but of course you can spend a good deal less... or more... depending on your tastes and interests...

If you mostly get around by bus, shop and dine in local spots, and stick to domestic beers when going out, you'll spend little on a daily basis. Those who prefer taking cabs everywhere, fine dining, and European wines will have a much higher bill.

In local tiendas and markets, you can easily stock up on essentials (fresh produce, eggs, rice, beans, tortillas, milk, coffee) for pennies on the dollar. For more specific or imported items, you'll have to head to a supermarket like Chedraui or La Comer.

When it comes to property prices, they run the gamut. In a popular spot like Zona Romantica you can expect to pay from $2,500 to $4,500 a month for a two-bedroom condo. Move a little farther from the beach to the Bucerias area on the far side of the highway and you can find rentals from $700 a month. In a residential community like Valle Dorado you could find a rental for as little as $500 a month.

Your utilities (electricity, gas, and water) will cost about $280 a month; Internet and cell phone will be $45; a couple should budget about $400 a month for entertainment; and $500 for your monthly grocery shop.

Puerto Vallarta is warm year-round. Temperatures range between an average high of 86°F (30°C) and an average low of 70°F (21°C), with humidity hovering around 75%. From June to October, it's hot and stuffy; from November to May it gets a little cooler, with temperatures dropping from 90°F (32°C) to 83°F (28°C).

There are only two seasons here: dry and rainy. The latter runs from June to October and can be muggy, sweaty, and wet. Rainy season is when many snowbirds get out of town or hole up in their airconditioned homes.

About 55 inches of rain falls here over the course of the year. Puerto Vallarta's rainiest month is August with an average 15 days of heavy precipitation. Expect 15 inches of rainfall, on average, throughout the month of September. In contrast, April, the driest month, experiences less than an inch of precipitation.

Despite being a relatively small city, Puerto Vallarta has an extensive health care system.

A private specialist consultation typically runs $40 to $80, routine doctor visits can be as low as $25, and overnight hospital stays in private rooms run from $300 to $900 depending on the complexity of your condition.

Doctors can provide basic consultations and write you a prescription to fill in the pharmacy next door. If you'd feel more comfortable going to an international clinic with English-speaking doctors, Sanmaré Health-Care Group offers consultations for about $45.

Prescription drugs are incredibly affordable here. Plus, many people travel to Puerto Vallarta simply to receive dental or medical treatment of some kind. Dentoamerica is a dentistry office popular among expats. It's run by a Canadian owner whose team is incredibly well-trained, qualified, and near fluent in English.

For hospitals, there are several options in the area. In the northern part of the city, you'll find Hospital Joya and the Vallarta Medical Center. These are state-of-the-art facilities with emergency rooms and ICU staffing 24 hours a day. Just east of the Hotel Zone is Hospital CMQ Premiere, which also has a location in the Romantic Zone. Another option downtown is Hospital Medasist.

One of the best things about living in Puerto Vallarta is the tight-knit expat community. It's hard to put a specific number to it, as many are snowbirds who come down just for the winter. During those busy months, there are probably some 40,000 to 50,000 expats here. That's a lot for a city with a population of 250,000.

There are some "gringo bubbles" around, but most expats live in close proximity and harmony with locals. While there's a substantial number of retirees in Puerto Vallarta, there's also a large community of expats who work for local companies or run their own business, such as managing vacation rentals or leading tours.

The digital nomad population has grown rapidly over the past few years with the rise in remote work. You'll encounter vacationers and retirees, business owners (bars, restaurants, and breweries, mostly), and countless nomads passing through for a month or two.

The result is an eclectic expat community. It's a diverse group in terms of nationality, age, occupation, etc. If you're a social being, then you're in for a treat when you move down here. This is a town where it's easy to make friends with both locals and expats.

These days, there are several Puerto Vallarta-specific Facebook groups. It's a good idea to join a few of these before you make the move, as you can get tips and recommendations from people already on the ground.

The bus system in the entire Banderas Bay area is excellent. It's the preferred method of transport for locals, and there are bus routes serving just about every neighborhood here.

Long-distance buses can take you to nearby cities in Mexico. Mexican buses are luxurious compared to the Greyhounds up north, with reclining chairs, a personal TV, clean bathrooms, and even a little snack pack and drink for the ride. The best companies are Primera Plus, ETN, and Vallarta Plus.

Puerto Vallarta is home to an international airport (PVR) with plenty of direct connections to the States and Canada. It's a three-hour flight from Los Angeles, four hours and 10 minutes from Atlanta, and six hours and five minutes from New York. From Toronto, it's almost six hours and from Vancouver it's a little under five hours.

PV is generally a safe place to live. Expats report feeling completely at ease traveling the city by day and night. That said, bad things can happen anywhere. You'll need to take basic precautions to prevent against pickpocketing and bag-snatching.

With the ocean on one side and the mountains on the other, there's a wealth of activities at your fingertips here. Add to that an active and growing expat population plus the super-friendly locals, and you've got a recipe for good times as a retiree in Puerto Vallarta.

Health Care In Mexico

In Mexico, there's a difference in the quality of medical care between public and private facilities. As an expat, you'll likely seek out private care, which is excellent.

The best facilities have first-rate technology, English-speaking doctors, and low prices. Private facilities are the best option for expats. They're similar to what you're used to in the States or Canada.

Medical tourism is a fast-growing industry, with more Americans choosing to cross the border to seek quality, affordable health care in Mexico every year, and many Mexican doctors are trained in the United States, Europe, or Canada and speak English fluently.

Costs here are low, typically just one-third the cost you'd pay for comparable care in the United States.

Residency Requirements

Mexico offers straightforward paths to residency, although it doesn't offer a retiree-specific, golden, or digital nomad visa.

You can apply for temporary or permanent residency. To qualify for temporary residency, you'll need to show that you receive $4,295 per month in income or have a minimum of $71,375 in savings.

Mexico is unique in that it allows you to jump straight to permanent residency, which is a more solid residency status. To do this, you'll need to show that you receive $7,075 per month in income or $284,089 in savings.

Note that the exact qualifying amounts can vary from consulate to consulate.

Our Latin American correspondent Lee Harrison is a permanent resident of Mexico, and he found the process to be simple, straightforward, and fast.

All it took to get a residency visa was a single consular visit, where he was helped by an English-speaking agent. And even better, they accepted his English-language documents at the consulate with no translations.

He also didn't need apostille certifications of his income, social security, or banking information... although if a couple applies as a family unit they will require that you apostille your marriage or birth certificate.

Best of all, there's no lawyer required... although if you do not speak English or Spanish, you'll need to bring a translator.

The biggest thing that stands out about Mexico is that they allow you to use savings in lieu of income when qualifying for a visa. This is great for people who have savings (like a 401k) but don't have a formal pension.

Qualification thresholds have become high, at least for now. This is because income requirements are based on multiples of the Mexican minimum wage, which has gone up dramatically in recent years. There are plans to correct this calculation, so that thresholds are more reasonable... but no timetable as to when it will happen.

Most of the people we hear from choose to qualify with savings, using an IRA or a 401(k). Then they switch to permanent residency after four years, with no required proof of income.

No minimum stay time is required to maintain your visa. You do not need to live in Mexico to maintain residency, however you do need to be there to renew your residency if you have a residency which expires.

Of course you may not even need residency in Mexico, thanks to their liberal tourist-entry policies. You get an automatic 180-day stay when you enter the country, which is usually enough for a part-year resident. And if you leave Mexico during your stay, you get another 180 days when you return.

You can import your household effects duty-free as a new resident. The nearest consulate will give you the permit upon request.

Mexico offers a clear path to citizenship, after either two years or five years of residency.

If you were born in Mexico, or born to a Mexican citizen outside of Mexico, then you already qualify for citizenship (Mexico recognizes dual-citizenship). Just grab your parents' birth certificates and head to immigration to begin the process.

If you have been a resident for five years, you can apply for naturalization. All time as a resident counts, including time as a temporary resident.

As part of the naturalization process you must take an exam on Mexican history and prove that you can speak functional Spanish. The history test can be waived if you are over 60 or under 18... there is no waiver for the Spanish test.

They offer a study guide to help you pass the history test. Definitely use the guide when the time comes.

Real Estate Restrictions

Mexico places some restrictions on foreign buyers when it comes to property ownership. Specifically, property ownership in areas that are 32 miles (50 kms) from the coastline and 64 miles (100 kms) from international borders is restricted.

There's a workaround, however. You can purchase properties in this area through a trust (a *fideicomiso)* with a Mexican bank.

You retain all ownership rights and can sell, give, mortgage, or lease your property as you wish, but you have to carry out this extra administrative step to do so, including added expenses.

Taxes

Mexico has a good tax treaty with their USMCA brothers in the U.S. and Canada, as well as a lax policy for categorizing you as a "tax-resident".

Mexico has the lowest tax burden among all OECD countries (a group of the world's 35 wealthiest nations).

You are a tax-resident of Mexico if you have established your primary home or center of business there. Unlike most jurisdictions, they do not use time-in-country to determine tax residency.

Non-tax-residents are subject to tax on their Mexican-source income only, paying zero, 15%, or 30%, depending on your income. Capital gains for non-tax-residents are taxed at either 25% of the sale, or 30% of the gain (the highest tax bracket), whichever is less.

Tax-residents are subject to tax on their worldwide income, although much of your income may be exempt for various reasons. (For example, any income that had tax withheld is considered final, and not declared on a Mexican return.) Also, Mexico has tax treaties with the U.S. and Canada, designed to prevent double-taxation.

Otherwise, tax brackets run from zero to 35%. Capital gains for tax-residents are taxed as ordinary income.

There is no inheritance tax or wealth tax in Mexico.

CHAPTER 2

PANAMA

Panama could arguably be called the world's best offshore haven. There is no doubt that the Central American country has serious pluses for those looking for a place with a cheaper cost of living than the United States. Panama is blessed with beautiful islands, ample coastline, beaches, mountain retreats, and colonial towns.

This little isthmus offers something for everyone, from culture vultures to adrenaline junkies to beach bums and everyone in between. Panama is home to dozens of attractive havens for expats and retirees.

The Panamanian people are friendly, and, outside of the city, the atmosphere is laid back and easy going. With a population of only 4 million, the country does not feel overly crowded.

This country is among our top-ranked retirement choices, regardless of the size of your budget. Panama City is no longer a bargain retirement destination, but elsewhere in Panama, specifically the Veraguas Province, can be.

Cost of living is important, but it's not everything, which is why it's worth noting that Panama also makes great sense for the would-be retiree abroad for many other reasons, too. Its health care facilities are top-notch, its currency is the U.S. dollar, local health insurance is a bargain, it's easy to get a retiree visa, and retirees living here enjoy lots of special discounts and perks.

Panama is bordered by Costa Rica to the northwest and Colombia to the southeast, and both its southern and northern borders are on the coast. The Pacific Ocean is to the south and the Caribbean Sea to the north. At its narrowest point, it's only 50 miles wide. Panama is Central America's southernmost country, and because of a bend in the isthmus, it gives the impression that the sun rises in the west (over the Pacific Ocean) and sets in the east (on the Atlantic).

Panama has a tropical climate, and being close to the equator, the temperature does not change much throughout the year. Different parts of Panama do have different climates though.

The daytime temperature in Panama City, for instance, is around 86°F (30°C). At nighttime the temperature drops to around 75°F (24°C).

In Boquete, on the other hand, the average daytime temperature is around 75°F (24°C). Although nights are cooler here, the temperature seldom gets below 50°F (10°C).

The country offers generous tax incentives to encourage foreigners to live there. Residents do not pay any tax on foreign-earned income. This means your pension cannot be taxed, nor can any other funds set up outside of Panama.

If you are looking to start a business in Panama, you will be given tax breaks from the government. Tourism investments have exemptions from import duties for construction materials and equipment. Exemptions are also applied to income and real estate taxes. Panama is actively looking to improve its economy and will assist you in your efforts.

The country is a safe place to live. Most Panamanians are friendly, especially in the rural areas. Generally, Panamanians are not money-orientated and not resentful of expats who are perceived as being wealthier. Armed policemen are a common sight in Panama City and tourist areas in particular are very safe.

The country is politically stable. Panama has had its share of political problems in the past, but nowadays things are more secure.

You can drink the tap water everywhere in Panama besides Bocas del Toro and the comarcas, like Guna Yala where San Blas is located. Plus, you can live car-free in Panama City. While you'll need a car in most parts of the interior (countryside), it's not necessary in the capital.

Panama is known as the Hub of the Americas, and the country enjoys consistent upgrades. Major undertakings in Panama City this year include progress on Metro Line 3 (phases 1 and 2 are already up and running), improvements to the Inter-American Highway, and key upgrades at Tocumen International Airport. In addition, port and logistics developments connected to the Panama Canal Authority are moving forward, further strengthening Panama's role as a regional logistics hub.

Many destinations have large, well-connected expat communities. Here you will find people to socialize with who will help you acclimatize to your new life. Living in a popular expat haven means you'll be surrounded by services that cater to expats. You can find restaurants, shops, and businesses all providing goods for expats.

Top Picks For A New Life In Panama

Panama City

When considering Panama City, it's important to keep a couple of pointers in mind. The city is huge, and each neighborhood is unique. If you are looking to live here, we recommend that you "thin slice" the city into the areas that best suit your lifestyle and tastes.

Panama City offers a different caliber of lifestyle experience—a more comfortable, well-appointed standard of living than anywhere else in Central America. It's changed drastically over the past 15 years or so as it pushes always for growth. This city is constantly under construction as it builds and rebuilds, expands, and develops... It's well on its way to becoming the brand-name city it has long aspired to be.

All of Panama but especially Panama City has been one of the greatest economic success stories of the past two decades. The massive growth has been due largely to foreign investment.

It's a strategic business hub with strong banking, excellent infrastructure, and an established track record of stability—even during global downturns.

My husband, Lief, and I were drawn to Panama 30 years ago. Our reasons for picking Panama at the time were all financial, but that's just one face of this little country.

The government is pro-business and foreigner-friendly, meaning outsized incentives for foreign retirees and investors, and the country offers more than a dozen visa options (including the Friendly Nations visa that grants work permits), making it easy to become a full time resident if that's something you'd like to do.

In Panama City, skyscrapers meet the Pacific Ocean, and a vibrant culture pulsates through every street. Whether you're seeking a new adventure, a change of scenery, or a place to call home, Panama City has something to offer everyone.

Panama City is more than just the capital of Panama; it's a thriving metropolis that boasts a blend of history, modernity, and natural beauty. As the only capital city with a rain forest within its limits, Panama City provides a unique backdrop for your expat life.

The city is made up of several neighborhoods, each with their own unique flavor. Some are closer to schools; others are closer to nightclubs and bars; and some are in historic areas.

The city isn't a budget destination anymore, but the cost of living is still less than what you surely pay back home. A couple could live in Panama City on a monthly budget starting at about $3,000. These numbers will vary significantly depending on what neighborhood you choose and your lifestyle choices (how and where you shop, how often you eat out, how you entertain yourself, etc.).

Here are a few neighborhoods in the city that are ideal for expats to call home.

Casco Viejo (Old Town) is laid out like a classic European city: It's on a grid with shady plazas complete with churches every couple of blocks.

Its narrow streets are meant to be explored on foot... Walk around and take in the colonial architecture, like the buildings with shuttered windows, balconies on every level overlooking the street, ornate ironwork and turned wood... these are the kinds of facades you see more often in the pages of coffee-table books than you do in real life. It used to be a slum, but it is now the hippest night spot in the city.

The Spanish-, French-, and American-colonial structures here have been remodeled. You could call one of these buildings your home if you dream of living surrounded by history and spectacular architecture.

Punta Pacífica is one of the areas where Panama's wealthiest citizens live and one of the more expensive areas of Panama City. The skyscrapers that typically appear in magazines and commercial videos are likely from this area or the neighboring Avenida Balboa. There are many high-end apartment buildings to choose from.

You could be closer to the bay and have an uninterrupted view of the water or live further inland. Punta Pacífica has all the amenities you could think of nearby—grocery stores, a hospital, and malls. If budget is no concern, then Punta Pacífica may be the best place for you. Its proximity to the Cinta Costera makes it perfect for someone who enjoys jogging or taking a stroll from time to time.

Marbella is a well-known neighborhood sitting between Avenida Balboa and Calle 50. It's a business hub, so it's filled with office buildings and corporate centers. One of the most attractive features of Marbella is its proximity to Avenida Balboa, Calle 50, Punta Pacífica, Paitilla, and Casco Viejo.

You could walk to each of these neighborhoods if you wanted to. Soho Mall, Multiplaza, and Megapolis Outlets are nearby. The John's Hopkins affiliate hospital called Pacifica Salud, and the Paitilla Hospital are also close. Keep in mind, though, its central location and proximity to the very busy Calle 50 means it can get noisy.

Albrook is a former military (Air Force) base converted to a residential area with homes and large yards. It features renovated former officers' homes, newly constructed houses, and condos. They enjoy greenery and a country feel, despite being just minutes from the city. One of Panama's largest and best-established private schools, St. Mary's, is in Albrook with more than 1,500 pupils taught in English-only classes. If you're moving to Panama with children, Albrook may be an appealing option for you.

The number and range of entertainment options in Panama City may not be as high as it is in other capital cities... but that doesn't mean that Panama City has nothing to offer. It has its own unique brand of entertainment that expats find out about after a few years of living here and getting to know the community...

The most charming part of town is undoubtedly Casco Viejo. At only four avenues wide, Casco is compact; a tiny treasure trove of historical structures best explored on foot.

Despite being full of visual reminders of the past, Casco is constantly evolving; old buildings are converted into private homes, condos, restaurants, funky cafés and bars, art galleries, shops, and more as it continues to be gentrified. It's where Panama City residents go when they want a night on the town, with trendy eateries and bars with carefully curated ambiances and international menus.

For a more casual dining experience, you could pay a visit to the fish market—a local staple where you can avail of cheap, freshly caught fish: yellow fin tuna, shrimp, red snapper, mahi mahi, octopus, and more. You can choose any fish and have workers cook it for you on the spot or sample some ceviche—a cheap and cheerful delicacy in Panama.

Vibrant cultural events take place in Casco Viejo constantly, from impromptu street concerts to pop-up artisan markets. A pickup baseball game might be taking place on the beach... A photography exhibition could be on around the corner... Gastronomic events like "Diner en Blanc" are hosted regularly... These unique cultural events are made more interesting by the fact that they're set within a UNESCO World Heritage Site, surrounded by centuries-old architecture.

One place where you're guaranteed to come across the arts in Panama City is Anita Villalaz Theatre. Previously a court, the building has been used as a place for performances since 1996. Here you can see plays, concerts, and folklore performances or attend seminars, workshops, and conferences, many of which are in English.

Just around the corner from Casco Viejo is the Amador Causeway, a 6-kilometer (3.7-mile) stretch of road that reaches out into the Pacific and leads to Naos, Perico, and Flamenco islands. On these islands you'll find shopping, bars and restaurants, and a harbor... but the causeway itself is an attraction. It's one of the best vantage points for watching large container ships enter and exit the canal.

With nicely paved roads and manicured sidewalks, it's also popular for walking, jogging, renting pushbikes, and so on. At the end of the causeway is the Biomuseo, an eye-catchingly colorful building that's dedicated to showcasing Panama's biodiversity. It has exhibitions on culture, geology, and natural history and is one of the city's best museums.

Panama is a shopping destination. It's a low-tax environment, making it a hub for many multinational corporations, and it has a reputation for trade and transport because of the canal. Many well-known and loved brands have bases here, like Adidas and Estée Lauder, and you can shop their products at a wide range of malls all over the city.

Albrook Mall is one of the biggest malls in the world, with hundreds of shops and thousands of daily visitors. More modern complexes like Multiplaza and AltaPlaza are home to luxury brands and a host of restaurants, shops, and cinemas. Going to the movies is a popular activity in Panama City. Movie theaters have luxury seating with fully reclining chairs and table service.

You can find any type of organized recreation activity you can think of in Panama City—sports leagues, running groups, yoga and pilates, boxing, MMA, and Muay Thai, Zumba and aerobics dance, running groups, cycling clubs, marathons, competitions, and more. You'll also find full-service modern gyms with personal trainers and facilities like saunas and pools.

Many people prefer outdoor recreation and get their exercise in at one of the city's many parks. Parque Omar, just behind the San Francisco neighborhood, is the biggest park in the city. It's full of people jogging, walking their dogs, playing with their kids, doing sports, and occasionally doing outdoor salsa lessons.

The Cinta Costera is a recently created public space along the oceanfront, stretching from Paitilla to Casco Viejo. It features running and cycling tracts, exercise equipment, playgrounds for kids, and spaces to play soccer, tennis, and basketball. Nearby, you can rent paddleboards and kayaks for mini excursions out to sea.

Panama City offers an incredible opportunity to be immersed in nature without leaving the city limits at Parque Natural Metropolitan, a 265-hectare park. It has several walking trails where you can spot rare bird species and tamarin monkeys. Another inner-city hiking opportunity is Cerro Ancón, a 200-meter (656-foot) hill that overlooks Panama City.

Panama is a great place for golfers, with five golf courses in close proximity to the capital and five more scattered across the country.

You can enjoy a comfortable lifestyle without breaking the bank here. On average, a one-bedroom apartment in the city center may cost about $1,000 to $1,300 per month, while dining out can range from $5 for a casual meal to $40 for a fine dining experience. A typical monthly grocery bill for a couple averages about $600.

As for utilities, water and gas are relatively cheap. Electricity, however, can be more expensive. Depending on the number of appliances, electronics, and use of air conditioning, you could pay up to $250 a month.

For transportation, a metro ticket costs just 35 cents, and taxi rides are reasonably priced. Overall, many expats find that they can enjoy a higher standard of living without the stress of exorbitant costs.

While Spanish is the official language, many Panamanians speak English, particularly in tourist areas. Learning some basic Spanish phrases will enhance your experience and help you connect with locals.

If you decide to settle in Panama, you'll find that learning basic conversational Spanish will help you when trying to get your point across to the building's security guard, taxi drivers, public sector workers, your cleaning lady, and more.

Moving to a new country can be daunting, but Panama City boasts a robust expat community that makes the transition smoother. Expats from various countries have settled here, contributing to a vibrant social landscape.

You'll find numerous expat groups and clubs that cater to different interests. Organizations like the American Society of Panama and InterNations host regular events, networking opportunities, and social gatherings. These platforms allow you to meet people, share experiences, and build friendships.

Social media groups are another fantastic way to connect. Search for expat forums or local Facebook groups focused on Panama City like Expats In Panama and Young Expats In Panama. These spaces are great for asking questions, sharing recommendations, and finding out about local happenings.

When it comes to health care, Panama City offers modern medical facilities and quality care. Many doctors and specialists speak English, making it accessible for expats. The cost of health care is often lower than in the United States, and many services are of high quality.

Major hospitals, like Pacifica Salud, a John's Hopkins affiliate hospital, and Hospital Nacional, have English-speaking staff, and you can often find specialists who understand your needs.

Before moving, ensure you have appropriate health insurance that covers your needs in Panama.

Panama City is increasingly recognizing the importance of accessibility for people with disabilities. Many public spaces, including shopping centers, restaurants, and public transportation, are becoming more accommodating.

The metro system is accessible for those with mobility challenges, with designated spaces for wheelchairs. Buses are also adapting to provide easier access. However, while major attractions often have ramps and accessible facilities, it's wise to check specific locations ahead of time.

Panama City is a two-season destination: its rainy season is from June to November and its dry season is from December to April. The rainiest month of the year is usually October, when you can get 20 rainy days throughout the month. The driest months are February and March, when you might get just one or two rainy days...

Temperatures in Panama City are warm throughout the year. They range from an average low of 77°F (25°C) to an average high of 88°F (31°C) with humidity hovering around 76%. It's hot and stuffy year-round here... The city sees a lot of rain throughout the year, too—usually about 75 inches.

Despite its long Caribbean coastline, Panama City is safely outside the Atlantic Hurricane Belt where Caribbean countries get battered by tropical storms. That said, it does get thunder and lightning during rainy season and certain neighborhoods are prone to flooding. Luckily, most parking lots in buildings and shopping complexes are above ground.

Panama City is known as the Hub of the Americas, and looking at the list of destinations its international airport serves across the globe, it's not hard to see why. It offers direct flights to key U.S. cities, making travel to Panama super convenient.

Panama City also offers domestic flights around the country, including to destinations like Bocas del Toro and David.

Panama City is safe, but like every city in the world, it has some rough areas and places you should avoid... As a rule of thumb, areas where businesses are set up, malls are located, and homes are built are safe. These are neighborhoods like Punta Pacífica, Avenida Balboa, El Cangrejo, San Francisco, Clayton, Marbella, Obarrio, and more, where you can enjoy walking around with minimum concern.

That said, it's not always easy to distinguish where one neighborhood ends and another begins, so you should be mindful as you're wandering around. If the look of the houses and streets changes, you may have stumbled upon a rough area and you should turn back in the direction you came from.

With a bit of common sense, you should be able to avoid crime-related problems in Panama City.

Panama City is a dynamic destination that offers an enticing blend of culture, convenience, and adventure. Whether you're drawn by the friendly locals, delicious food, or the promise of a new beginning, this vibrant metropolis welcomes you with open arms.

If you decide to settle in Panama City, embrace the unique experiences it has to offer. From the colorful streets of Casco Viejo to the breathtaking views from Ancon Hill, every corner of the city has a story to tell.

Boquete

Boquete is one of the most famous retirement havens in the world. This district in western Panama's Chiriquí Province features a large and well-established expat community, almost perfect weather, and lush green surroundings.

Back in 2000, I made my way to this small town in the mountains of Panama. There, I met with a developer who showed me the valley he intended to purchase to create the world's first expat retiree community. That same day he closed on the deal.

Back then, the idea of moving overseas was far from mainstream and even those ahead of the curve were following more familiar trails to Mexico or Costa Rica. Selling up in the U.S. to set up home in the highlands of Panama wasn't on most retirees' radars.

But I knew my readers weren't your average retirees and I knew that this developer was on to something big. I reported on the project, named Valle Escondido, in real time and named Boquete the world's best place to retire overseas a year on from my first visit.

The mainstream caught up over time with everyone from the *AARP* to *Fortune* magazine highlighting this little town's big charms. More than two decades on from my recommendation, Boquete is perhaps the world's best-known expat haven. It's home to some 25,000 people, over a fifth of whom are expats primarily from the U.S. and Canada, but a good number of Europeans, too. Living here you'll never want for English-speaking company.

Chiriquí is the breadbasket of Panama, and in Boquete you'll find a selection of local fruits and vegetables available year-round. This is also where some of the best coffee on Earth is produced like the Geisha variety—the world's most famous and most expensive variety.

If you're looking to relocate someplace surrounded by nature, with spring-like weather, a large expat community, and a place where you can try your hand at growing your own fruits and veggies, Boquete is worth your attention.

Boquete may be small, but it has an active social scene and busy calendar of events. The Flower and Coffee Fair is the biggest event of the year here. Local florists and farmers showcase their produce. People from all over the country head over to Boquete for this event.

Boquete Jazz and Blues Festival is another big yearly event and draws local and international acts.

It's also a great place for nature lovers. If you're into hiking, Cerro Artillería trail, the Lost Waterfalls trail, and Piedra del Musgo trail offer the chance to observe Panama's magnificent plant and animal life. Parque El Explorador has five acres of trails with stunning views of coffee plantations and mountains. You'll see hundreds of kinds of flowers in as many colors, streams and ponds, nurseries, eclectic and quirky sculptures, and recycled car license plates painted with motivational quotes.

Though the cost of living is rising rapidly in Boquete, it's still more affordable than the United States and Canada. A couple should budget about $2,400 a month for their new life in Boquete.

As with anywhere, though, your cost of living will depend on the lifestyle you choose. If you rent a casita, shop in local markets, and use public transport, you could get by on a little less. If you choose to live in a large villa, dine out often, run a car, buy imported goods, and enjoy mornings on the golf course or afternoons at the spa, your monthly budget will easily exceed $5,000.

You can rent a two-bedroom apartment for $1,250, and utilities like electricity, gas, and water will cost you about $140 a month. Budget $400 a month on entertainment if you plan on eating out twice a week, have drinks twice a week, plus other social activities. Groceries will cost you $400 a month for basic items. These are all costs for a couple. Household help will run $12 per hour.

Wander through the Boquete Tuesday Market where you'll find all kinds of locally sourced fruits and vegetables, prepared foods, meats, and artisanal crafts for less. It's held weekly at the fairgrounds and is an ideal way to get acquainted with the Boquete community.

For those looking to buy, property prices range widely depending on location and amenities. A modest two-bedroom home can cost about $150,000, while luxury properties in gated communities like Valle Escondido run from $350,000 and up.

As for health care, Clínica Especializada del Dr. Chen is a private clinic and the preferred choice among expats. Another private option is the Policlínica de Boquete. A general appointment at a private clinic will cost between $20 and $50.

Boquete's clinics are reliable for regular check ups, minor emergencies and wounds, suturing, and other conditions that don't require surgery or specialized care. For serious emergencies, specialized care, and treatments for any underlying or preexisting conditions, seek care in David (about 45 minutes away).

Boquete also has public and private dentists. You'll pay $20 to $25 for a cleaning at a private clinic and no more than $40 for a filling or other specialized treatment.

Boquete is the only destination in Panama where you can thrive with no Spanish. Almost everyone working in the service industry—in hotels, restaurants, tour agencies, grocery stores, etc.—speaks English proficiently. The only time it's truly necessary to speak Spanish here is if you're having housework done. Many gardeners, maids, plumbers, and handymen don't speak English.

Boquete's climate is one of its biggest draws. Perched at an altitude of about 3,900 feet, the town enjoys a mild, spring-like climate year-round. Daily temperatures typically range from 65°F to 75°F (18°C to

23°C), making it a haven for those looking to escape extreme heat or bitter cold.

Boquete is peaceful and safe. Violent crime is essentially unheard of, and offenses are limited to random petty thefts.

This town has everything you could want for your retirement lifestyle... and it's for all those reasons and more it's the place we've named the world's best for an overseas retirement in 2026 in our annual Overseas Retirement Index.

Veraguas Province

Veraguas Province is an emerging haven for expats and retirees who seek an affordable, culturally rich lifestyle that's mostly tranquil but offers a hint of adventure.

This is the heart of Panama, and it's full of incredible landscapes, from secluded beaches to virgin rain forests to verdant highlands. It's the only province in the country with coastlines on both the Pacific Ocean and the Caribbean Sea, so it's not surprising that some of Panama's most beautiful beaches are found here.

Located in Panama's Azuero Peninsula, the drive from Panama City takes anywhere from five to eight hours. You could also choose to fly to one of the regional airports on the eastern side of the Azuero Peninsula, or the one in Santiago, the capital of Veraguas Province.

Veraguas is ideal for expats who want to escape the hustle and bustle of urban living and just get away from it all, surrounded by the best of nature. Here, the troubles of the rest of the world feel far away and unimportant.

There are a scattering of towns and villages across the province that offer different lifestyles. Los Islotes, at the southwestern tip of the Azuero Peninsula, is a one-of-a-kind option. It's a private residential community spread out over 215 acres of undulating terrain, multiple beaches, far-reaching views, and five-star amenities.

Los Islotes is our passion project, and along with my husband, Lief, we're layering amenities and conveniences of 21st-century living over the best that Mother Nature can offer. Los Islotes is my forever beach, the one I plan to grow old with... where Lief and I have committed to a lifelong legacy of creating a private escape on a secret shore.

Another place to settle on Veraguas' Pacific Coast is Santa Catalina, an expat town that features colorful houses, golden-sand beaches with surfable waves, and a friendly community made up of people from all over the world. Santa Catalina is the base for explorations of Coiba National Park, a UNESCO World Heritage Site that's home to remarkable flora and fauna.

Entertainment options in Veraguas are limited to going out for meals at local- and expat-run bars and restaurants, shopping at malls or open-air markets, and attending local festivals and events.

This is a place for self-starters—people who can entertain themselves or are content with a simple, low-key lifestyle. You won't find museums, theater performances, or many live shows, for example.

Veraguas' natural world is spectacular, so for nature lovers, there's no better place to be based.

Some of Panama's most pristine beaches are found here thanks to the dual Pacific and Caribbean coastlines. Los Islotes, Mariato, and Santa Catalina are some of the most-loved beach spots, with long, uninterrupted sandy stretches and surfable waves.

Go to Coiba National Park to snorkel or scuba dive where you might spot humpback whales, hammerhead sharks, turtles, manta rays, whale sharks, and more.

The interior of the province is covered by dense rain forest that's ideal for hiking and trekking. Cerro Hoya National Park and the hills around Santa Fe are popular places to commune with nature and see wildlife like toucans, monkeys, and even jaguars. Birdwatchers come to see rare scarlet macaws and harpy eagles.

The economic and cultural center of Veraguas is Santiago, the capital and biggest city. If you settle in Veraguas, you'll inevitably visit Santiago often—any time you need to achieve an administrative task or run an errand. Santiago has amenities like hospitals, supermarkets, malls, and more. It's convenient and charming in some sections, but not many expats opt to settle here.

Regardless of where in Veraguas you settle, you'll be surrounded by incredible nature, including virgin forest and unspoiled beaches. Plus you'll have the safety, space, and privacy to live your life according to your own rules.

Costs of living in Veraguas Province vary wildly depending on the size of your house and your lifestyle. The average cost of living for two people is about $2,200. The most common type of rental you'll find is small, Panamanian-style homes, which rent for $500 to $1,000 per month.

To cool your home using air conditioning (something you'll definitely want), you'll pay anywhere from $200 to $450 per month, depending on the size of your home and how often you run it.

For internet, you'll pay $55 per month for Starlink, which recently arrived in the province and provides super-fast and reliable connections.

Groceries can be expensive, depending on where you shop. At open-air markets, you can buy bags of fresh produce for next to nothing. At Costco-style superstores that sell imported products, a couple's grocery bill could easily be $1,000 per month.

Veraguas is a big region with diverse geography, so it has multiple climate zones, each with their own weather conditions. If you don't like the weather in one area, you can drive an hour or so in another direction and find completely different weather.

It's hard to summarize the entire province's climate, but generally, you can expect warm weather and high humidity year-round. The rainy season is May to November, when the downpours can be significant. Dry season is from December to April.

Panama has excellent medical facilities where most health care needs can be taken care of to a high standard... but they're in Panama City.

Locally, you'll find public hospitals and private clinics scattered across the province. Public health care is affordable, but facilities and equipment are basic, and wait times are often long.

Private clinics provide care for everyday ailments and offer faster access to care, plus better facilities and a higher probability of English-speaking doctors.

The biggest public hospital, Luis "Chicho" Fábrega Hospital, offering general and emergency care, is in Santiago. It can treat most ailments, but if you have a serious medical condition, Veraguas may not be the right choice.

You'll need to speak Spanish to live in Veraguas Province. You might encounter the odd local who speaks a smattering of English, but for most day-to-day things, you'll need to take the initiative language-wise. Veraguas offers a real-deal authentic Panamanian experience, which means that Spanish is a must.

There's a range of options when it comes to community: you can settle into an established expat town (like Santa Catalina or Torio), or you can settle into a remote area with no other expats for miles.

In an expat town, you'll socialize with people from back home. You'll make connections quickly, but you may end up discussing the same old stuff that you did back home—politics, the economy, etc.

In a remote area with no other expats, your life will look completely different to your life back home. You'll have to work harder to make friends with your local neighbors, and you may not have as much in common with them, for better or for worse.

Public transportation consists of small buses that connect cities and towns, but services can be unreliable. You'll want your own car to live well in Veraguas.

Veraguas has a rural, small-town feel. Locals are friendly and look out for one another. There's a bit of petty crime, particularly if you have a vacation house that you leave unattended for months at a time. You can avoid problems by burglar-proofing your home or hiring a caretaker.

In Veraguas, you'll have the safety, space, and privacy to live your life according to your own rules.

Health Care In Panama

The standard of care in Panama's public system is decent, but in the private system, it's exceptional.

As an expat, you'll almost certainly choose to be cared for in the private system by enrolling in a low-cost insurance plan.

Panama's best medical facilities are in Panama City... But all over the country there are high-quality public and private hospitals and clinics, with more to come.

Panama's health care system has three levels, giving people options. And, expats can access quality care at MINSA facilities, but the private hospitals are excellent and offer services on par with those in the U.S. or Europe.

Panama City is home to Punta Pacífica Hospital, the only hospital in Latin America affiliated with and managed by Johns Hopkins Medicine International. Other renowned hospitals can be found in the city, for example, Punta Paitilla Hospital, which is generally less expensive than Punta Pacífica.

Like everything, medical costs are higher in Panama City than elsewhere in the country, but, even in the capital, a doctor's visit costs $50 or less.

Private health insurance and prescription drugs are readily available and much less expensive than their U.S. equivalents. American private health insurance policies are accepted in some Panamanian hospitals.

Throughout the country you'll find dentists, orthodontists, optometrists, physical therapists, massage therapists, and more.

Alternative therapies have been popular in Panama for centuries. Today, herbal medicine, indigenous medicine, and traditional medicines and therapies are as prevalent in Panama as modern medicine. You'll find many homeopaths, homeopathic pharmacies, acupuncturists, and chiropractors (most of whom are trained in the States).

Residency Requirements

Panama offers a wide range of unique and enticing residency options, including investor visas and innovative new programs like its digital nomad visa.

Its retiree-specific visa, the Pensionado Visa, is the gold standard of retirement visas, providing special perks like discounts on hotel stays, doctors' bills, and more.

Here are three of your best residency options in Panama:

Friendly Nations Visa

This program was designed for citizens of countries that maintain strong economic and professional ties with Panama. The list includes the United States, Canada, the U.K., much of the EU, Australia, and dozens of others.

When we applied, the Friendly Nations Visa granted immediate permanent residency upon approval. That made it especially attractive. With proof of economic ties (at the time, that included forming a company, employment, or other professional connection) you could move directly into permanent resident status.

That has since changed.

In 2021, the program was restructured. Today, applicants are granted temporary residency first, typically for two years, before becoming eligible to apply for permanent residency.

This is an important lesson: residency programs evolve. Governments tighten requirements, minimum investments increase, categories disappear altogether. If you're considering applying, don't assume today's terms will still be available tomorrow.

Currently, to qualify for the Friendly Nations Visa, you must demonstrate economic ties through one of three routes:

- Employment with a Panamanian company

- A real estate purchase of at least $200,000
- A fixed-term deposit of at least $200,000 in a Panamanian bank for a minimum of three years

You'll also need a clean criminal record, proof of good health, and standard identity documentation. Spouses and dependent children can be included.

Despite the changes, it remains one of the most popular residency pathways in Panama.

The Pensionado Visa

If you're retired or planning to be, Panama's Pensionado Visa may be even more attractive.

This program grants permanent residency upon approval to those with a lifetime pension income of at least $1,000 per month. U.S. Social Security qualifies, as well as many private and government pensions.

If you own property in Panama valued at $100,000 or more, the income requirement can drop to $750 per month.

You can include dependents with an additional $250 per month per person.

The Pensionado program is also famous for its benefits, which include:

- A one-time duty-free import of household goods and a vehicle
- 50% movies, concerts, and entertainment
- Up to 30% off public transportation
- 25% off airline tickets
- 30% to 50% off hotel rates
- 25% discount on restaurants
- 20% off medical consultations

- As well as additional discounts on utilities, professional services, and certain financial products.

The Qualified Investor Visa

With a real estate investment of at least $300,000, you can qualify for permanent residency in as little as 30 days.

We've invested in real estate in 24 countries and we've invested more in Panama than anywhere else. The reason is simple: This market offers opportunity across multiple property investment classes from pre-construction and tourist rentals to historic restorations, land banking, and more.

If you're not a retiree looking for a second home but instead looking for a Plan B residency destination through a profitable investment opportunity, Panama should, again, be on your list.

Real Estate Restrictions

You can legally own property in Panama as a foreigner and have the same legal rights as Panamanians in property ownership. Panama also offers a golden visa with a property investment option to encourage foreign buyers.

That said, foreigners are subject to a few restrictions... You cannot own land within 6 miles (10 kms) of international borders or islands under the jurisdiction of Panama.

Special laws apply to rights of possession land, which requires extra due diligence on the buyer's part. Rights of possession land must be owned by a Panamanian for two years before it can be sold to a foreigner. After two years, it can be titled and sold again without restriction.

Neither Panamanians nor foreigners can purchase property located within *comarcas*, which are sovereign indigenous reserves.

Taxes

Panama is one of the world's most tax-friendly countries. It's a tax haven and only taxes its residents on locally sourced income. Relocating here is an opportunity to minimize your tax burden.

Capital gains tax applies to real estate sales. There are two options to calculate this tax: you can pay 10% of the taxable base (the difference between the purchase and sale value) or pay 3% of the taxable base (the sale or cadastral value). There are no net wealth or worth taxes in Panama, nor are there inheritance, estate, or gift taxes.

CHAPTER 3

BELIZE

Welcome to a country full of diversity, from its people to its natural environments. Belize may be small and may not be well-known to the outside world, but don't underestimate the country. You could say this small-fry rookie packs a big punch.

The combination of Central America and the Caribbean unique to Belize is unlike anywhere else. Once you experience the laid-back lifestyle, cost of living, and welcoming people, you'll have a hard time saying no to Belize.

The unmeddlesome government and financial jurisdictions may also provide the opportunity for investment. Although not for everyone, Belize is all about finding the right fit for each individual.

Belize is a small country. A land mass of 8,867 square miles makes it roughly the same size as Massachusetts. The country is approximately 180 miles from north to south and 70 miles from east to west. Although small in size, it is rather diverse in environment. The northern half of the country is more flatlands whereas the southern half is a low mountain range.

The Maya Mountains, as they are known, reach a little over 3,500 feet above sea level at their highest.

Just offshore from the mainland, Belize has the second-largest barrier reef in the world, including the famous underwater atoll known as the Great Blue Hole.

Belize is divided into six districts: Belize District, Cayo District, Corozal District, Orange Walk District, Stann Creek District, and Toledo District.

This little country is a true melting pot of races, cultures, and socioeconomic classes. A total population of only 397,000, and yet Belize is extremely diverse. Mestizo, Creole, Garifuna, and Maya are the largest subsets of peoples and, as if these weren't overflowing with cultural richness, add in Germans, Chinese, East Indians, Lebanese, Palestinians, North Americans, British, and South Africans. Instead of clashing, all things blend together to take on a new identity—Belizean.

Since 2005, the rate of expats leaving their home country behind and putting roots in Belize has been on the rise. But with more than a few people who like to fly under the radar, it is likely there are more than are accounted for. This gringo population is substantial and increasing as it becomes easier for interested foreigners to see others paving the way.

Belizeans are extremely welcoming people. They will want to get to know you; they will want to be your friend. For the vast majority this is simply genuine and without ulterior motives.

Belizeans enjoy life. The people are honest and hardworking and take pride in everything. They are proud of their country, community, family, and home, but it is a humble pride. Life is simple and good.

You'll know you have begun converting to Belizean life when your habits and approach to life begin to change. Maybe you'll take a nap, a siesta, during the hottest part of the day. Or maybe you'll discover the joy of preparing a meal including fish you've caught and fresh-picked fruit.

But Belize also draws people in for practical reasons. English is the official language, so there's no need to struggle with a language barrier. Locals speak English as well as Spanish and Kriol at home. Its currency, the Belizean dollar, is fixed to the U.S. dollar at a rate of 2:1 (BZ$2 = US$1).

It also uses common law, it has a stable government, and it's part of both the British Commonwealth and the Caribbean Community (CARICOM).

Its visa options are some of the most user-friendly in the world, including its retiree-specific visa that comes with special perks and incentives (like the ability to import your household effects without paying duty fees).

Belize is also a tax haven, with extremely tax-friendly policies for retirees and other residents whose income is sourced from outside the country.

Just a handful of decades ago, only scuba divers, sport anglers, and independent free spirits were attracted to Belize. Back then, Belize was pretty rough around the edges. And both Belizeans and expat residents preferred it that way...

Nowadays, Belize is a haven for everyone from software millionaires to humble farmers, retirees to world-famous movie directors, volunteers to eco-adventurers.

The common denominator among these people from diverse walks of life is the desire for a simpler, freer, more private way of life. With everything going on in the world these days, Belize's back-to-basics lifestyle is almost irresistibly appealing...

Top Picks For A New Life In Belize

Ambergris Caye

Ambergris Caye is a slice of Caribbean heaven—perfect for retirees who seek a relaxing tropical lifestyle in the sun.

Here, shorts and flip-flops are the standard attire, neighbors wave hello to each other as they walk down the street, and people wake up to the sound of waves gently lapping white-sand beaches every day.

The stress and worries of the rest of the world feel far away and unimportant. Instead, a laid-back atmosphere pervades...

At 26 miles long and 1 mile wide, Ambergris is Belize's biggest island, found just offshore from the mainland. It's surrounded by clean turquoise waters that invite you in for long swims and water sports—snorkeling, diving, boating, fishing, and more.

The island's eastern side is flanked by the Belize Barrier Reef—the longest reef in the Western Hemisphere. It protects Ambergris from rough waters and provides a safe haven for countless marine species.

On land, San Pedro is the main settlement and hub of activity on the island. This colorful, quirky little town combines local charm with modern conveniences. It boasts open-air bars and restaurants, art galleries, wine shops, and bakeries.

It's also where the majority of Ambergris's expat community is based. The island is a mini melting pot, home to people from Latin America, the States and Canada, Europe, Asia, the Middle East, and beyond. This diversity is reflected in the variety of dining and entertainment options available in San Pedro.

The main appeal of a Caribbean island like Ambergris Caye is the lazy, laid-back beach lifestyle. But there's more to do here than just hang out in your hammock.

San Pedro is the beating heart of Ambergris Caye. It has beach bars and restaurants, art galleries, wine shops, and bakeries. There are no fast-food franchises, U.S. clothing store outlets, or Cancun-esque, Caribbean-themed establishments. Ambergris is the real deal—the prototype of all those themed restaurants.

Day-to-day life is familiar, friendly, and informal. Entertainment consists of potlucks, live music, and happy hours on the beach. There isn't much to offer in terms of highbrow entertainment—no opera, orchestra, or fine art museums, for instance.

With warm weather, sunshine, and the sea, Ambergris Caye is perfect for outdoor recreation. The Caribbean Sea is at your fingertips. You can go for walks or swim at white-sand beaches with clear waters on any given day.

You can snorkel and scuba dive at the Belize Barrier Reef. The Great Blue Hole, a collapsed underwater cave, is a once-in-a-lifetime snorkel and dive spot.

Boating, fishing, sailing, and most other water sports are very popular among Ambergris residents. Sailing is excellent, and there are plenty of sheltered places to take a break and enjoy a snorkel or dive with turtles and stingrays. Sportfishing for tarpon, snapper, grouper, barracuda, and other species is huge.

On land, there are sports bars where you can catch the game... or partake in quirky live sports. Ever seen a hermit crab race? You can at Crazy Canucks Beach Bar.

If you like golf, the 18-hole Greg Norman-designed White Shark Golf Course is a short boat ride away.

Island living is always going to be more expensive than mainland living because all goods and consumer items need to be imported—in Ambergris Caye's case, by barge. These extra logistics incur extra expenses. The average monthly cost of living for two is $3,320.

Ambergris Caye is also Belize's top tourism destination, so prices are often geared to that market. Day-to-day prices are comparable to what you might spend in small-town Canada or the U.S., but they're a bargain compared to other Caribbean islands, like Turks and Caicos or Barbados.

Rent can vary from $1,000 to $2,500 per month depending on the style of home and proximity to the beach. Utility bills are impacted by how often you use your air conditioning.

The most reliable method on Ambergris Caye to find a long-term rental is word of mouth. Book a short-term rental for a month or two, get out in town, talk with your server, other diners in a restaurant, or the people working at the gate to a community... they will know about available units. Facebook groups will occasionally have postings as well.

Groceries can be expensive if you shop for imported goods rather than local ones. Imported goods from the U.S. carry a hefty duty on top of their travel costs, and if they come in a refrigerated container, it's even more exorbitant. For example, a pint of Ben & Jerry's ice cream is going to be $22 to $26. Oreos and Cheez-Its are $20 to $24. Transversely, a pint of Western Dairies Ice Cream from the mainland is only $8.

Costs vary widely when dining out. If you "live like a local" and enjoy rice and beans with stewed chicken, expect to pay $12 at a stall or small restaurant and $15 at a larger restaurant or one with a view.

Local breakfasts like fry jacks (a deep-fried flour tortilla stuffed with cheese, refried beans, and pulled chicken) can be had for under $8, or four small pork or chicken rolled tacos for $3. On the flip side, just like at the grocery, if you order meals that have imported ingredients like fancy cheeses, quality steak, or out-of-season vegetables, a dinner will easily run $70 to $100 per entrée.

Wines are expensive, too—a bottle of basic wine will be $26 to $32 in a grocery store here and higher in a restaurant. A local rum drink can be had during Happy Hour for $3 to $5 and $5 to $7 the rest of the day.

To get around the island, most expats opt to rent a golf cart on a long-term basis, which costs about $500 per month. If you use taxis instead, you'll pay about $275 per month. You can also easily get around on a bicycle.

If cold weather is not your cup of tea, you will bask in Ambergris Caye's tropical climate; you can depend on temperatures between 75°F and 95°F year-round and a comfortable water temperature in the low- to mid-80s.

It is sunny most days and humid—you will appreciate the trade winds off of the Caribbean Sea. There aren't "four seasons" that you find in a moderate climate; instead, there's a "wet season" (May to October) and "dry season" (November to April). Even when it rains, it seldom does so all day—a brief rain shower may roll through, then clear up to a beautiful, sunny day.

Belize experiences a small number of hurricanes compared to other Caribbean islands. Only about 5% of hurricanes that form in the Caribbean ever make landfall on Belize.

Health care standards on Ambergris Caye have improved greatly since a private hospital, Ambergris Hope, opened its doors in February 2024. It offers a range of services including an operating theater, CT scan, and ultrasound. It offers 24-hour emergency care and has radiology and X-ray services and a pharmacy and dental clinic.

Two miles north of the bridge, you will find San Pedro Urgent Care, which is open Tuesdays through Saturdays, 8 a.m. to 5 p.m. A general consultation is $69, and walk-ins are welcome. Specialists visit occasionally.

The Dr. Otto Rodriguez San Pedro Polyclinic II is just south of town, by the Tropic Air Cargo Depot. It is a walk-in, government-funded clinic where care (including dental) and medicines are free for residents.

For dental services, a routine cleaning will be around $120 to $150, and a tooth extraction is about $150 in most private clinics. The island has a handful of dentists who can perform root canals and offer orthodontics.

Unfortunately, a person with limited mobility will struggle on Ambergris Caye. There is no handicapped parking in town, nor are there more than a few ramps into buildings; the roads are cobblestone or dirt in many areas, so using a walker or wheelchair is difficult.

Belize has been popular with U.S. and Canadian expats for decades. It's a well-established expat haven, and Ambergris Caye is its most popular destination. If you're looking for a place where it's easy to settle in socially, Ambergris Caye could be it.

The population is about 20,000 people, and about 15% of that number are expats. Most expats come from the States and Canada, but there are also some folks from Europe, South Africa, the Middle East, and Asia. An array of restaurants, bars, and shops reflects the diversity of the expat community and keeps life interesting for residents.

Opportunities to socialize abound, from charity meetings and rallies to barbecues and house parties. Ambergris Caye Community group on Facebook is a good place to connect with people, ask questions, and find out about upcoming events.

It's easy to reach Ambergris Caye from the States and Canada with plenty of quick direct flights to Belize City's Philip S.W. Goldson International Airport. To get to Ambergris Caye from there, you can take a ferry or "puddle jumper" (small plane).

Locals say that Ambergris is the safest place in all of Belize. There's little risk of violent crime, but petty crime is possible if you're not mindful of your possessions.

Don't make it easy for would-be petty thieves by leaving your cell phone and wallet on your towel when you go for a swim. With common-sense precautions, you should be able to avoid trouble.

You'll love Ambergris Caye if you are looking for a gentle transition to expat life. You won't have to learn a new language, deal with fluctuating exchange rates, or experience drastic cultural changes.

Cayo

In the Cayo District of Belize, the burdens, stresses, and concerns of the rest of the world feel far away and unimportant...

It doesn't take long for any other reality you've brought with you to fade once you get here...

The Cayo District is a rugged, sprawling region of the Belize mainland that's full of rivers and rain forests, as well as rustic small towns and villages with strong community spirit.

It has long held a kind of mystique... Its rich history dates back thousands of years to the Maya empire, with relics and ruins strewn about the vast natural landscape.

Today, Cayo's population is made up of an eclectic community of expats and locals who appreciate space, freedom, privacy, the outdoors, and back-to-basics values.

The biggest of Belize's six districts, the Cayo is paradise for nature lovers, containing some of the country's best opportunities for exploring rivers, caves, mountains, tropical forests, and wide-open spaces, including several nature reserves.

It has a scattering of small towns and villages—San Ignacio town is the nucleus. Over the years, it has developed from middle-of-nowhere outpost to charming, well-appointed hub.

It's home to a town square lined with boutiques, restaurants, and cafés, tour companies, and real estate agencies, as well as a pedestrianized thoroughfare. It's a market town, with lively fruit and vegetable markets a few days per week, and it's the commercial center of the country.

This is a benefit because it offers the widest selection of goods and materials... which can be difficult to source in other parts of Belize.

San Ignacio offers an unmatched level of convenience.

Just down the road from San Ignacio is Carmelita Gardens, an eco-focused community made up of a couple dozen expats with a shared interest in simple, self-sufficient living.

Many choose to live here because they appreciate the down-to-earth nature of the place... It doesn't take long to become a part of the community in the Cayo...

You'll soon know the shop owners, farmers, schoolteachers, yoga instructors, artists, and your expat neighbors. A friendly smile and nod of the head are the standard greetings around here.

The Cayo is rural, and its appeal lies in its simplicity... It lacks formal or organized cultural entertainment options.

Your options for entertainment include down-home events like community art shows, cultural heritage festivals, Christmas tree lightings, open-mic nights at bars, and the like.

For a dose of history, there is a scattering of ancient Maya archaeological sites nearby, but not much by way of museums.

One way to connect with local culture is to try the local cuisine. Popular local dishes include corn-based recipes like *tostadas, garnaches*, and *salbutes*. You can try these at any mom-and-pop restaurant, which are plentiful in Cayo.

Cayo provides unlimited opportunities to get active, with wide-open spaces, country roads, and river access around every bend.

Swimming, tubing, floating, and kayaking in the river are top pastimes. Plus, sandy beaches and the bright blue waters of the Caribbean Sea are just a few hours' drive away.

On land, you can trek, horseback ride, or garden. This is a horticulturalist's dream location and a great place to go off-grid or become self-sufficient with your food supply.

All of Belize is a bird-watching mecca, with Crooked Tree Wildlife Sanctuary being a world-class bird-watching destination.

There are organized sports, like La Ruta Maya (a canoe marathon), as well as running and cycling events throughout the year.

Cayo has a relatively low cost of living. The average cost of living for two is $2,000. One reason why you're likely to reduce your spending is that there's not much to spend on: there are no malls, outlets, or big shopping centers.

That said, certain things, like electricity, fuel, and electronics, cost more in Cayo than in the States. Other things (water, internet, and basic utilities) cost much less.

Your monthly grocery bill, if you shop for local products, will be about $400 a month. You could rent a two-bedroom home with Western finishes for $800 a month. Electricity costs $49 to $150 depending on air-conditioning use, an internet and cable bundle will cost $70, and monthly entertainment for a couple would be about $250.

You'll likely need a car in this rural, sprawling part of Belize. The alternatives are taxis or informal buses.

You'll go through an adjustment period as you learn where to find local alternatives to the products you normally buy.

The Cayo District is warm all year, with slightly cooler, less humid weather than the rest of the country thanks to breezes coming off of the Maya Mountains.

You could get by without air conditioning since most houses in Belize are designed to be self-cooling, but you'll be more comfortable with air conditioning.

Rainy season hits Cayo from June to November. Dry season is November to May.

Cayo is fortunate to have one of the best private hospitals, La Loma Luz, and one of the newest public hospitals, San Ignacio Hospital. While the private facilities charge more than the public facilities, the cost is low. Many generalists and specialists also have private offices.

No need to grapple with a language barrier here. Many locals also speak Spanish and Belizean Creole, an English-based Creole language.

Cayo's expat community is a mixture of North American retirees, young adventurous homesteaders, and Brits who served in the army in years past.

Here, socializing and integrating into the expat community come easy. Casual social events are always on, from volunteer groups to women's groups to hang-outs at the local pub.

Belize is about as close to the States and Canada as you can get—so close you can drive here. The international airport in Belize City offers plenty of direct flights to both countries. You'll need to drive for about two hours to get to Cayo from Belize City.

Belize has a negative reputation for crime, but much of the commentary and statistics come from Belize City. The crime that takes place there doesn't affect the average person living in Belize.

Cayo in particular is a safe, quiet region. Petty crime can be an issue if you're careless—for instance, if you leave your bicycle on your front lawn overnight... there's a possibility it won't be there when you wake up. Basic precautions can curb most issues.

Whether you plan to relocate full-time, part-time, rent, buy, start a business, or simply get off the grid and relax a while, Cayo is a great option. It's a largely untouched natural paradise where you can settle into a welcoming community and forget the world's troubles.

Health Care In Belize

Belize's reputation for health care is mixed. Public facilities generally aren't up to expats' standards. They suffer from underfunding, which can mean long wait times, limited services, and outdated equipment.

Private facilities offer higher standards, and many expats feel comfortable and confident having their health care needs met in Belize. This will depend on your needs and preferences. Some expats maintain national health coverage from back home and travel back when needed. Others travel to Mexico, right next door, where there's a wider range of facilities.

In Belize City, you find a range of facilities, including the biggest hospital in the country, Karl Heusner Memorial Hospital as well as modern, private facilities including Belize Medical Associates and Belize Healthcare Partners.

For a general doctor visit you'll pay around $25, a consultation with a specialist will be around $35, and a routine dental cleaning will be about $30.

Life insurance companies in Belize offer plans to expats for both local and regional coverage at reasonable rates. We recommend that your policy covers emergency air evacuation. In the event of a serious emergency, the nearest port of entry to the States is Miami, Florida, which is an hour flight by air ambulance.

Residency Requirements

Belize offers an excellent retirement visa through its Qualified Retirement Program (QRP). It's one of the most user-friendly visa programs in the world.

The basic requirements are that you're at least 45 years old and earn $2,000 per month. It also comes with perks, like exemptions on import duty for household effects.

The downside to the QRP is that it does not lead to permanent residency.

The cost to gain QRP Status includes a $150 program application fee per person; $1,000 program fee per person or $750 per dependent (can be a spouse); ID Card ($200 per card); and the annual renewal fee is $25 per card. These fees must be paid in U.S. currency.

In order to gain citizenship, you must have permanent residency for five years. In that time, you cannot have been out of the country for more than 30 consecutive days or have accumulated more than three months out of Belize over a 12-month period.

Real Estate Restrictions

No restrictions are imposed on foreigners when it comes to buying property in Belize. Belize allows foreigners to own property outright, and with contracts written in English, the terms are easy to understand. Bank financing is not offered to non-Belizeans, although some properties offer seller or developer financing. As they say, "cash is king."

Taxes

Income tax is only due on income earned in Belize, regardless of your residency status. Income can be from employment, business ownership, or investment and rental vehicles. Belize will not levy taxes on foreign-earned income.

Belize has a flat-tax system, rather than income brackets. Should you earn more than $26,000 per year, income tax is assessed at a flat 25%. If your income is under $26,000, no tax is due.

Value-added tax, or VAT, is essentially sales tax on goods and services. This rate is 12.5%.

There is no wealth tax, inheritance tax, or capital gains tax in Belize.

Belize doesn't have a tax treaty or totalization with the U.S., so you will be liable to pay taxes in both countries, as well as contribute to Social Security in the U.S. and Belize. Check with your U.S. accountant; your tax payments in Belize may be able to offset what you owe in the States.

Property taxes are incredibly low—about $600 per year for a small villa.

III

SOUTH AMERICA

South America offers a host of lifestyle options for the retiree.

Your choices include Spanish-colonial old towns bursting with culture, laid-back Caribbean beach locales, vibrant cosmopolitan cities... even a wine-growing region where you could own your own vineyard.

This region of the world has safe cities, developed infrastructure, unspoiled culture, good health care, easy residency, and friendly people—all combining to create an idyllic lifestyle overseas. Your cost of living will be affordable too—as little as $1,800 a month for a couple.

In the top retirement destinations featured below, you could spend your days skiing, hiking, playing golf, bird-watching, kayaking, or swimming in tepid Caribbean waters. Or maybe you'd prefer to live in a big city full of colonial charm, with tons of culture, bustling markets, trendy cafés, restaurants, and shops.

These kinds of experiences are already a reality for millions of expats...

No matter what kind of lifestyle you're after... No matter what size budget you have to play with... There's a place with your name on it in South America.

CHAPTER 4

ARGENTINA

Economic issues aside, Argentina has a lot going for it. The capital, Buenos Aires is one of the world's best cities. It would draw people to the country even if it were the only city in Argentina.

Entrepreneurs claim that it's a great place for hiring a workforce, with its skilled, highly educated population. (College education is free in Argentina.)

And entrepreneurs also claim that Argentina is in the perfect time zone for doing business with the U.S. and Europe. At GMT-3, they're two hours ahead of New York, and three hours behind London.

Argentina is crypto-friendly, currently enjoying a high adoption rate, wide acceptance, and legal recognition.

If you're pursuing citizenship, Argentina has a strong passport, with visa-free entry to most of the world's countries.

The country is intrinsically beautiful, with an extremely diverse landscape. From the snow-capped Andes, to world-class wine regions, to the high deserts of the north, and several first-world, livable cities... plus 2,900 miles of Atlantic coastline.

Argentina has a strong European influence which sets it apart from other Latin American countries. The culture is predominantly Italian, with 62% of the population of Italian ancestry.

For wine lovers, it's a wine and culinary paradise with reasonable prices for an elegant lifestyle.

The cost of living is low, with properties being an exceptional bargain.

You'll spend a fraction of what life would cost you in the U.S. or Canada.

Top Picks For A New Life In Argentina

Buenos Aires

Buenos Aires, the bustling capital city of Argentina, is home to over 15 million people and is a veritable melting pot of cultures.

Most people here have European origins, mainly from Spain and Italy. Buenos Aires also has one of the largest Jewish communities in the world, as well as a substantial Chinese population.

All of these cultures come together here under the blue and white flag of Argentina with the Sun of May in the middle—a reference to the day the sun poked through the clouds in May of 1810 at the start of the War of Independence.

The name Buenos Aires translates as "fair winds," dating back to the arrival of the Spanish conquistadors in the 16th century.

These days, you'll hear people refer to the city as CABA, meaning *Ciudad Autónoma de Buenos Aires* (Autonomous City of Buenos Aires). The city earned its autonomous status through an amendment to the nation's constitution in 1994, allowing residents to elect their own mayor.

Prior to this amendment, the mayor of Buenos Aires was appointed by the President of Argentina.

Residents of CABA are known as *porteños*—the people of the port. This name dates back to the 1880s when a huge wave of European immigrants arrived here via the port.

At the time, the name helped to distinguish this group from the indigenous, mestizo, and criollo populations that already inhabited the city.

Nowadays, everyone embraces the *porteño* identity in this melting pot of a city.

While the city may be named for the "fair winds" that brought early settlers here, it's all about the *buena onda* these days.

That phrase translates as "good vibes," and it's often heard in conversations here. For example, a restaurant or a bar can have a *buena onda*, as can an event like a concert or *fútbol* match.

Sometimes you find the good vibes, and sometimes the good vibes find you...

This city and its residents are passionate and welcoming. Whether it's tango or *fútbol*, Buenos Aires provides that *buena onda* and invites visitors to share in it.

Of course, no place is perfect—especially no urban area crammed with 15 million people.

Buenos Aires, like any other capital city, has its share of problems. During the summer months, the city can be stifling hot, which can lead to power outages.

Protests are also a common occurrence here. Many are upset about the economic situation in the city and country at large. People may be frustrated with their political leaders, but all agree that football legend Lionel Messi is a hero.

As with most cities of this size, which neighborhood you call home in Buenos Aires is crucial to your enjoyment of the place. The city is home to 48 different *barrios*, each with its own unique vibe.

A few blocks can mean a whole new world here, and not always in a good way...

For example, the San Telmo neighborhood is a popular choice among tourists and expats and is generally a safe place.

Meanwhile, neighboring Constitución is one of the most dangerous parts of the city and is best avoided. This isn't the city for aimless wandering, as you do not want to end up in the wrong part of town.

San Telmo is a fun place to live and has a great Sunday market. It's also a quick trip to areas like Puerto Madero and La Boca. La Boca is one of the most popular places to visit in Buenos Aires. Meaning "The Mouth," this port area is one of the oldest neighborhoods in the city. It's famous for its colorful houses that you can admire along the *Caminito* (Little Path)—a traditional alleyway and street museum.

However, while La Boca is fine to visit during the day, it's not the best place to be after dark.

The Recoleta neighborhood gives you easy access to the airport and ferry terminal. It's a more upper-class, conservative area. Staying here is convenient for visiting the art museums and the famous cemetery, but there's not much else going on, and it's more expensive than most areas.

Without a doubt, the top choice for expats, digital nomads, and tourists is Palermo. This is actually a huge neighborhood that's broken up into a few smaller districts, with Soho and Hollywood being the most popular to stay or live in.

Both are trendy areas with tons of cafés, restaurants, shops, bars, and clubs. If you're trying to live the socialite life, look no further than Palermo. That being said, this is, not surprisingly, one of the more expensive addresses you can have in Buenos Aires.

The nearby neighborhood of Villa Crespo is a cheaper option. It's close enough to walk to Palermo Soho, but it's far enough away to have a bit of peace and quiet. Plus, it feels more like you're actually living in Argentina, as there are more locals than tourists.

Here you'll find a metro station, supermarket, money exchange, shops, restaurants, and bars.

Other *barrios* that are close to Palermo and worth your consideration include Chacarita, Colegiales, and Belgrano.

There are plenty of places to find long-term accommodation and a good way to find them is through Facebook and WhatsApp groups. Many posts in these groups are from agents, so you can expect to pay a fee if you work with them.

The local way to rent apartments in Buenos Aires is unfurnished for a period of three years. That's the only way you'll really get a great deal on a place and pay something closer to the local rate than the tourist one.

Money can be a complicated subject in Buenos Aires. If you're arriving with a stash of dollars or euros and leaving a more expensive address, you'll find the cost of living to be quite low here.

Even on Airbnb, you can find a fully furnished studio or small one-bedroom apartment for $600 to $800 a month. If you can commit to three to six months, you can shave a few hundred off that price. Chances are all utilities, including high-speed Wi-Fi, will be included in the rent.

If anything, an extra charge for electricity might be incurred, especially in the hot summer months.

Once you manage to find a SUBE card, your costs for getting around the city will be virtually zero.

Trips on the local buses and metro are heavily subsidized and cost around 25 cents. The public transport system is so extensive that you can go anywhere in the city and surrounding areas with a transfer or two.

Taxis are everywhere here and their rates are very reasonable—typically about $3 to $5 for shorter trips around town and only $10 to $15 for getting to and from the airport. It's about the same price or even a bit less using rideshare apps like Cabify.

The best deal you'll get here, though, is on eating and drinking out. Lunch of a couple of fresh empanadas costs only a few dollars. A rib-eye steak and a few glasses of Malbec in the evening will cost $30 to $40 for two people.

With so much amazing wining and dining to do in this city, you won't have to cook a lot. Supermarket shops will set you back about $150 a month. For little things, there are tons of local markets throughout the city.

You can get a ticket to a new release in a modern cinema here for about $5 to $6 and refreshments are equally affordable.

There are also all kinds of art galleries and music venues, many of which host free events. Places that have a cover charge or minimum spend are usually quite reasonable, including jazz clubs and house music bars.

You can also attend big ticket events here like Lollapalooza, which is affordable compared to its American and European counterparts.

If you want to experience tango dancing in Buenos Aires (and you should), you have a lot of options. There are people dancing in touristy areas like the San Telmo market and restaurants in La Boca. If you enjoy their performance, you can toss some pesos (or dollars) in their tip jar.

You can also visit the city's famous *milongas* where locals gather to dance the night away. Many of them host dance classes early in the evening before the pros arrive, so you can learn a few moves in a relaxed environment.

People here really take their tango seriously, with the most dedicated dancers arriving at the *milongas* well after midnight and dancing well into the morning.

If you're a bit hesitant to hit the dance floor during those busy hours, it's perfectly fine to just sit back and watch. It's quite an impressive performance and one of the quintessential Argentine experiences.

Fútbol is more than a sport in Buenos Aires. It's a way of life. The city is home to 18 professional clubs, including the Big Five of Boca Juniors, River Plate, Independiente, Racing Club, and San Lorenzo.

These teams have supporters not only in Buenos Aires but throughout the country. With so many clubs here, there are games quite often. Attending one is a great way to experience the local culture.

Argentina operates a mixed health care system that combines public hospitals and clinics, government insurance plans, and employer-sponsored plans with private health insurance.

With Argentina's universal health care system, everyone is guaranteed access to public health care, regardless of residency status. Those who can often choose private health insurance providers, as public hospitals are often overwhelmed.

Buenos Aires has excellent health care facilities, both within the public sector and private sector. The city is home to many of Argentina's best hospitals, with top class equipment and English-speaking doctors—many who have trained overseas.

Public hospitals are perfectly fine, but many expats opt to use private hospitals where wait times are way shorter and the cost way cheaper than the U.S. The top private hospitals in the city are Hospital Aleman, Hospital Italiano, and Hospital Britanico.

Buenos Aires is, for the most part, a rather safe place to visit. As with any capital city, it's advisable not to wear flashy clothes or jewelry and don't walk around with cell phones out all the time.

Just keep your wits about you and be aware of your surroundings here. Speaking a little Spanish and wearing an Argentina national team jersey also help you blend in...

Buenos Aires has two main airports serving domestic and international flights. Ministro Pistarini International Airport (Ezeiza Airport, EZE) is the largest and main international airport in Buenos Aires, located about 14 miles (22 kms) southwest of the city center. It serves a wide range of international flights, connecting Buenos Aires with cities across North and South America, Europe, Asia, Africa, and Oceania.

For North Americans, you can find direct flights to EZE from New York (JFK), Dallas-Fort Worth, Houston, and Miami. From Dallas, the flight time is 10 hours.

To get to the city center from the airport you can take a taxi, private transfer, uber, or bus.

The second airport, Aeroparque Jorge Newbery (AEP) is situated about five miles north of downtown Buenos Aires, and serves primarily domestic flights and some regional and international flights within South America. If you plan to do some traveling around Argentina or neighboring countries, you'll likely end up going in and out of AEP. If you're traveling to or from neighboring Uruguay, you can also take the ferry. There are a few companies operating ferries between the two countries, with several options per day.

Buenos Aires has an extensive public transportation system, with commuter trains, buses, and several metro lines. It's efficient and convenient, so long as you can get yourself a SUBE card and figure out the routes. You can buy SUBE cards at the airport, so it's not a bad idea to just grab one there before heading into the city.

It's good to have a working smartphone on the bus so you can check the route. You need to tell the driver your stop when boarding the bus so they know how much to charge you. Just tap your SUBE card, and you're good to go.

Public transportation is generally safe, but there are issues with pickpockets and people stealing phones. Be aware of your surroundings, and don't hold your phone carelessly.

There's also a large network of public bikes in the city called Eco-Bici. You need to download the app and create an account with a payment method, then you can use the app to unlock a bike. There are stations all over the city, so it's definitely an efficient way to get around.

Buenos Aires certainly isn't for everyone, especially in the often brutally hot days of summer. The best months living here are April to June or September to October where you'll enjoy more moderate weather.

If you enjoy the big city life and the excitement that comes with it, from the intensity of the football games to the all-night music festivals, then Buenos Aires could be ideal for you. This is not exactly the city for the peace-and-quiet kind of crowd.

It's a fascinating city to explore, and it's much easier to enjoy it to the fullest when it's not putting a New York-sized dent in your wallet.

For those doing the digital nomad thing or recent retirees who want to get out and see this part of the world, Buenos Aires is a fantastic choice.

Mendoza

Mendoza is Latin America's first wine-growing region, and where vines grow, the living is generally good. Here in the interior of Argentina, food, wine, and interesting conversation are the priorities of life.

This region's laid-back atmosphere, safe cities, developed infrastructure, unspoiled culture, affordable cost of living, and friendly people combine to create an idyllic lifestyle.

This is a good choice for active retirees who aren't ready to sit back and rock on the front porch. You could spend your days skiing, hiking, climbing, playing golf, bird-watching, white-water rafting, kayaking, and even kite-surfing, and your evenings practicing tango.

Mendoza has an effect on people. They come as tourists and end up extending their trip... and eventually decide to make Mendoza their home for good.

It's the name of both a city and a province in northwestern Argentina. Mendoza City offers real cosmopolitan distractions, including five-star restaurants, shopping, and performing arts... But it's not only lively and bustling; it's also livable.

This city's streets are shaded by sycamore and acacia trees, making rambling a pleasure. The whole city is clean and well-kept. Cycling is the preferred mode of transportation.

Malbec and mountains have long been the draws to this part of Argentina, both for investors and visitors. In Mendoza, you'll find more than 350,000 planted acres and 500 wineries that are responsible for two-thirds of total wine production for the entire country...

Mendoza is wine country, and much of the culture and local attractions revolve around its wine industry. It's one of the world's 11 Great Wine Capitals and a growing enotourism destination, known for being the birthplace of Argentinian malbec.

Aside from its wine culture, Mendoza is a historically significant city. It features charming architecture and beautiful plazas in its city center, along with several historical buildings, landmarks, and museums, like the Mendoza Museum of Modern Art and the Wine and Harvest Museum.

Argentina is famous for its *asados*, which are essentially barbecues over open grills. Many of the restaurants in Mendoza serve excellent-quality *asado* meals, which pair perfectly with local malbec. Restaurants range from casual joints to high-end eateries.

This region is famous for its festivals, like the National Grape Harvest Festival in March, which celebrates not only grapes but all harvested fruit. It includes a beauty pageant, a parade, salsa and tango in the city's squares, and fireworks.

For total relaxation, you can indulge in spa treatments in Mendoza and even combine them with wine culture.

Mendoza is a haven for adventure sports and a dream destination for hiking enthusiasts. Set in the foothills of the Andes Mountains, the landscape is perfect for hiking expeditions, mountain biking, cycling, horseback riding, whitewater rafting, camping in mountain bungalows, wind sports, and more.

One way to experience the landscape is to do as the *gauchos* (Argentinian cowboys) do and hop on a horse to explore the hills and valleys. You can arrange day trips or multi-day excursions. Night rides are especially atmospheric and allow for the best view of the stars.

If you feel more comfortable on two wheels than on four legs, this is prime cycling and mountain biking territory. Mendoza is a great city for biking thanks to the Vuelta Ciclistica, the primary road for cyclists. You can even bike from vineyard to vineyard, wine tasting as you go, or go mountain biking in the foothills.

Easy access to the Andes makes Mendoza an important ski destination. The province offers 55 miles (89 kms) of trails, with slopes as high as 11,975 feet (3,650 meters). Outfitters offering all the necessary gear are scattered around the region.

A handful of golf clubs that feature spectacular views is found in the area. Algodon Wine Estates Golf Club combines a golf resort with an Argentinian winery. The championship course plays through the estate's lush vineyards, all against the backdrop of the snow-topped Sierra Pintada Mountain Range.

Other fringe activities that you can do in Mendoza are paragliding in the canyons and valleys, whitewater rafting, and kitesurfing and windsurfing at Potrerillos Dam.

Mendoza has a reputation as one of the cheapest places to live in Argentina, so for North Americans, it's super affordable. The average cost of living for two people per month is about $1,800.

The cost of buying or renting property is a bargain. You can rent a semi-furnished, two-bedroom apartment for $400 to $1,000 per month. Your monthly utilities will be very low—about $30 for electricity, gas, and water. Internet and cell phone will total $44. Budget $400 a month for two for your entertainment and another $320 for your monthly grocery shop. If you own a car, you'll pay about $85 a month.

The city has a fairly well-organized public transport system, so technically you don't need a car (although having one to take full advantage of Argentina's wide-open spaces is recommended). The average bus fare is about 50 cents.

Argentina is famous for beef, empanadas, and red wine, and you can enjoy a good meal out for $10 to $30. A coffee or beer is $2, a movie ticket $10 and a visit to the doctor is $20. Groceries are similarly budget-friendly, with staples like beef, bread, and milk far cheaper than back home.

The catch? Argentina's high inflation and fluctuating peso mean you need to be savvy with money, especially if you're navigating the gap between official and unofficial exchange rates, although recent reforms have narrowed the gap between official and blue dollar (Argentina's informal exchange rate for U.S. dollars used when people buy or sell dollars outside official channels) rates.

There are public hospitals where care is free or low cost, but resources are limited and wait times are long. Most expats prefer to use private clinics like Clínica de Cuyo and Hospital Español. The care is good quality, the equipment is modern, and professionals are well-trained and often speak English.

Hospital Español offers a wide range of services, including emergency care, outpatient consultations in more than 20 specialties (including cardiology, neurology, dermatology, and urology), high complexity diagnostics (imaging, clinical laboratory), and advanced surgical units. A general consultation will cost around $15 to $20.

If you opt for private health insurance, you can have your health care needs taken care of comfortably in Mendoza.

For dental care, there are several well-regarded private clinics in Mendoza offering a full range of services including routine cleanings, fillings, whitening, implants, root canals, and cosmetic work. A routine appointment will cost around $25, a filling will cost around $40, a root canal will be around $100, and a crown around $250 to $300.

Note that certain prescription medications are not available in Argentina's pharmacies because of government limitations on imports. Be sure to fill your prescriptions before coming here.

Mendoza has an arid, four-season climate, although the seasons operate differently than what we're used to in North America. Argentina's summer is from December to March, and winter is from June to September.

Mendoza can get hot in the summer, but low humidity makes conditions more comfortable. Still, you'll probably want both heating and air conditioning at home.

Argentina's English levels are some of the highest in Latin America. The younger generation is the most fluent, as English is a mandatory subject in schools.

That said, you should learn Spanish to live well in Mendoza. This will help you integrate into the local community, which has a reputation for being traditional.

Expats are attracted to Argentina for its cultural richness and natural beauty. Strong foreign investment in the wine, tourism, housing, and hospitality industries has helped develop a small but diverse expat community.

Expats in Mendoza hail from Europe, North America, and beyond. Business opportunities are one of the motivators for relocating here. You can socialize with the help of community groups like Mendoza Expat Community on Facebook, which has 3,500 members. There's also a local InterNations chapter, which organizes meetups and social events.

Mendoza is an agricultural region; it's not as cosmopolitan as Buenos Aires, for example, and locals have a reputation for being traditional and closed off. It might take some time to be accepted by the local community.

There are no direct flights to Mendoza from the States or Canada. To get here, you'll likely fly to Buenos Aires and then catch a domestic flight to Mendoza or connect through a city in another country, like

Panama City, Panama, or Santiago, Chile.

Mendoza is considered safe, and it has a high police presence. There are areas of Mendoza that are best avoided, however, and economic woes may have made opportunists of some people. Be mindful of bag-snatching and pickpocketing.

Violent crime is rare.

Mendoza is best suited to people who want to enjoy the unique lifestyle available... one that's far away from the troubles of the rest of the world where you can sample wine, go on outdoor adventures, and enjoy the blend of natural beauty and sophisticated lifestyle.

Health Care In Argentina

Argentina operates a mixed health care system that combines public hospitals and clinics, government insurance plans, and employer-sponsored plans with private health insurance.

With Argentina's universal health care system, everyone is guaranteed access to public health care, regardless of residency status. Those who can often choose private health insurance providers, as public hospitals are regularly overwhelmed.

Overall, the health care in Argentina is excellent, particularly in Buenos Aires. Hospitals, both public and private, have good quality standards, the equipment is modern, and professionals are well-trained and often speak English (many were trained overseas).

Foreigners are often in awe of how many procedures are covered and provided for free in Argentina. These include dental fillings, extensive prenatal care, surgeries, hospital stays, and more.

You will easily find doctors across all disciplines who are bilingual and practice in English—and some are even proficient in third and fourth languages.

One thing to note is that certain prescription medications are not available in Argentina's pharmacies because of government limitations on imports. Be sure to fill your prescriptions before coming here.

Real Estate Restrictions

As a foreigner, you can buy property in Argentina without any restrictions. To be able to purchase, you'll need a *Clave de Identificación*, or tax ID.

If you're a non-resident, you'll need to appoint a local representative to pay your property tax on your behalf.

Residency Requirements

For visitors from North America, Europe, and Oceania, you're allowed up to 90 days visa-free in Argentina. No need to apply, no need to pay, and no hassles.

The Pensionado Visa (retirement visa) is intended for those who are receiving a stable pension. The required amount is around $1,500 per person. Although the threshold is the same as the Rentista visa (see below), a Pensionado visa is easier to obtain approval for, since the income is guaranteed.

The Rentista Visa is intended for those with passive income from outside Argentina. You'll need an income of around $1,500 per month, per person (including children). This visa does not apply to digital nomads. You must demonstrate that this amount is being transferred into Argentina, routinely, through normal banking channels. You'll need to lay the groundwork for this before applying, so you'll have a history of transfers to show them.

Note: The exact income requirement is five times the minimum wage in Argentine pesos, and subject to exchange rate fluctuations.

Argentina has also joined the ranks of many nations in rolling out a digital nomad visa. This allows you to stay in the country for 180 days and is then renewable for an additional 180, giving you a full year in Argentina.

You need to apply for this visa in advance and prove sufficient income.

There's no specific number given, but we've seen $2,500 per month set as a benchmark.

The process for obtaining residency is fairly simple. Argentina has a valuable passport, and offers several fast paths to citizenship. You must have health insurance to enter Argentina—even as a tourist—and past criminal convictions could cause denial of entry.

Taxes

Residents of Argentina are taxed on their worldwide income, although some foreign pensions are eligible for exemptions.

The provinces of Argentina set their own rates for things like property tax, stamp duty, wealth tax, and so on. Argentina doesn't impose inheritance tax unless you're a resident of Buenos Aires Province, in which case, it's 1.6% to 8% depending on the relationship between benefactor and donor.

A wealth tax is levied on a resident's worldwide assets. This ranges from 0.5% to 1.75% on assets that exceed the threshold ($27.3 million pesos or about $21,000). Assets held abroad are taxed at a higher rate: 0.7% to 2.25%.

CHAPTER 5

COLOMBIA

Colombia is a big country with varied geography and a culture that is far from homogenous.

It's a land of many capitals... Each major Colombian city is known for something unique and offers its own blend of local history, geography, climate, and micro-culture.

For expats, this translates to multiple lifestyle opportunities across the country, from Spanish-colonial environments to Caribbean beach towns to cool-weather cosmopolitan living...

Colombia is a naturally beautiful, unspoiled country. Known for its "megadiversity," it harbors a high number of the Earth's species. Meanwhile, its landscape boasts mountains, rain forests, grasslands, and beaches. The climate is, broadly speaking, warm all year. However, due to the scale of the country, there is a wide variation in temperature. Otherwise, rainy season runs from May to November and dry season through the rest of the year.

The cost of living is low, and you have a huge stock of natural produce to eat. Colombian coffee is among the best in the world. Though it's taking the rest of the world some time to catch on to, Colombia is also much safer now than in the past. Though some rural and ghetto areas still experience drug-related crime, tourist and expat areas are generally as safe as major U.S. cities.

The health care is world-class and low cost—about a quarter of what you'd pay in the United States... and, plenty of English-speaking doctors can be found in most big cities.

Colombia is quietly becoming one of the world's top overseas havens. From bustling cities to Caribbean escapes, this corner of the world is shedding the stigma that has lingered since Pablo Escobar's death over 30 years ago.

Top Picks For A New Life In Colombia

Medellín

Medellín is a high-tech, highly sought-after city. It's been named one of the best places to retire in the world, the most innovative city in the world, and the world's smartest city, to name but a few of its accolades...

What is it about Medellín that has it topping all the charts? It's a combination of its unique infrastructure, well-used and much-loved public spaces, and the accessibility of technology and internet throughout the city...

Medellín is a place where things work—the internet, the Metro, street-cleaning, garbage-collection... you can count on these services day to day. Taxis are metered, shop-keepers are well-mannered, and the people you pass on the street are well-dressed.

Despite being the second-largest city in the country, Medellín's public transit system and infrastructure are superior to those of capital Bogotá. They play an integral role in shaping the fabric of the city and its development by connecting high- and low-income neighborhoods.

Medellín is competitive with the world's best-known metropolises when it comes to cultural entertainment. With modern movie theaters, shopping, vibrant nightlife, impressive galleries, museums, venues for theater and music, plus soccer stadiums... and the intoxicating city-wide attitude toward fitness and health culminating in the weekly pedestrianization of its main avenues, Medellín really does have something for everyone.

With tree-lined streets, and a law that requires creation of a green space equal to the footprint of each new building constructed, Medellín is a big city without the big-city environment. That said, it suffers from poor air quality due to its location at the base of a valley.

This city has a special energy, which emanates from the fun-loving locals, known as *Paisas*. They're undeniably proud of their city and famous for their friendliness.

Paisas are also famous for their colorful regional culture. As an expat, you can experience this culture simply by sticking around for a year and living out its jam-packed events calendar.

In fact, Medellín is Colombia's capital of culture. It offers so much to do, see, and enjoy that it's impossible to be bored here.

The city boasts festivals, fairs, museums commemorating the region's culture and history, galleries, shopping malls and boutiques, and a diverse culinary scene, with everything from laidback local joints to fine dining. It has modern movie theaters with English-language movies and VIP seating.

Festivals take place throughout the year, but *Feria de las Flores*, the flower festival held each August, deserves special mention. Already a verdant region, Medellín comes alive with eye-catching colors when a myriad of plants bloom in its springtime. There are also festivals dedicated to music, literature, dance, and more.

Medellín's culinary scene is vibrant and multifaceted, and a handful of events dedicated solely to food take place year-round. Medellin Gourmet Month, when local restaurants offer fixed menus at bargain prices, is held each spring and fall.

As a family-oriented culture, there's a host of activities designed just for entertaining little ones, too. At the Universidad Metro Station, you'll find *Parque Explora*, an interactive educational museum; the Planetarium; a water museum; and *Parque Norte*, featuring an amusement park for kids...

Medellín is an active city, and locals are generally health and appearance conscious. On any given day, you'll see people out exercising—doing sports, Zumba, running, cycling, dancing, or working out at outdoor gyms.

Group exercise is popular here, and you can easily join running groups, bodybuilding teams, hiking groups, yoga classes, and more. There are also modern, air-conditioned gyms with high-quality equipment and trainers.

The local sport is without a doubt soccer, and two local teams play at the stadium in Laureles: *Nacional* and *Independiente*. The most exciting time is when the two home teams meet in "*El Clásico Paisa*." There's always a sold-out crowd of 40,000 for this, and all the bars in the area are packed with fans.

Medellín sits in a valley, so it's surrounded by green hills where you can walk, cycle, or hike. Parque Arví is one famous example. Perched on a hill, you reach it by cable car. It's a sprawling nature preserve and archaeological site with 54 miles of trails through the forest ideal for nature tours, cycling, and outdoor adventure sports.

When you consider the standard of living in Medellín, all of this adds up to incredible value. For the retiree or expat looking for a new life in a cosmopolitan setting, Medellín offers a Euro-chic lifestyle supported by modern comforts.

Lifestyle and location have a huge effect on the cost of living here. Neighborhoods (or *estratos*) are ranked from one to six by wealth, with six being the wealthiest.

Medellín can be an extremely affordable place to live if you choose to go local and live in a lower *estrato*, shop local brands, and eat at local restaurants.

On the other hand, Medellín also offers luxury-level lifestyle opportunities. You can live in a higher *estrato*, dine at fine-dining establishments, shop at high-fashion boutiques, and purchase imported goods such as Peter Pan peanut butter and French wines. You just have to be happy to pay for it and have a cost of living that's closer to what you pay back home.

The two most popular neighborhoods for expats in Medellín are El Poblado and Laureles. El Poblado has many places in *estratos* five to six and is home to the most expensive and luxurious options. Residences in Laureles are primarily in *estratos* three to four, so it's a bit cheaper.

Taking a middle-of-the-road approach, expect to pay about $850 for a comfortable two-bedroom apartment (in El Poblado or Laureles), about $370 on monthly groceries, and about $30 on the average nice meal out for two. A couple's basic monthly budget here should come to about $1,800.

Electricity bills stay low because the weather is so comfortable, you never need to turn on your air conditioner or heater. Your utility bill (electricity, water, and gas) will be about $75 a month. Budget $300 for entertainment for two and $315 for your monthly grocery shop.

Colombia is a regional leader when it comes to health care, and some of the best hospitals in Latin America are found in Medellín. This is a city where you can have your health care needs taken care of to a high standard and affordably.

Medellín is home to several top-tier hospitals, including the JCI-accredited Hospital Pablo Tobón Uribe and Clínica Medellín. Both public and private facilities are available, although expats pay for private insurance to use the private facilities where standards are highest.

Medellín has become a hub for medical tourism because of the affordability, quality, and advanced equipment and services. Many medical professionals have international training.

Medellín's José María Córdova International Airport offers direct flights to several cities in the States but not to Canada.

Public transportation is excellent, with the Metro, Metro Cable (cable cars), buses, taxis, and shared bikes. Medellín has some of the best-organized public transport systems in Latin America. You won't need a car here. The standard fare for a person over 60 is about 60 cents.

Medellín is famous for having some of the best weather in the world. The temperature never strays far from a baseline of about 74°F (23°C). Most people consider this to be about perfect. The climate is so stable because of its elevation. It sits at 4,900 feet (1,495 meters) above sea level, which prevents big swings in temperature.

It gets two rainy seasons and two dry seasons. The rains hit from March to May and October to November. December to February and June to August are the dry seasons.

As it rises in popularity as a tourist destination, more English is spoken in Medellín every year. There are pockets of the city, like El Poblado, where you could maybe get by without speaking Spanish...

But to live a full life here, you need to learn at least the basics. And this is a great place to learn, so don't worry if your español isn't up to par.

There are plenty of Spanish schools offering reasonably priced lessons. There are also free language exchanges on a near-nightly basis where you can interact with locals looking to improve their English. It's a fun way to meet people and improve your skills.

Medellín's expat community has grown in recent years. Thanks to its low cost of living, excellent infrastructure, and reputation as an interesting place to spend time, Medellín has become more popular, particularly among remote workers and digital nomads. It's also popular with retirees, single women, couples, and young families with children.

There are certain areas of the city (El Poblado, first and foremost, but also Laureles, Evigado, and other areas) where you're almost guaranteed to bump into fellow expats as you go about daily life.

You can have it both ways in Medellín: you can settle into an expat *barrio* and socialize with other expats, or you can settle into a neighborhood that has a higher concentration of locals and opt to have a more culturally authentic living experience.

If you decide to socialize with other expats, you'll find plenty of opportunities to meet up. There are websites (Medellín Living and Medellín Guru, for instance) and Facebook groups that can help you get connected.

Colombia has a reputation for crime, and violent and petty crime are still risks here. This might take the form of fairly innocuous scamming (such as not getting the correct change in the grocery store—always count it) to more serious offenses, like a purse-snatching or mugging.

You'll need to be mindful of safety on a day-to-day basis living here. That said, the longer you live here, the more awareness you'll develop about how to stay safe.

With its vibrant art, music, and culinary scenes, the city's energy is infectious. It's easy to feel this and be a part of it, whether by checking out the street art, sitting down at a new restaurant, or signing up for salsa lessons. No matter what your interests are, you'll never be bored here.

Cartagena

Located on Colombia's northern coast, Cartagena's principal attraction is its Ciudad Amurallada, or walled city, which was named a UNESCO World Heritage Site in 1984. The area is steeped in history. The Spanish arrived in the early 1500s, laying the foundation for the charming colonial atmosphere as well as for its future prominence.

Today, this part of the city is a colorful land of colonial architecture, narrow cobblestone streets, bougainvillea-filled balconies, and shady patios. Wandering leisurely and enjoying the street life, as well as the many plazas, shops, restaurants and bars, is the best part of life in Cartagena.

Despite its historical ambiance, Cartagena also has modern amenities, including a growing number of high-rise condos with spectacular water and beach views in addition to modern shopping centers. It offers a fashionable, modern lifestyle that can be challenging to find elsewhere in Latin America.

There are lots of ways to keep yourself entertained and active living in Cartagena.

You could go salsa dancing at the popular Café Havana and dance the night away. If you want a more low-key place with less crowds, go to Bazurto Social Club for live music.

Free walking tours are a great way to explore the Old City. With the guides you'll be able to see and learn about the city in a way that you wouldn't be able to do on your own. Even though it's free, make sure to give them a nice tip.

Get some drinks, enjoy the park and any performances going on, buy some fruit from the *palenqueras*, and finish the evening with a nice dinner.

The great thing about living in this coastal city is that it has a completely swimmable city beach. There're several areas along the Bocagrande coast where you can enjoy a day in the sun. Some areas are more touristy than others so you might have to actively avoid vendors, but a simple "no, thank you" is enough for them to leave you alone.

Hop on a boat and discover the Caribbean islands near Cartagena, where you'll experience some of the best white-sand and turquoise water beaches around. If you take a private tour the guides will take you to the least crowded areas... and it's still affordable.

Cartagena is a modern city with plenty of conveniences that you can find back home. If you enjoy golf, tennis, padel, paddle board, kayaking, basketball, and more... you'll have no issue finding clubs, courts, and equipment to do so.

Probably the most iconic neighborhood in Cartagena, the Walled City (*Ciudad Amurallada*) is alive at all times of day. Throughout the historic center you'll see street food vendors, fruit vendor ladies with colorful outfits, and artisans and artists selling their creations...

The architecture of the Walled City evokes the feeling that it's stuck in time. The many churches, palaces, and plazas speak of the period when Cartagena was one of the main sources of commerce and culture in the Caribbean.

Inside the walls of the historic center, you'll enjoy restaurants that are affordable as well as some high-end dining experiences. This is the main source of Cartagena's vibrant nightlife. Here you'll find famous bars and nightclubs, such as Café Havana, La Jugada, and Alquímico.

During the daytime you can stroll around the cobblestone streets and enjoy boutiques, ice cream parlors, bookstores, and its parks. In the Historic City you can find the famous *Portal de Los Dulces* or "Candy Portal." In this area you'll find cart after cart of local handmade pastries, candies, and anything sweet.

Cartagena and its *Ciudad Amurallada* are a Gabriel García Márquez magical realism novel come to life. Understandably, as this is the city that saw him bloom as a writer and the inspiration for his greatest works, such as "Love in the Time of Cholera." He loved Cartagena so much that he came back many times throughout his life and even built a property with a rooftop overlooking the ocean.

Getsemaní is one of the most charming neighborhoods in Cartagena. It's full of narrow, cobblestoned streets, colorful architecture, vibrant street life, music, and dancers.

You know you are in Getsemaní when the streets become incredibly narrow. During the day, this neighborhood is pretty quiet. By nightfall, the area completely transforms and these narrow streets are filled up with plastic tables and chairs. Bar carts set up outside, and many of the residential houses turn out to also be restaurants and bars.

Street food can be found on every corner, and in the main square, Plaza de la Trinidad, dancers, musicians, and fire performers put on a show most nights. The neighborhood is still a little rough around the edges, but it's bustling and full of Caribbean flow.

Even though the historic center and Getsemaní are the most fun areas to be in, these are neighborhoods to visit, not live in. Not far from them, about a 10-minute drive away, are the Bocagrande, El Laguito, and Castillogrande neighborhoods.

The area is reminiscent of the city skyline of Miami or Panama City. This is the most cosmopolitan area of Cartagena, with rows of modern oceanfront sky-high buildings. Many have been built in the last couple of years, but you also get your mix of mid-rise and low-rise buildings that have a couple-decades-old look.

This is where you want to live if you want to be close enough to the hustle and bustle of this city, but outside the tourist-heavy environment. The carnival vibe is great for a weekend or for a night out, but not many would want to live right by such busy streets.

Bocagrande, El Laguito, and Castillogrande are made up of lots of commercial plazas, a long boardwalk by the sea, green areas and parks, coffee shops, restaurants, clinics, a hospital, supermarkets, pharmacies, vets, and everything to meet your basic needs in a radius of a few miles.

If you want to live or stay in a more low-key and relaxed environment, go to Manga. This neighborhood is popular with couples and families, and it has some great affordable restaurants, as well as the popular seafood eatery, *Club de Pesca.* Manga has some of the largest yacht moorings in Cartagena and has a beautiful boardwalk overlooking the bay.

This was one of the first neighborhoods built outside of the Walled City, when at the end of the 19th century, its wealthier residents started to feel trapped within the historic center.

The area has a mix of modest homes and mansions, all built in the republican style, an architecture style developed at the time when Colombia became a republic. The style mimics European designs, as the wealthy residents were traveling to Europe and the United States and bringing with them inspiration for the development of their city. Here you'll find properties on large lots, with a greater amount of space and a lower density of people.

It's possible to get the best of life in Cartagena for under $1,850 per month. For a little more luxury, you'll be paying about $2,500 a month. To many potential expats, vacation-home buyers, snowbirds, investors, and workers with portable careers, Cartagena can be a lower cost and viable alternative to most Caribbean-beach locations in other countries.

The city is home to several chains of grocery stores, such as Éxito, Carulla, Olímpica, Jumbo El Castillo, La Estrella, and more. Éxito is a big department store that's also a supermarket, and along with Olímpica, locals say that these are two of the most affordable. Carulla supermarkets are a little more high-end, so some items might have a premium, especially the Carulla convenience stores called Carulla Express. A monthly grocery budget of $300 would easily cover a couple here.

You can find internet packages starting at about $20 per month.

This includes 250 MB of internet, a basic cable plan with 34 channels, and a landline plan with unlimited local calls. Your monthly phone bill will be less than $20.

Rent can vary greatly depending on what neighborhood you decide to live in.

Bocagrande and Castillogrande can be expensive neighborhoods for big, modern, oceanfront buildings. You can find ocean view apartments from about $930 all the way up to $5,000 a month, depending on size, finishes, location, and building amenities. Lower rents are available too, starting at $700 for buildings that don't have a direct ocean or city views.

In Manga, you'll mostly find houses for rent. These houses are big, usually with three or more bedrooms and range from 100 square meters to 500 square meters. You could rent a house here starting at around $675, but you won't find many at this bargain price. Most start at about $1,000.

For electricity in Cartagena, you will pay around $60 to $70 per month, largely because air conditioning is a must for the majority of expats who live here.

Eating out is much more affordable than in big cities in the United States. Portions are big and cost no more than $15, including drinks and perhaps an appetizer.

It can be a lot more in high-end restaurants, but you have plenty of options that fit well if you're on a budget, and not just street-style food but traditional Colombian food and Afro-Caribbean dishes, middle eastern eateries, and many other types of international cuisines.

For health care, The Nuevo Hospital de Bocagrande offers 24/7 care for people of all ages. Many doctors speak English. They have a well-rounded team of medical specialists, such as cardiologists, gynecologists, and more. They have an ER wing and offer services such as surgery, radiology, clinical labs, a blood bank, and more.

Cartagena's most modern hospital, Hospital Universitario Carlos Haime, was inaugurated back in 2019. This is the first specialized institution for cancer treatment in the region. The hospital carries an intensive care unit, cardiology, endoscopy, MRI, delivery rooms, chemotherapy, radiotherapy, and more.

It's about 30 minutes by car from the Bocagrande neighborhood and they have a special office for international patients to ensure they receive information in their native language. The care here is top-notch, and as this is a private hospital, prices may be higher than in others in the city, but it's still far less expensive than in North America.

For less urgent medical care, several clinics are available in the city. One is Clinica Medihelp Services. At one point during its run, it was ranked as the best in Cartagena and one of the top 50 in the country.

Cartagena is a coastal city with a humid and tropical climate. It is warm year-round, and temperatures range between their lowest at about 23°C (73°F) and their highest at 33°C (91°F). The city goes through a dry season from December to April and a rainy season from May to November.

Currently, you can find seasonal non-stop flights to Cartagena with Avianca from Miami and New York City and American Airlines from Miami. JetBlue offers year-round flights from New York City and Delta offers them from Atlanta.

If you're coming from Canada, Air Transat is the only airline flying nonstop to Cartagena from Montreal and Toronto, with seasonal flights.

You'll arrive in Rafael Núñez International Airport and you can get to the center of town for less than $10.

You can get around the city on foot, but Cartagena is hot, which can make walking tough at times. Ubers cost around $2 to $4 around the city.

Taxis and buses are also available and affordable. Official taxis are yellow and should have a *servicio público* label on them. Before getting in, tell them where you are going and ask for the fare, as they don't have meters like they do in Medellín. A taxi ride has a minimum fare of about $2.50 with a nightly extra fee of about $0.23.

If you plan on retiring to Cartagena or making it your second home, we recommend you learn Spanish. This will get you a long way with locals and will allow you to connect better with your new community. It will also help not to feel like a tourist in the place that is supposed to be your new home.

Locals speak fast in Cartagena, so be patient, you'll get the hang of it. If you can understand a Cartagenero easy, you'll be fine in any other Spanish-speaking country.

A considerable number of expats call Cartagena their home. There's a big community of Americans, Brits, and Latin Americans. Many are teachers, retirees, digital nomads, and businesspeople.

Cartagena feels very much like a small town, and you'll likely run into people all the time. You can join the many expat Facebook groups available where you can learn about meetups and activities the community takes part in together.

Crime here is a mixed bag depending on where you are—much as it is other cities in Latin America and around the world.

Touristy El Centro and the Walled City are considered the safest areas with petty crime such as scams and pickpocketing posing the biggest risk to tourists.

Other tourist areas in the city like the beach neighborhoods of Bocagrande and El Laguito are likewise considered relatively safe areas. As with every other big city, exercise caution after dark when the streets are quieter.

Cartagena is the jewel on Colombia's Caribbean coast. Mixing Old World charm with Caribbean culture and beach lifestyle, it packs an unbeatable combination that entices visitors from around the world.

Santa Marta

You've just read about the charms of colorful Cartagena, but not many people have heard about Santa Marta, a laid-back beach town about 150 miles up the coast.

Santa Marta is Colombia's oldest colonial city—in fact, it's one of the oldest cities in all of South America, founded by the Spanish in 1525.

The city is more geographically diverse than Cartagena, with the Caribbean Sea to the north and west, Tayrona National Park to the east, and Colombia's Sierra Nevada mountain range to the south.

It offers excellent beach- and water-based activities, like boating, snorkeling, and diving... but it also offers mountain-based activities, like hiking, trekking, and biking. The Sierra Nevada even has snowy peaks at certain times of year.

On top of this, Santa Marta has an upbeat and energetic culture and a diverse selection of lifestyle opportunities...

There's the historical center, with its quaint, narrow lanes, white-washed Spanish-colonial architecture, and squares lined by everything from pizza joints to burger bars to more upscale Italian and Mediterranean food.

The newer part of the city features an attractive seafront park, plenty of small cafés and bars, as well as boutique hotels, excellent seafood restaurants, and a cruise-ship port. There's a 256-slip marina and new, tasteful condo projects all around.

The most popular beach is Rodadero Beach, which boasts soft, golden sands, warm Caribbean waters, and a long boardwalk.

Rodadero has a friendly, laid-back feel... It's always bustling with people enjoying the beach, shops, and restaurants... but come sundown, its boardwalk becomes a hub of activity, with people exercising, strolling, or simply peoplewatching.

Entertainment in Santa Marta consists of enjoying its historical ambiance... You can dine at diverse restaurants in the city square, surrounded by Spanish-colonial architecture.

There are also malls nearby where you can shop, have a meal, or go to the movie theater.

Santa Marta is a mid-sized city, so it's fairly well-appointed, but its cultural entertainment options aren't extensive. The city's Caribbean beaches are its main appeal. At Rodadero you can rent jet skis and arrange boat trips from the beach.

The area that surrounds Santa Marta offers many off-the-beaten-path recreation opportunities. It's right next to the Sierra Nevada mountain range—one of the highest coastal ranges in the world.

The mountains provide opportunities for hiking, trekking, mountain biking, splashing in waterfalls and rivers, and wildlife spotting. There are mountain villages you can visit to enjoy slightly cooler weather, as well as coffee farms where you can sample Colombia's high-quality brew.

Santa Marta is also next to Tayrona National Park, one of the most famous nature reserves in the country. It has untouched Caribbean beaches and dense jungle with wild monkeys and other wildlife. You can hike, horseback ride, and camp in the park.

A couple's average monthly cost of living comes in around $1,700 to $2,000. You could rent a two-bedroom apartment for $880 a month. Transportation will cost a couple $60; gas and electricity (including air-conditioning) costs about $126 a month; groceries will come in at about $300; and eating out twice a week, including drinks for two will be $350 a month.

Note that electricity is not very reliable... Outages happen often, although they're usually short-lived.

Colombia is already very affordable by North American standards. Because the dollar is strong against the Colombian peso, everything comes at a further discount. Plus, Santa Marta is priced for the local tourism market.

This is definitely a place where you can reduce your monthly cost of living.

Colombia's overall standard of health care is the best in Latin America—better ranked than both Canada and the United States.

It has high-quality medical facilities with state-of-the-art equipment and a reputation for caring bedside manners.

In Santa Marta, there are over a dozen hospitals, clinics, and health centers, both public and private. You should be able to meet all your medical needs within the city, but finding an English-speaking doctor will be a challenge.

Medical care in Colombia is not only high quality; it's also extremely affordable. Most medical procedures and medications are one-third to one-tenth the cost of comparable U.S. prices.

It's always hot in Santa Marta... You'll definitely want air conditioning in your home. The average high is 91°F (33°C); average low is 75°F (24°C); and average humidity is 76%.

Santa Marta's rainy season is May to November, when the surrounding mountains turn lush green. It doesn't receive much rainfall throughout the year, but the rainy season can be intense.

There's less English spoken in Santa Marta than in other Latin American beach destinations. You'll need to pick up some Spanish to facilitate day-to-day living.

There isn't a substantial expat community here. This provides an opportunity to have an adventure and live a more authentic Colombian lifestyle rather than a replica of the lifestyle you had back home.

It's best suited to people who are self-reliant, adventurous, and open to learning Spanish. That said, its star is on the rise, and the small expat community that is here is growing.

Public transportation includes buses, which operate semi-informally (don't expect to find timetables publicized anywhere) but work well once you get the hang of them, and taxis.

There are currently no direct flights to North America, so you'll need to make a stop on the way here, but domestic airlines are low-cost. While slightly farther than our other Latin American havens, Colombia is still easy to reach from North America. To get here, you'll likely take a direct flight to Bogotá and then catch an onward connection to Santa Marta.

Santa Marta is generally a safe place to live, and Colombian people are some of the world's friendliest... but you'll have to be mindful of safety in your daily life here.

Petty crime is fairly common—phone or bag snatching, for instance. You shouldn't walk around with your cell phone in your hand or hanging out of your back pocket.

The longer you live in Santa Marta, you'll develop awareness and fine-tune your instincts to largely avoid issues.

Santa Marta is our favorite spot on the Colombian Caribbean coast. If you're looking for a colonial Caribbean city with less bustle and more bargains than the famous Cartagena… then Santa Marta could be right for you.

Health Care In Colombia

Colombia is home to some of the best hospitals in Latin America. In the most recent WHO study including 191 countries, Colombia ranked #22 for quality of care, surpassing both Canada (#30) and the United States (#37).

Many clinics and hospitals are accredited by U.S. organizations, including the Joint Commission International. Physicians enjoy excellent education in Colombia and often receive at least part of their training in the United States.

Medellín has some of the continent's best medical facilities and most highly skilled doctors. Long known as a destination for cosmetic surgery, Medellín is now established as a destination for complex procedures and advanced technology. This includes transplant surgery.

Costs for procedures can be 50% to 90% less than for comparable procedures performed Stateside. If you reside in Colombia, you can use the basic, government-subsidized health plan, called EPS. With no Colombian income, this will cost you 12% of the minimum wage. From there you can buy add-on plans, many of which require that you have EPS as a prerequisite.

These entitle you to faster service and better, more-upscale facilities. Not every insurance company offers add-on coverage to people over 60. You may need to shop around if you're older.

The cost of your plan will depend on your age, lifestyle, and any existing medical conditions. Private health care is known in Colombia as *Perpagada*. Private health costs range from $180 to $325 per month.

While the standard of Public Health care is good, there are some benefits to going private. These include private bedrooms, and more choice of hospitals available. You are also likely to get an appointment faster through private insurance.

Residency Requirements

Americans, Canadians, and citizens from many European countries can visit Colombia visa-free and stay for 180 days in a year, continuously or discontinuously. If you wish to stay longer than 180 days, you need to apply for a visa.

Colombia offers three types of visas: Visitor, Migrant, and Resident visas. Each has several subcategories.

Two common subcategories under the Visitor visas are the Rentista Visa and the Digital Nomad Visa.

For the Rentista Visa you need to earn a monthly income of $4,000, and for the Digital Nomad visa you need to provide bank statements of at least $1,100 a month. For the DN visa, you'll also need to provide an employment contract and the visa application letter.

Visitor visas don't accumulate time towards permanent residency, and they can't be changed to Migrant or Resident visas within the country.

Two common Migrant visas are the Pension Visa and the Investor Visa.

You need a monthly pension of $1,100 for the Pension Visa. You can apply for the Investor Visa by making a real estate investment of at least $120,000, a capital contribution to a Colombian company for $35,000, or a direct foreign investment of at least $225,000.

Migrant Visas will be granted for one up to three years and the granted time is very much random depending on the official who takes your case. You can renew your visa once it expires. The minimum stay in the country to keep your Migrant Visas is one visit every 180 days.

If you hold your Migrant Visa for five continuous and uninterrupted years, you can apply for a Permanent Visa. You can also apply for permanent residency by holding a Spouse Visa for three continuous and uninterrupted years. The Permanent Visa will be given for five years to an indefinite amount of time. To keep your Permanent Visa, you will need to visit at least once every two years.

If you do decide to reside in Colombia most of the year, it's important to note that after staying in country 183 days in a rolling 365-day period (continuous of discontinuous), you become a tax resident of Colombia.

After acquiring a Permanent Visa and five years of continuous domicile in Colombia you're eligible for citizenship. A foreigner is domiciled in Colombia from the moment the Permanent Visa is granted. Domicile is interrupted if the foreigner remains outside of Colombia for more than one continuous year.

Real Estate Restrictions

No restrictions are imposed on foreigners when it comes to buying property in Colombia.

Taxes

Colombia taxes worldwide income, and its income tax rates are moderate, at between 0% and 39%.

It offers an exemption on foreign pension income up to a certain threshold. Capital gains are taxed at a general rate of 15%. Property taxes are low.

A permanent equity/wealth tax was recently introduced and applies to net worth above a certain threshold.

CHAPTER 6

URUGUAY

Bordered by Argentina to the west and Brazil to the north, Uruguay has a long coast, with the Atlantic Ocean to the east and the Rio de la Plata to the south.

While it may be a small and often overlooked country, there's a lot that makes Uruguay stand out. For one, it's considered the strongest democracy in the Americas. It's refreshing to see a government functioning with a diverse array of political parties.

Uruguay also ranks towards the top of the heap in South America for peace, economic freedom, innovation, and income equality. It has the lowest poverty rate in Latin America, making for a much more stable situation than many of its neighbors.

For water enthusiasts, it's important to note that Montevideo, the country's capital, is on a freshwater river, while nearby Punta del Este is on the ocean.

The latter is known as more of a beach destination, and it's where the well-to-do from Montevideo prefer to head on weekends and holidays.

The highest point in the country is Cerro Catedral, at 1,685 feet (513 meters). No one moves to Uruguay for hiking, that's for sure.

The entire country is a part of the larger region known as the *Pampas* (from the Quechua word for "plains") that includes parts of Argentina and Brazil.

With all this vast, empty land, it should come as no surprise that agriculture plays a major role in Uruguay's economy. Around 70% of the land in Uruguay is used for the 12 million head of cattle that graze on the nation's vast plains.

Cattle farming is a huge part of the economy here, as it is a major exporter and consumer of beef. The country produces about 600,000 tons of beef per year—450,000 of which is exported.

While often neglected or flat-out ignored, Uruguay is a fascinating, beautiful, and welcoming country.

It's home to just under 3.5 million people, making it the 10th most populous country in South America and #132 in the world.

Montevideo is home to about 40% of Uruguayans (1.3 million). The second-biggest city is Salto, with 104,000 residents, followed by Ciudad de la Costa (which is basically a Montevideo suburb) with 95,000.

For a small country, Uruguay has a lot going for it. There's a high standard of living thanks to a strong social safety net with a developed health care system and progressive policies with legalized same-sex marriage, abortion, and cannabis.

Football (soccer) is practically a religion here, and everyone is passionate about *La Celeste* (The Sky Blue)—a nickname given to the men's national team.

Going to the beach is a big part of life and living here you'll experience unique Carnival celebrations, which are said to be the longest in the world. There's also a noticeable European flair This is because most Uruguayans have Spanish or Italian ancestors.

With its abundance of rolling plains and its thriving agricultural sector, *gaucho* culture is alive and well here in Uruguay. This culture is celebrated with special events throughout the year, including the *Patria Gaucha* festival held every March in Tacuarembó, a city in the north of Uruguay. The festival features traditional music and dance, along with parades, horse races, bonfires, and plenty of meat and wine.

Uruguay may live in the shadows of Brazil and Argentina, but it outshines them when it comes to standard of living, safety, and infrastructure.

Everything works as it should here, from its public transportation system to its U.S. dollar-dispensing ATMs. That user-friendliness makes it an ideal destination.

The official language of Uruguay is Spanish. However, it's unlike what you would may have learned in school or spoken elsewhere in Latin America. Uruguayan Spanish shows a strong Portuguese influence, with a lot of words that simply don't exist in other Spanish-speaking countries.

But don't worry. If you already speak Spanish, you'll do fine with whatever version you've learned. If you don't know a word of Spanish, you will need to learn at least the basic, as English is not spoken widely in Uruguay, especially outside of the bigger cities.

Top Picks For A New Life In Uruguay

Montevideo

Montevideo, Uruguay's capital, truly is the beating heart of the country.

Founded in 1724, this colonial city has seen Spanish, British, and Portuguese influence over the centuries. Over the years, Montevideo has consistently ranked as having the highest quality of life in Latin America.

There's plenty to see and do here—from learning about the *guacho* culture and attending barbecues to watching soccer matches and enjoying *mate* (tea made from the yerba mate plant).

For beach enthusiasts, Montevideo is on a freshwater river. Going to the beach is still a big part of life here, though. *Playa Pocitos*, within walking distance of the city center, is a great place to lay your towel down on the beach in the middle of a capital city and relax for a bit with a picnic.

History buffs will love the beautifully-preserved 18th century buildings you'll see all around Montevideo. And if you like to socialize, you're in luck. There are numerous bars, restaurants, and cafés all over the city where you can go to enjoy the finest steaks and the best wine.

Yerba *mate* is regularly enjoyed by locals and expats at cafés or in one of the many sprawling plazas around the city. It is such a big part of the culture of this part of the world, and it's something you'll become very familiar with if you move to Montevideo.

For those not in the know, yerba *mate* is a caffeinated herbal tea that's native to South America. People of all ages drink it, and sharing your *mate gourd* with friends and family is a huge part of the culture. If a local offers you a sip of their *mate*, it means they like you, so go for it!

Go to a football match at the *Gran Parque Central* in Montevideo—the oldest stadium in the Americas. As is the case across much of Latin America, *fútbol* is much more than a sport in Uruguay—it's a way of life. Having hosted a few matches in the inaugural World Cup, it's a historic venue for the sport.

Even if you're not the biggest soccer fan, it's such an important part of the culture that it's worth it to at least feign an interest.

It might not be the most famous (that goes to Rio) or the rowdiest (hello, New Orleans), but *Carnaval* is a big deal in Uruguay as well. The Uruguayan Carnival is a much more family-friendly affair. The main thing to do is attend a performance at the *Teatro de Verano* (Summer Theater) in Montevideo, of which there are many throughout the season. Their version does have one claim to fame—it is the longest Carnival celebration in the world, lasting up to 40 days.

Hire a bike and go for a cycle around the city. Dedicated bicycle lanes are now a common sight. The city also offers a bike-sharing system called "*Movete en Bici*," which allows residents and visitors to rent bicycles for short trips.

For the most part, Montevideo is a pedestrian-friendly city with many sidewalks and pedestrian zones. Of particular note is the city's famous Rambla, a 13-mile-long promenade that runs along the coastline. Along the Rambla, there are several beaches, parks, and recreational areas. Head there to enjoy days on the beach, long walks at sunset, and watching local *fútbol* or volleyball matches.

Take a stroll around *Ciudad Vieja* (the Old City), which perfectly blends the old and new. You'll see historical monuments and centuries-old structures. There are cafés, shops, and markets to explore here, too.

At some point, you'll also have to try a *chivito*. The national dish of Uruguay, it's a sandwich with *churrasco* (sliced beefsteak), ham, mozzarella, tomatoes, and black and green olives.

Although Uruguay is not the cheapest country in South America, it's still more affordable than living in parts of the U.S. or Western Europe. A couple should budget about $2,500 to $3,000 a month for a comfortable lifestyle.

Going out for something simple, like a *chivito* with fries and a beer, costs $10 or less. You can always find street food like *arepas* for a couple bucks. Even ones that are stuffed to the brim with beef and cheese only cost $3.

For fine dining, expect to pay around $30 per person for dinner with a bottle of wine and dessert. Tickets for a movie costs less than $10 per person. If you plan on going out regularly, plan on spending about $350 a month on entertainment.

Enjoy a coffee or a craft beer in the many cafés and beer joints in the city from $2 to $6.

You can get a solid home Internet connection for about $40 a month. If you switch to a local SIM card for your phone, you can expect to pay around $15 to $20 a month for a reasonable amount of data.

Your utilities will come in around $180 a month and your grocery bill will be about $350. If you shop at local markets and hit the *ferias* (street markets), you can load up on fresh food for very little.

For rentals, if you hit the pavement and speak a decent amount of Spanish (or get local help), you'll be able to secure a place for $800 to $1,500 a month.

While things like electronics are certainly more expensive, you'll generally pay less for the most important things—housing, transportation, and health care.

For city dwellers in Montevideo who are able to get by without a car, your transportation costs can be very minimal. It only costs about $1.50 to take the bus anywhere in the city. The occasional cab won't break the bank, either, at $5 to $10.

Everyone in Uruguay is entitled to quality medical care via the national health care system… and this includes foreign residents. There are no restrictions on this system, and we've even known nonresident visitors who've used it.

For health insurance, most who relocate to Uruguay end up enrolling in a plan known as a *mutalista.* This costs around $70 a month and allows you to visit a specific hospital and associated clinics. You only need to pay a small copayment each time, and you can also add an emergency response plan for around $30 a month.

If you'd prefer the extra services that the private system offers, you can also join one of the many higher-end private hospital associations. The cost for these is reasonable, plus you'll have fewer people waiting and more-pleasant conditions.

Your options for initial signup in private health plans will be fewer after you reach age 60, and will diminish further as you pass 65 and 70.

There are a number of hospitals and medical clinics in Montevideo. Many Uruguayans and expats believe that the British Hospital is the best medical facility in Uruguay—and that's located in Montevideo.

The British Hospital is where you'd go for serious illness or major surgery—and you'll find English-speaking medical professionals there.

There is a large, thriving expat community in Montevideo, so you won't be stuck making new friends or finding things to do. InterNations has an active website and forum, where you can connect with fellow expats, get information in their expat guides, join events, and exchange tips about expat life in Montevideo.

The climate in here is sub-tropical. Wintertime is June to August and the weather is mild at this time of year. Summers (December to March) are hot. The temperature varies throughout the year from 45°F to 80°F. April is the rainiest month.

Uruguay is a bit isolated, nestled in a corner of South America between two giants, Brazil and Argentina. As a result, your options are somewhat limited for traveling here, at least directly and conveniently.

On the bright side, this means that Uruguay isn't overrun with tourists. Far from it, in fact—only the intrepid travelers seem to make it here.

If you're flying into Uruguay, the primary gateway to the country is Carrasco International Airport (MVD) located to the northeast of Montevideo in Ciudad de la Costa.

Direct flights to Montevideo may vary depending on the time of year, as many airlines offer seasonal flights. For those in the States, American Airlines offers direct flights to Montevideo from Miami.

There are no direct flights from other cities in the States, nor are there any from Canada. You can go with AA by connecting in Miami or opt to fly with Copa from Panama City.

LATAM, the largest airline in South America, operates direct flights from São Paulo, Santiago, and Lima.

From the airport, you can catch a local bus to town. They pull up right in front of the terminal every 10 to 15 minutes. Make sure you know your stop so you can alert the driver in advance. These buses cost about $1.70.

For those who prefer a more comfortable journey, you have several other options... There are always local cabs waiting outside the terminal. You can also book a *remis* (private transfer) in advance or just use Uber. Expect the trip to cost around $30 to $40, depending on where you're headed.

Many travelers choose to fly into Buenos Aires. From there, you can easily travel to Uruguay by ferry. Ferries depart from the Buenos Aires terminal located in Puerto Madero and travel across the *Rio de la Plata* to Uruguay. From the Argentine capital, you can hop on a ferry bound for Montevideo or Colonia del Sacramento.

Public transportation in Montevideo is generally efficient and affordable. The city offers several options for getting around, including buses, official taxis, rideshare apps, and a growing network of bicycle lanes.

As in many big cities, Montevideo has been making efforts to promote cycling as an eco-friendly mode of transportation. Dedicated bicycle lanes are now a common sight across the city.

If you're living in Montevideo it's quite easy to get by without a car. Most neighborhoods have a market, bakery, pharmacy, butcher, and a few *tiendas*.

Montevideo is one of the safest cities in Latin America. However, while walking around the Old Town at night, be vigilant of your surroundings and exercise the usual cautions you would anywhere else in the world.

Montevideo is a fascinating, beautiful, and welcoming city. Whether you're a traveler, a digital nomad, or a retiree looking to relocate, it's time to put this capital on your radar.

Punta del Este

Uruguay has a spectacular coastline, featuring some of the continent's most luxurious beach resorts—one of the most popular being Punta del Este. The city is situated two-hours east of Montevideo, on the Atlantic Coast.

Punta del Este's population of about 10,000 swells to five times the size during the summer months of December to February, such is the popularity of the city.

It is one of the most famous beach towns in South America and attracts the elite from around the world. In fact, it has a reputation as being the playground of the rich and is often referred to as the St. Tropez or Monaco of South America. You'll find high-end developments with stunning penthouses and multi-million dollar yachts docked in its marina.

Punta del Este is an incredibly popular destination for tourists—mainly from Argentina and Brazil, but also increasingly from the

States. And because of the glamorous lifestyle here, it has gained the attention of many celebrities.

Spend your days in Punta enjoying the beaches, browsing the main shopping avenue of Avenida Gorlero or looking at local handmade crafts at the fair. The beachfront boulevards coupled with the lighthouse and the yacht harbor are also worth a visit.

Renowned for its white sand and clear water, Brava beach is a local and expat favorite. The beach is lined with restaurants, cafés, bars, and shops—so if you need a break from the sun there's plenty of other things to keep you entertained for the day.

The Punta Shopping Mall has an array of stores and restaurants... plus entertainment venues where you can watch a movie or go bowling.

You'll find water sports in abundance here, including swimming, sailing, kayaking, and surfing. If you are a golfer or tennis player, there are plenty of courts and courses in the area, too.

The city has a number of parks, including the Punta del Este Botanical Garden which is perfect for an evening stroll.

For culture vultures, there are museums and art galleries dotted around the city. The Ralli Museum is home to a collection of paintings, modern sculptures, and lithographs by Latin American artists. *Guera Galeria de Arte* has contemporary works by local and international artists, and *Galeria Sur* features works by prominent Uruguayan artists.

Festivals and events are held throughout the year. The biggest is the Festival of Las Llamas which celebrates the regions ancestors and features street dancers, drumming, and parades.

Other festivals include Day of the Dead (November 1), a Jewish Film Festival, and an International Jazz Festival.

You'll find more fine-dining establishments than you could experience in a year... plus high-rise casinos, big-time shows, high-fashion expos, and concerts. The shopping is also world-class.

Not too long ago, Uruguay had one of the cheapest costs of living in Latin America.

Fast forward to nowadays, and life here is not so cheap. That's not to say it's not good value for money. Punta del Este offers a high quality of life for less than you would pay in the States.

One of the biggest costs in Uruguay is owning a car. If you choose to buy a car, expect to pay more than you would in the U.S. or Canada due to Uruguay's high automotive import duties.

On the flip side, health care is relatively cheap, so these costs more or less balance out.

A couple's monthly living costs will likely cost about $2,800 to $3,700, including rent. You could get a two-bedroom apartment with a balcony close to the beach for about $1,800 to $2,200 a month.

Your monthly grocery bill will come in at about $600. Utilities, including internet, electricity, water, heating and cooling will be $210 a month. Other costs include entertainment...and in Punta del Este, the sky is the limit. But, if you're only eating out a few times a month, budget about $300.

There are several hospitals and clinics and emergency services in Punta del Este that are reliable. The major hospitals include Hospital Británico, Hospital Punta del Este, and Clínica Punta del Este.

There are also several pharmacies where you can get your prescription medications and over-the-counter drugs. If you have a serious illness, the British Hospital in Montevideo (two-hours away) has an excellent reputation for its standard of medical services.

Punta del Este attracts expats from around the world and you'll find a number of social clubs and expat groups that host gatherings and events, giving you the opportunity to meet like-minded people.

There are lots of cafés, bars, and restaurants in the city too—and this is where you'll also meet expats.

The high season in this coastal resort town is mid-December through February. The number of visitors to Punta del Este at this time of year swells. You should feel comfortable in Punta del Este, with its European ambiance and laid-back seaside life. It has drawn a steady stream of expats for a long time.

As a whole, Uruguay enjoys one of the lowest crime rates in Latin

America, the culture is honest and hard-working, and levels of corruption are low. Overall, this country is safe, stable, peaceful, and friendly. Punta del Este is considered a safe place to live with many expats having no problem walking around alone at night.

The weather in Punta del Este is fantastic during the summertime months of November through March—with little rain and a pleasant average high of 76 degrees F (24.4°C), thanks to the ocean's moderating effect. (It's pretty nice in the wintertime too, but not warm enough to draw many to the beach.)

In mid-winter, highs run around 60°F, with the lows near 42°F. Frost is rare in Uruguay, and it never snows. Few people use air conditioning due to the cool evenings and ocean breeze, but you'll want to use the heat in the wintertime.

To get here, you'll need to fly into Montevideo and make the journey to Punta del Este by car or bus, which takes about two hours.

Punta del Este is a naturally beautiful place. The beaches are wide and long, bordered with dunes, and are beautiful and well-maintained. The infrastructure is impeccable, the roads are well-kept, and the beaches are groomed daily.

Health Care In Uruguay

Medical care here is of a high standard, and everyone in Uruguay is entitled to quality medical care via the national health care system... including foreign residents. There are no restrictions on this system.

If you'd prefer the extra services that the private system offers, you can also join one of the many higher-end private hospital associations. The cost for these is reasonable, plus you'll have fewer people waiting and more pleasant conditions.

Quality public health care is readily available throughout Uruguay, although most of the best health care services are in or near Montevideo.

ASSE is the main provider of state-covered health care, with a network of services throughout country that offers integral health care, including promotion of healthy practices, prevention, diagnosis, timely treatment, and rehabilitation.

ASSE oversees a network of hospitals, health centers, polyclinics, and family physicians throughout the country. Membership in ASSE is not mandatory, and regardless of pre-existing conditions or age, access to health care services is available to everyone and is free for the unemployed and low-salaried workers.

As a resident-in-process, you have the right to be treated at any public hospital in Uruguay in case of an emergency. However, long or repeated treatment is only available for those who cannot afford private cover. The standard of public health may be lower than what you are used to in your country of origin. In the public system the free clinics can be slow and crowded.

For private care, you can obtain hospital-based coverage through two programs, *La Asistencial* and *Sanatorio Mautone*. As a member of either of these programs, you are covered for all in-patient treatment, surgery, emergencies, tests, even after-care in your home.

This is hospital-based care, meaning this program does not follow you to any other hospital or medical facility within Uruguay and provides no coverage outside the country.

Private, non-profit organizations cover more than 52% of Uruguay's health care needs. They consist of independently operated associations and vary in size from a single hospital to a network of hospitals, clinics, and doctors' offices.

If you just walk into the emergency room for treatment in a private hospital (without a plan), you'll typically spend about $80, which will include doctor fees and lab work.

There are about 50 medical centers, 12 of which are based in Montevideo. Pre-paid monthly premiums entitle patrons use of their facilities, ambulance service, pharmacy, and specialists in accordance with the plan that is selected.

With about 1,100 pharmacies in Uruguay, 40% are in Montevideo. All medicines must be dispensed by pharmacies. Before you leave home, check that your prescription medication is available in Uruguay.

Residency Requirements

Travel to Uruguay is visa-free for North Americans and all EU countries. A passport with a validity of six months is all you need to spend up to 90 days here, and that can be extended for an additional 90, giving you half a year.

Just make sure to head to an immigration office while your initial stay of 90 days is still valid to start the application for an extension.

Alternatively, you could just hop on the ferry or take a quick flight over to Buenos Aires for a weekend, then come back.

Making one of these "visa runs" here and there is fine, but immigration officials might not like it if they see you doing it every three months, and we don't recommend it as an option.

If you're considering a long-term move to Uruguay, the good news is that it's relatively easy to establish residency here.

Of course, there are plenty of forms that need to be filled out, translated, notarized, and all that red tape that comes along with moving to a new country...

You can get the process started with just your passport, vaccination certificate (MMR and tetanus), and a photo.

As it may take a few months to get an appointment, it's good to get the ball rolling even if you don't have all the other documents ready. You can submit these as you go, which takes some of the stress out of the whole process. There are no special requirements or benefits to applying as a retiree.

Unless your Spanish is more than decent and you have a high tolerance for bureaucracy, you may want to enlist some professional help in applying for residency.

The process for residency takes about a year to 18 months. In the meantime, you'll be issued with a temporary residence card. Once it's approved, you'll receive your permanent residence card (called a *Cedula*).

The benefit of having a *cedula* is that you are allowed the same luxuries and facilities available to any other national of the country.

The easy residency also allows you to import your household items before residency has even been granted.

Once you're a resident in the country you can apply for citizenship.

Citizenship is relatively easy to get when you move to Uruguay, given the low financial requirements for doing so (great for retirees).

It usually takes around three (for married couples) to five years (for a single person) to get approval for citizenship. You'll need to prove that you've integrated into your new life in Uruguay and that you can speak conversational Spanish.

There are some caveats to this easy residency and, later, citizenship. You must stay in the country more than 183 consecutive days in a given year. This is known as the Days Test.

However, if you have family ties in the country you can apply for residency. For example, if your spouse and children live there and your children go to school in Uruguay.

Or, if you make a business or real estate investment and stay in the country for at least 60 days in any given year, you can also apply. The minimum real estate investment amount is $390,000. The minimum amount to invest in a business is $1.7 million.

Uruguay recently joined the growing list of countries that offer a digital nomad visa, which allows you to stay and work there for six months. This visa is called *Hojas de Identidad Provisoria* (Provisional Identity Card).

You can apply in your home country before arrival or wait until you get there to do so, and it only costs about $15 from abroad or $30 if you apply from within Uruguay. Then it's an additional $30 to extend that to a full year.

To get that six-month extension, you will also need proof of a clean criminal record in all of the countries where you have lived for more than six months in the last five years.

Not only is the process simple and affordable, but Uruguay isn't imposing any strict requirements when it comes to proving your income.

This is likely to change, but since the program is quite new, it looks like they are being very welcoming for the moment.

Real Estate Restrictions

Anyone can buy property here. There are just a few minor restrictions when it comes to purchasing rural property... This is because the government is trying to encourage more locals to move to rural areas, and thus a government organization has the option to purchase these properties first.

Whether urban or rural, you'll still need to use a public notary for all of the paperwork. You typically get charged 3% plus the VAT from a notary if you're buying property and 1% if selling.

This isn't the only expense associated with buying real estate here. At the end of the day, you can count on paying around 8% of the total price in the various fees, taxes, and expenses you'll encounter.

Once you've settled on a place, you need to sign a contract that's known as *boleta de reserva.* This is a legally binding contract, and it's custom to pay 10% at the time of signing. There is also a penalty clause that is usually the same amount as the deposit in case either party defaults.

All real estate purchases in Uruguay are done in U.S. dollars, which may be a blessing or a curse, depending on where you're moving from. Taxes, meanwhile, are paid in the local currency of UYU (Uruguayan pesos).

Should you decide to invest in property in Uruguay, it's essential to have professional, Spanish-speaking help.

Realtors can represent both the buyer and seller here, which you may think of as a conflict of interest. That's not the case here.

Taxes

Uruguay does not tax on outside income or investments, making it an ideal place to run a business abroad from anywhere.

Tax-resident foreigners in Uruguay enjoy tax exemption on foreign-earned income only during their first five years in the country. After that, certain types of income, specifically dividends and interest, are taxed at 12%.

In short, until the end of the five-year exemption, dividends in Uruguay are tax free, whether they're foreign or locally sourced.

For many items, VAT runs at 22% of the selling price. But some goods like medicines have a more reasonable 10% tax imposed on them.

Personal Income Tax is only payable on income earned within the country. Income tax ranges between 10% to 25% and just like in the U.S., certain expenses may be subtracted. Tax on income earned inside the country is paid by Uruguay nationals and any foreign nationals who spend more than 183 days in the country for that tax year.

The capital gains tax rate is 12% for individuals, 12% for foreign corporations, and 25% for Uruguayan corporations.

While Uruguay has no inheritance tax, the country does impose a wealth tax on the difference in assets and certain liabilities year over year.

IV

THE CARIBBEAN

If your dreams of a new life overseas are all about white sand and swaying palm trees, the Caribbean should be at the top of your list.

Imagine living in a sunny Caribbean destination, where no one is in a hurry, the sea is every shade of blue you can imagine, and the evenings are spent with cold drinks and neighbors...

Turquoise waters and swaying palms, gentle breezes and sunset cocktails... Few places on Earth are quite as dreamy as the Caribbean. The region has an irresistible charm that has drawn tourists and escape seekers for decades. But in recent years, the Caribbean has emerged as more than just a place to get away from it all...

With its generous residency and citizenship programs, quality construction, and enduring tourism appeal, the Caribbean has become not only the ultimate safe haven but also a prime property investment destination.

It's true that the cost of living in the Caribbean can be pricey, but there are certain places where your dollar still stretches and the cost of living is attainable. We've included those places in this section.

It's easy to fit in with your new life in the Caribbean, especially if you can abandon attitudes about having everything you want and need right away. Learn to live island style... Relax, slow down, enjoy life, and make family more important than the daily grind of back home.

Read on to find out more about your best options for living the quintessential Caribbean lifestyle at an affordable cost.

CHAPTER 7

THE DOMINICAN REPUBLIC

The Dominican Republic is quintessential Caribbean: sand, sun, and fun. The great part about it is that it offers the best of the Caribbean at bargain prices compared to other island nations in the region.

The DR has long been a favorite holiday destination for Europeans, North Americans, and South Americans, with regular direct flights from all three of these continents.

This isn't some new fad getaway destination... It's the most popular Caribbean vacation destination in all of the West Indies.

Christopher Columbus established Hispaniola as the predominant land in the New World... Five hundred years later, it's still the best place to base yourself in the Caribbean.

The quality of life is an undeniable benefit to living in the DR. Dominican culture is warm, welcoming, and strongly family-oriented.

Plus, it's easy to get to. The country has seven international airports and all major U.S. airlines and many of the low-cost ones fly here. Latin American carriers and major European airlines fly directly to the DR, too. The island also has 10 major ports and several smaller ports that cater to the cruise ship industry.

On top of that, it's affordable. With $2,000 a month you can live a comfortable and enjoyable life here. The DR offers several residency visa options that are easy to apply and qualify for. It also offers quick paths to residency, and it's increasingly sought out by people who'd like a second passport.

Everything from real estate to food to services is more economical in the DR. Best of all, your health, and therefore your quality of life, will be enhanced by eating local fruit, vegetables, seafood, and meat. Buy local, buy fresh, and enjoy great meals.

Here you'll find an eclectic multicultural community that blends Dominican and international culture.

For those who want to live on or near the beach, the DR is the perfect destination for you. With over 800 miles of beach to lay down your beach towel, the challenge is deciding where you want to do it.

As well as pristine white-sand beaches, palm trees swaying in the tropical breeze, and crystal clear turquoise blue waters, the island also offers lush forest, breathtaking mountains, beautiful waterfalls, and many national parks.

Top Picks For A New Life In The Dominican Republic

Las Terrenas

Las Terrenas is located on the Dominican Republic's Samaná Peninsula, a finger of land that sticks out from the country's northeast coast.

Settled by French expats in the 1970s, Las Terrenas has been attracting foreigners ever since—among them Germans, Italians, Swiss, Brits, Poles, and Russians.

This helps explain the diverse shopping and dining options around town that include everything from a German meat shop to an authentic French boulangerie to an Omaha beef store and an Italian clothing boutique.

While this goes far beyond the selection available at your average Caribbean destination, none of the natural tropical appeal has been lost in Las Terrenas. It remains a pastel-washed Caribbean beach town, with swaying palms and beach vistas around every corner.

In recent years, mostly thanks to its infrastructure developments, more Americans have been arriving. Aside from the beautiful beaches and welcoming cosmopolitan community, they're attracted by the affordable, active lifestyle, ease of access from the States and Canada, and user-friendly residency options.

The main source of entertainment in Las Terrenas is going out for meals and drinks. There's not much in terms of historical or cultural entertainment—not a lot of museums, theater, performances, or the like.

That said, Las Terrenas' restaurant scene is exceptional. It boasts a wider selection of high-quality restaurants than your average Caribbean outpost thanks to the diverse expat community.

There's everything from multi-course French cuisine to simple grilled fish at Dominican restaurants. Likewise, the bar scene is eclectic and affordable, with daily happy hours where you're sure to bump into fellow residents.

Beyond the restaurants and bars, there's a small art scene as well as a growing reputation for dance. Las Terrenas draws professional and semi-professional salsa, bachata, and merengue dancers.

Living here, you'll find some of the best beaches in the world on your doorstep. White sands, gentle waves, curving palms, and soft breezes... inspiration for ultimate relaxation.

There are five main beaches, two within walking distance of Las Terrenas' dining and nightlife. Some beaches are more active. On Playa Bonita, you can take surf lessons, and at Playa Portillo, there's kitesurfing.

For land-based recreation, you can cycle around town or join a group with fellow Dominican, French, Swiss, Canadian, and Italian participants.

There's a local tennis club and sailing club, both with similarly diverse memberships. January through March, there are whale-watching tours led by a local marine life expert. Further afield, you can hike in national parks, go on quad tours, or splash in waterfalls and natural pools.

The average cost of living for two is around $2,100, making living here 58% cheaper than the cost of living in the United States.

So, Las Terrenas offers the Caribbean lifestyle at a bargain price. Costs for day-to-day expenses—things like groceries, dining out, and transportation—are inexpensive.

Rent prices vary widely... from a couple hundred dollars per month if you're willing to live in a humble, Dominican-style home to $1,500 per month for a well-appointed, luxury-level home.

Real estate is affordable, and construction standards are high, with quality finishes available locally and highly skilled general contractors. You can buy a two-bedroom, two-bathroom home with a pool for around $275,000.

For utilities (electricity, gas, and water) you'll pay about $100 a month (if you run an air conditioner around the clock, you could face a higher-than-average electric bill). Cell phone and internet costs are $75. Budget $425 for entertainment for two and $450 for your monthly groceries. If you own a car, will it cost you about $75 a month.

Las Terrenas has a public health center and several small private clinics.

Most expats keep private insurance plans to gain access to the private clinics where wait times are shorter and the facilities are better. The quality of care is adequate, fine for everyday health needs, and many of the staff speak English.

For an emergency or for specialized care, expats go to Santo Domingo, a two-hour drive away, where more facilities are available, or back to their home country.

Las Terrenas has a tropical climate, with hot and often overcast summers and warm, clear-skied winters. Temperatures don't fluctuate much throughout the year.

Las Terrenas doesn't experience seasons beyond wet and dry. It gets significant rain, especially May and September to November. Then again, it also gets lots of sunshine. February to April are usually the sunniest months.

The town is perfect if you're seeking a tropical climate—warm weather, high humidity, lush vegetation, and lots of sun.

You should learn the basics of Spanish to live well in Las Terrenas. That said, service staff in hotels, resorts, tourist-oriented restaurants and bars will speak a bit of English.

Outside tourist and resort areas, you'll hear a variety of languages as you go about daily life since Las Terrenas is home to people from a variety of nationalities.

There's a unique expat community here that's made up of people from many different backgrounds—locals, Americans, Canadians, French, Germans, Italians, Swiss, Brits, Poles, and more.

One expat explains how building a house in Las Terrenas showed him how multicultural the community is. His developer was French, the kitchen designers were Italian, and the electrical contractors were Swiss.

Some drawbacks of life here is that power outages are relatively common, especially during bad weather. Outages are short-lived most of the time, but many people rely on backup generators.

Public transportation is limited to moto-taxis and shared vans. Most expats have their own car so that they can go where they want, when they want. That said, you can get around town by bicycle or on foot.

To get here you'll fly to Samaná El Catey International Airport in Samaná Province, where Las Terrenas is located. There are several direct flights to cities in Canada but none to the States.

If you're traveling here from the States, you can either fly through a city in Canada or fly direct to Santo Domingo, the DR's capital.

Crime is a risk in the Dominican Republic, but expats report feeling safe in Las Terrenas. That said, you should take basic precautions against petty crime while living here, like making sure your home is burglar-proof, especially if it's in a remote area. Don't leave valuables unattended on the beach or at the bar, and so on.

Whether you're looking for a second home in the sun... a full-time option for your retirement that offers an attractive lifestyle... or a chance to earn rental income in a growing tourist market, Las Terrenas is worth checking out.

Santo Domingo

The Dominican Republic's capital, Santo Domingo, is where the Spanish—Columbus himself—first landed in the New World, and this city is home to the first cathedral, first university, first real street, and many other European imports that hadn't existed on this side of the world previously. Established in 1496, it is undisputedly the oldest continuously inhabited city in the Americas.

It's the Caribbean's only medieval Spanish city... but it's also a truly cosmopolitan capital. It has plenty of history and culture, but also diverse dining options, entertainment, and modern shopping along its cobbled streets. In Santo Domingo, you can enjoy theaters, museums, and stadiums (*béisbol* is a national obsession).

Santo Domingo's extensive Zona Colonial, a UNESCO World Heritage site, offers countless Spanish-colonial buildings—interesting prospects for both investment and lifestyle—plus, it hasn't yet become populated with expats like many of the typical colonial city options.

Founded by Christopher Columbus' brother Bartholomew, colonial Santo Domingo might best be described as dignified. The structures at the heart of this old town are classic Spanish colonial but simpler, statelier, and somehow more refined than their counterparts across the region.

Calle Las Damas, the first street of the original city and therefore the oldest street in all the Americas, is lined with 16th-century pale stone facades and runs into Plaza de España, the expansive open square at the harbor.

The highlight here is the colonial city's first palace, the private home of the first governor of the colony, Diego Columbus, Christopher's son. It's an exceptional example of classic Spanish-colonial architecture.

In colonial Santo Domingo, the Columbuses built a customs house, a hospital, a cathedral, a university, a library... everything required to launch a new Spain.

During its golden age, this city's colonial structures stood as testament to the riches flowing through their benefactors' coffers.

The city's coastline is a buzzing, energetic strip, popular among locals and foreigners alike. From kids and teens riding bikes and boards to families and tourists out on walks along with the health-conscious jogging back and forth, this pleasant pedestrianized byway is one of the most popular (and beautiful) hangouts in the city.

Plenty of ice cream and pizza stands dot the way, along with playgrounds, outdoor workout areas, playing courts, pavilions, and artistic graffiti that liven up the route. If you're in the mood for a sit-down meal, you'll find several excellent local joints at which to take a load off.

There's a lot more to the city than just the Zona Colonial. Other neighborhoods of note include Gascue, Naco, Piantini, Paraíso, Evaristo Morales, Arroyo Hondo, Bella Vista, and Mirador Sur.

Piantini is the heart of the business district, but it's becoming one of the trendier new residential neighborhoods. You'll find an increasing number of boutique and luxury hotels, restaurants, and stores here, including some of the city's premier new residential developments (mostly in the form of midrise condo buildings).

There certainly is no lack of entertainment in Santo Domingo, particularly in the Piantini district, which has several good malls, theaters, and fantastic restaurants, and in the Colonial Zone, the heart of the city's pedestrian and café culture.

For the best sightseeing, the Colonial Zone is not to be missed. Visiting Parque Colon and strolling Calle de Las Damas is something residents never tire of, and you'll find several galleries and small museums throughout the colonial city.

The vestiges of the Spanish Colonial period offer many pursuits... Fort Ozama, Plaza de España, La Atarazana, the Royal Shipyards, the Convent of the Dominican Order, and Calle El Conde top the list. Take a tour through the ancient ruins at Monasterio de San Francisco, or, for a more modern tour, visit Kah Kow Experience to see chocolate production from the pod to the bar.

You should also take a jaunt to the Columbus Lighthouse, a fascinating structure said to contain the remains of Columbus.

If you're looking for upscale activities, Plaza de la Cultura in Gascue is where to go. This cultural headquarters and community center complex offer a wealth of education and entertainment, including the National Theater, National Library, National Film Library, the Gallery of Modern Art, the Museum of Natural History, the Museum of History and Geography, and the Museum of Dominican History... all set among bucolic gardens and splashing fountains.

The capital is also home to the National Symphony Orchestra of the Dominican Republic, which hosts many events throughout the year.

For a taste of the great outdoors within the city limits, take a wander through the National Botanical Garden, ranked by England's Kew Gardens among the 10 best in the world, or head to the National Zoo.

The malecón is a great place for a jog or long bike ride, as are any of the city parks: the Centro Olímpico (full of playing fields and courts, plus track and field), Paseo de los Indios (more commonly called Mirador Sur), Núñez de Cáceres Enviromental Park, and Iberoamérica Park, which is also home to the National Conservatory of Music, the Nuryn Sanlley amphitheater, an open-air gym, a children's area, and an iguana farm.

This is a city... to enjoy the best of Dominican nature, you'll have to head out of town. Mountains, jungle, pine woods, mangrove swamps, coral reefs, immaculate beaches, and fertile land... this island packs a biodiverse punch.

Spend a day at the beach at Boca Chica (just under an hour from the city), or Juan Dolio (just over an hour), or go further afield to enjoy this country's famous white-sand beaches.

A couple's basic monthly budget here should come to about $1,500 if you own your home. If not, factor in another $600 or so for rent, putting your budget at about $2,100. If your goal is to live as cheaply as possible (but you still have to rent), you could cut your budget down to about $1,800 a month.

With a budget of $2,500 to $3,000, you could afford more entertainment and extra household help, for example, and really enjoy the good life.

Invest in a place of your own, and your monthly living costs would be much less. This is a realistic and appealing option, as property prices are a bargain, certainly relative to elsewhere in the Caribbean. You could buy an apartment for as little as $100,000.

Services are good, with cable, internet, and phone services cheap and reliable. The Wi-Fi is fast enough to support calls and video streaming.

Santo Domingo has four private hospitals with good reputations—more than any other city in the country. Doctors at these hospitals would speak English.

If you have mobility issues, this city may not be for you. The streets in and around town are paved and in fairly good condition; sidewalks are another story... They are typically in disrepair and not maintained.

The city's metro is the second oldest metro system in the Caribbean and Central America, as well as the most extensive by both length and number of stations.

It's clean, fast, and safe. Unfortunately, it only goes in two directions, running parallel to the two most used thoroughfares: Avenida Máximo Gómez and Expreso Kennedy, so it's not hugely useful unless you're a commuter.

Buses are a great option for getting out of the city, with three private lines (with clean and modern vehicles, even including a movie as entertainment on long rides) running from the capital to all the popular beaches daily.

With the airport about 30 minutes from the city center, getting in and out of the DR is easy from the capital. At just an hour-and-a-half from Miami, it's a close hop to be back in the States.

The average annual temperature is just under 80°F (26° C), with humidity hovering around 84%, and variations from those averages are determined more by altitude than anything else. From May to

October it's hot and stuffy, but from November to March it gets a little cooler in the city just based on wind patterns.

Learning Spanish will certainly increase your quality of life, and we recommend learning the local language no matter where you want to live, but it's not an absolute necessity living in Santo Domingo. This capital city is home to many well-educated Dominicans doing business, plus a thriving service industry that often caters to tourists. If you don't wander far from the mainstream hangouts, you'll be fine getting by in English.

Santo Domingo is not yet a mainstream expat destination, but, historically, it's even less of a retirement destination. The expat community that does exist here are a working bunch. The majority of foreigners who live here were placed by a corporation and relocated for a job. The rest of the North Americans in Santo Domingo are mostly English teachers.

InterNations hosts many functions throughout Santo Domingo and joining this global network is a great way to break into the local social scene and meet other expats with similar interests. Hash House Harriers also has a chapter here and is always eager for new members. And The International Women's Club (IWC) has a chapter here, open to all English-speaking women living in the Dominican Republic, regardless of nationality. This super-active group hosts regular get-togethers for members and also works to help the local community, hosting many charity events throughout the year.

When it comes to safety, petty theft is the main issue you need to be alert for. Avoid walking alone and stick to tourist zones at night. In the parts of Santo Domingo an expat would spend time in, there are cops on every corner—all eager to welcome foreigners and make sure they feel safe. This is the case even outside the Zona Colonial, but within the ZC it's even more so.

Today, Santo Domingo is chasing a new prosperity. The streets are lively, the harbor busy. From real estate to the general cost of living, it can be hard to believe you're in the Caribbean. You could live well here on your monthly Social Security check alone.

Most of the world knows the Dominican Republic for its white-sand beaches. But, for many, the real appeal of the Dominican Republic is Santo Domingo, the oldest European city in the Americas.

Health Care In The Dominican Republic

In the capital, you've got access to the best health care the country has to offer. Emergency services exist, in fact, a 911 service was instituted 10 years ago and is operating effectively.

Santo Domingo has four private hospitals with good reputations—more than any other city in the country. Doctors at these hospitals would speak English, though you can't be sure of that in smaller, more rural facilities.

Almost all expats get health insurance, are treated privately, and rate the personal treatment they receive by medical professionals very highly. We know one expat who's saving $72,000 a year on his health bills thanks to free treatment at his hospital in Santo Domingo.

It's worth noting that, although public health services in the Dominican Republic are extremely affordable, the standard can be poor.

Residency Requirements

The Dominican Republic offers several paths to residency, including user-friendly investor visas. Its retirement visa is known as Residencia por Inversión en Calidad de Jubilado o Pensionado.

The basic requirement is that you receive a monthly pension of about $1,500. This grants a one-year residence permit that can be renewed.

The DR offers immediate permanent residency through investment in real estate. You must invest at least $200,000 in real estate or in term deposits in DR banks or securities traded in the DR. You can also make a capital contribution to a DR business. This makes you eligible for citizenship in just six months, although the process can take up to two years. The DR has one of the most affordable invest-for-residency options in the world as well as offering one of the fastest paths to citizenship available in the world.

Real Estate Restrictions

You can buy property without restrictions as a foreigner in the DR. It has an open-door policy, which is one of the reasons it's so popular with foreigners. It also has no short-term rental restrictions, and it's easy to find property management. Many condo residences have management in-house and come furnished, making an investment here as turn-key as they come.

Taxes

The DR follows a territorial tax system, meaning that mainly Dominican-sourced income is subject to tax. Foreign-source income is generally not. That said, after three years of being a resident in the DR, you start being taxed on your worldwide income.

There are no net wealth or worth taxes in the DR. Gifts are taxed at 27%, payable by the recipient.

CHAPTER 8

THE CAYMAN ISLANDS

The Cayman Islands are beautiful, tax-free, English-speaking, and friendly... Its pros are clear to see: It is an easy place to live and get around. Things work. People care. It enjoys a small-town feel with a strong sense of community.

Plus, it's a safe place to live—it has one of the lowest crime rates in the Caribbean. Even the lively capital of George Town has a very low crime rate.

Legend has it that in February 1794, 10 merchant ships sailing from Jamaica to England struck the reef off Grand Cayman. The Caymanians saw the ships sink and, without hesitation, headed into the sea and bravely rescued those on board, saving almost all their lives. This moment in history has been named the Wreck of the Ten Sail. As the story goes, one of the passengers rescued was a royal prince. To reward their courage and express his gratitude, King George III declared the people of Cayman should forever be free of taxes and the draft.

Caymanians explain their valor and compassion as "Caymankind." A reflection of their goodwill toward all people. And global investors are happy to use the friendly Caymans as a tax haven. They've found a home on these islands for centuries.

A philosophy of kindness and financial freedom are both solid reasons to consider the Cayman Islands, but there's something for everyone here... quiet, secluded beaches with blue, pristine waters and world-class scuba diving, rollicking nightlife, rich history and culture, active retirement communities, excellent schools, and family-oriented activities like kite festivals and snorkeling with stingrays. With year-round sunshine, a safe and clean environment, lively community spirit, and a stable government, how could you not love these islands?

It was Christopher Columbus who put the Cayman Islands on the map, recording the Sister Islands on May 10, 1503, when his ship was blown off course during a trip between Hispaniola and Panama. The turtles crawling the islands prompted him to name them "Las Tortugas." Sir Francis Drake, who spotted them 80 years later, called them "Caymanas," the Carib name for crocodiles. That name stuck—even though most believe it was rock iguanas he saw, not crocodiles. Plenty of iguanas still roam the islands today—especially on Little Cayman, where the speed limit is 25 mph to assure their safety.

Pirates promptly scared off early settlers, who arrived from Jamaica in late 1660, and the islands weren't permanently inhabited until the 1730s. The Cayman Islands were officially a dependency of Jamaica until that island's independence from England in 1962, after which the Caymans voted to become a self-governing Crown colony of the United Kingdom.

Today, each of the three Cayman Islands has its own personality. There's Grand Cayman, the largest and most boisterous of the group with a bustling capital of George Town and world-renowned Seven Mile Beach. And then there are the Sister Islands Cayman Brac and Little Cayman, with populations of around 2000 and 160, respectively.

Top Picks For A New Life In The Cayman Islands

Grand Cayman

Grand Cayman offers excellent schools, world-class doctors, fantastic restaurants, developed infrastructure, and everything you could possibly need for a comfortable life.

Grand Cayman's western side is home to touristy Seven Mile Beach, with active nightlife and world-class dining, as well the busy port of George Town. The cliffs and marshland on the island's East End and North Side are quieter. The island appeals to lots of tourists—you can holiday at the luxurious Ritz Carlton or stay in a low-key West Bay Airbnb. And it is safe, friendly, and family oriented—there is no gambling here or casinos.

Beyond a multitude of bars and restaurants, entertainment includes the National Gallery, Latin Dance Festivals, and Capella Music Festival. The Turtle Center, Crystal Caves, and Parrot Sanctuary are fun for kids of all ages, and unique aquatic adventures include the annual Flowers Sea Swim and Stingray City, home to more than 90 stingrays.

The island is breathtakingly beautiful, and even though it's the most developed of the three (with a population of 67,000), naturalists will be happy here as well.

Visit the 2.3-mile Mastic Reserve Trail for views of mangrove wetlands and wild banana orchids, and parrot-, and woodpecker-watching. You'll also see the silver thatch palm, Cayman's national tree, called "the money tree" by locals. Back in the day, they traded its leaves for goods from local merchants, who in turn exchanged them for goods imported from Jamaica. The leaves are so strong that historically they were used to construct thatch roofs. Today, ropes and baskets are still made from them.

Little Cayman

Little Cayman is the quietest and smallest of Cayman's three islands—about 10 miles long and a mile wide. Turtle fishermen, ready to supply passing ships with turtle meat and fresh water, were the first to set up camp on Little Cayman. Tiny Blossom Village, one of its original settlements, is still here today; the school, stores, and post office are located in the village. Its residents lean into the quiet of the place. After all, busy Grand Cayman is only a short flight away.

The Salt Rock Nature Trail, winding around orchid and mahogany trees, is home to blue land crabs and iguanas, of which reputedly as many as 2,000 roam the island. Signs warn drivers: "Iguanas have the right of way." Little Cayman also protects the hawksbill sea turtle and the black-billed whistling duck, both in danger of extinction.

Additionally, the Booby Pond Nature Reserve is home to the largest red-footed booby population in the Caribbean. The Cayman Islands National Trust building there has telescopes on hand and is open weekday afternoons.

Little Cayman's Bloody Bay Wall is the area's most famous dive site. Covered with coral and teeming with fish, you can dive with reef sharks and hawksbill turtles here, as well as shrimp, drummer fish, and eagle rays. Parrotfish, angelfish, and schools of tiny silversides dart among the coral.

It's small, but Little Cayman knows how to party, and the island's Point of Sand beach is a popular gathering spot. The island also hosts such fun as the Little Cayman Cook-Off and Agriculture Show.

Cayman Brac

Five miles west of Little Cayman, Cayman Brac is the easternmost island of the Cayman Islands. It's not much bigger than its little sister—12 miles long and a little more than 1.2 miles wide—but it undeniably has more going on.

Cayman Brac, likely named by Scottish fishermen for its most prominent feature, a limestone bluff, or "brac" in Gaelic, has the most diverse terrain of the Caymans. Blackbeard and Captain Henry Morgan were among the many pirates who allegedly hid treasure in its caves and crevices. (Many believe Blackbeard's is still somewhere on the island today.)

The three-week-long Pirates Fest, held in November on all three islands, celebrates their history. It's a wonderland for spelunkers as well, with some caves so remote that ladders provide access for those who dare treasure hunt deep.

The island's bluff runs the length of the eastern end of the island and rises more than 40 meters. A lighthouse sits at the top. You can spend a night or two up here at Bluff View, which has two apartments surrounded by banyan trees, agave, and cacti. It's rustic—with shared outdoor showers and no Wi-Fi—but on-site coconut trees provide fresh coconuts. There's a sports facility nearby too, with a 25-meter pool that hosts national competitions.

Like neighboring Little Cayman, Cayman Brac's reputation for plentiful turtle meat and freshwater springs made it a hunting ground for turtlers and a place for ships to replenish their galleys for centuries. Today Cayman Brac has a few small communities, with schools, tourist centers, and cozy restaurants offering local fare. Bussy's is one especially popular nightspot among locals and visitors. For a more highbrow experience, take the farm tour at the Soleil D'Or and enjoy a farm-to-table feast.

The island has extensive hiking trails for birdwatching, and the 282-acre Brac Parrot Reserve is home to the endangered Cayman Brac Parrot. Look for brown boobies, peregrine falcons, and the rare, black-billed whistling duck as well. And it, too, offers some of the best scuba experiences in the Caribbean.

Off Cayman Brac lies one of the Caribbean's most famous wreck dives, the 100-meter MV Captain Keith Tibbetts, the only warship of its kind in the Western hemisphere. You can swim here from Cayman Brac's northwest side. Sponges and coral cover parts of the wreck, barracudas live in its hull, and moray eels and bottlenose dolphins have been known to make appearances.

These islands are an aquatic paradise. They offer year-round sunshine (even the rainy season only sees brief showers) and truly some of the best diving in the Caribbean.

There's a lot more to the Cayman Islands than scuba diving, even on tiny Little Cayman. Fun-loving islanders enjoy impromptu and scheduled gatherings like beach cleanups, storytelling festivals, and Easter egg hunts, as well as island-specific events like Cayman Brac's

Brac Fest and Braccanal. The islands' turtles have inspired such festivals as Cayman's national Carnival Batabano, which takes place every May and is named for the footprints that turtles leave in the sand.

Grand Cayman celebrates a two-weeks-long Cayman Arts Festival and Red Sky at Night to recognize Caymanian arts and Culinary Month and Taste of Cayman food festival. Each island's museum also offers their own local historical accounts as well. Further examples of Caymanian heritage include Grand Cayman's Miss Lassie's House, an authentic wattle and daub house built in the 1800s.

Living here, you'll pay for your beautiful views and tax-free status. As on most islands where everything has to be imported, prices are high. Import duties (the government's primary source of revenue) are about 22%, and, while items like baby formula may be exempt, others are taxed at a higher rate based on their value.

A couple will need about $5,000 a month to live on the islands. Rent for a two-bedroom place will cost about $2,800. Utilities will run about $500 and your groceries will be about $500 a month if you shop local and cut back on imported goods.

You can still find ways to save, and some expats even say they find it more affordable than they expect. The best way to cut costs, obviously, is to eat local foods and cook them yourself; restaurants are expensive. Buy the day's catch from the fishermen who anchor their boats offshore and display their fish on tables on the beach. They charge per pound and sell the fish on the bone, or fillet by request.

Also, shop farmers' markets; Grand Cayman's Camana Bay Local Harvest Market and the market at the Cricket Grounds sell locally farmed items like eggs, mango, breadfruit, bananas, papaya, and jams. Buying in bulk at stores like Priced Right and Cost.U.Less can also save you money.

Expect slimmer pickings on the Sisters Islands, where your grocer's selection will be based on whatever comes in on the weekly food supply by sea or air. If you plan ahead, however, you can order additional items from caymangroceryonline.com and get deliveries to either island in a day or two.

Most places take both Cayman dollars and U.S. dollars (although you'll get change in Cayman) and most ATMS offer both currencies as well.

It's a little harder to find inexpensive housing. A well-situated and appointed studio for rent will average $1,740 per month on Grand Cayman, while a three- or four-bedroom house could be $6,000. Facebook sometimes posts good deals on housing, as well as on appliances and household goods.

You'll need deep pockets if you plan to buy. A three-bedroom, two-bathroom on Seven Mile Beach was recently listed at $1,995,000. A one-bedroom condominium with pickleball courts and a kids' play area was listed for $551,169, and a three-bedroom luxury waterfront condo for $2,400,000.

The Sister Islands are a little cheaper. Recent listings include a 1.26-acre property on the Cayman Brac Bluff situated almost 15 meters high with sea views for $354,237. A 0.52-acre waterfront property on the island's southern side was $225,000. A 1.73-acre, beachfront property was recently for sale on Little Cayman at $1,799,000, and a 0.52-acre, beachfront lot for $539,000.

Grand Cayman is an easy place to get to, and its Owen Roberts International Airport has direct flights everywhere from London and Toronto to Los Angeles and Atlanta, as well as several one-hour flights daily to Miami. Cayman Brac's Charles Kirkconnell International Airport offers direct flights to Miami as well. Cayman Airways connects Grand Cayman to Cayman Brac for $168 and Little Cayman for $187, and a flight between the Sister Islands is $78.

Public transportation on Grand Cayman and Cayman Brac consists mostly of a public mini-bus transport system. It's pretty relaxed: You can flag down a bus and let the driver know when you'd like to get off. Fares are $2.40 to $3 for short trips and up to $9.60 for longer ones on Grand Cayman, and $3.60 on Cayman Brac. If you ask your driver for any sort of detour (which is totally OK to do), it'll cost you $1.20 to $3.60.

Public transportation is more limited on Little Cayman, but it's not difficult to arrange travel in such a small community. Its cheerful 11-seater mini-bus taxi service provides pickups and drop-offs to beaches, bars, restaurants, and the airport, as well as land tours and food delivery.

If you plan on getting a car be warned that gas is expensive, locals have a reputation for bad driving, and Grand Cayman's traffic can be heavy during peak hours. Bikes, scooters, and mopeds can also be rented easily, and electric scooters are available on Grand Cayman.

Reliable internet is one of the many reasons there are lots of digital nomads living on the islands.

As for meeting people, there is a variety of social groups, including club sports, religious organizations, and community service organizations meet regularly. Special interest groups like Cayman Brac's Sew-n-So Ladies Club are also heartily enjoyed.

Most Caymanians are multiracial. While it's generally agreed that there is very little racial divide, sensitivities around class do exist. Additionally, some Caymanians are starting to feel pushed out by the white-collar expats moving to town. Be sensitive to that if you decide to move here.

Grand Cayman's terrain is flat, and the majority of places have good sidewalk ramps. Most people who use wheelchairs can get around pretty easily here. The Sister Islands are more challenging, although Cayman Brac's South Side Public Beach has a mobi mat, and Carter's Taxi & Tours has a wheelchair accessible van. The dive companies on all three islands, however, offer superb diving packages for people with varying needs.

The islands enjoy a tropical climate with warm temperatures year-round, typically ranging from 77°F (25°C) to 88°F (31°C). The island experiences a rainy season from May to November, which also coincides with hurricane season, though severe hurricanes are infrequent.

With year-round sunshine, a safe and clean environment, lively community spirit, and a stable government, how could you not love these islands?

Health Care In The Caymans

Every resident is required to have health insurance, and you're in good hands with the Cayman's health care system. Grand Cayman has world-class doctors. In addition to Grand Cayman's three fully equipped hospitals (Cayman Islands Hospital, Doctors Hospital, and Health City Cayman Islands), you'll find everything from mental health services, hearing centers, and wellness clinics to school health screenings, art therapy, and acupuncture.

There's a doctor's clinic on Cayman Brac and the island's Faith Hospital serves both Cayman Brac and Little Cayman; a consultation will cost you about $180. Little Cayman also has a clinic staffed by two nurses.

Residency Requirements

Technically visitors can legally stay for six months, after which they can apply for an extension. However, most visitors are in fact only given permission to stay 30 days when they arrive, unless they own property on the islands and can prove they can take care of themselves financially. If you'd like to settle in for a while, your best bet is to arrive with a letter demonstrating financial security, health insurance, and your island address. Frequent visitors are often granted six months, but will have to show a return ticket.

After you've been a permanent resident 12 months and have lived in Cayman for at least five years, you can apply for naturalization as a British Overseas Territories Citizen (BOTC). Once naturalized, you'll receive a BOTC passport and can register for British citizenship. Note: Living "off island" for more than 90 days in a year, or 540 days over five years, could affect your application.

After five years as a BOTC (or you've been 15 years in Cayman—whichever comes first), you can apply for the Right to be Caymanian.

This is decidedly *not* the same as being naturalized. The Right to be Caymanian officially grants you the right to reside and work in the Cayman Islands, while naturalization simply declares you a BOTC and allows a Caymanian passport, which only functions as a travel document.

You can apply for Permanent Residency with the right to work after eight years of living here, or immediately if you are the spouse or child of a permanent resident or Caymanian.

This is granted through a fairly complicated point system based on exigencies like age, community involvement, and education, as well as financial stability. There's even a history and culture test.

If you are willing to invest significantly in a business or property, however, you can apply straightaway to the Director of Workforce Opportunities and Residency (WORC) for permanent residency with or without the right to work in four different ways.

The Certificate of Permanent Residency is the easiest way to acquire permanent residency and the right to work. This option has no expiration date, but it's expensive: You are required to invest at least $2,412,000 in developed real estate and prove you can support you and your family financially. You'll also need to confirm your good health and good character. Only 250 of these certificates are granted annually.

If you want to live here and not work, you can apply for a Residency Certificate, renewable and valid for 25 years; the initial application fee is $600. You're required to show proof of an annual income of at least $144,000 (or deposit at least $481,000 in a local bank) and invest at least $1,202,000, half of which must be in developed real estate. (Applicants typically buy a property that meets that entire requirement.)

It's a little less expensive to live on Little Cayman or Cayman Brac, where you'll need proof of an annual income of $91,000, as well as to invest $601,000, half in developed real estate. Wherever you live, expect a one-time fee of $24,000 and an additional $1,202 for each dependent.

Your third option is to obtain the Certificate of Direct Investment, valid for 25 years and renewable and intended for investors interested in investing in employment that specifically generates business in the Cayman Islands.

You're required to demonstrate an existing or planned investment of $1,206,000 in such employment. Before you apply for a full certificate, you are permitted to obtain an Approval-in-Principle Certificate, valid for six months, which allows you to reside in the Cayman Islands and work in the business in which you've invested. The application fee is $1,202, with an additional $24,000 due upon receipt of the certificate, plus $1,202 per dependent.

Finally, the Residency Certificate (Substantial Business Presence), valid for 25 years, is designed to be more amenable than the Certificate of Direct Investment, and allows residency to anyone who owns at least a 10% share in an approved category of business in Cayman (these are listed online) or will be employed at such a business. You must prove you and your spouse have no criminal record and are in good health. The fee is $6,015, with an additional $1,202 per dependent.

Real Estate Restrictions

The Caymans make it easy to buy property. There are no restrictions on foreign ownership, and anyone can and even is encouraged to buy property here. You do not have to live here to do it. It's no surprise that many expats already have: It's safe, clean, and beautiful, and, of course, owners do not pay property, income, or capital gains tax.

Really the only fee you'll encounter is a one-time stamp duty fee, currently 7.5% of the purchase price or the market value of the property, whichever is higher. (Market value is determined by a Valuation Office and is open to review.) If you require financing, be aware that although banks in the Cayman Islands do offer mortgages to foreign buyers, they often have strict regulations concerning deposits and income verification. Secured mortgages are subject to a one-time stamp duty at 1% or 1.5%, depending on the amount of the loan.

You can purchase a property yourself or through a company or trust.

Still, it's always safest to work with a local real estate agent and attorney. CIREBA (Cayman Islands Real Estate Brokers Association) manages the Multiple Listing Service (MLS) where most properties are listed. Have your lawyer doublecheck any restrictions that could potentially affect the property and possible licensing requirements for, say, non-residential or rental properties.

Taxes

Cayman residents are not subject to local income, capital gains, corporate, sales, death, or annual property taxes. Although some argue that it wasn't King George III they should thank (rather, that most Caymanians were simply subsistence farmers or fishermen until the mid-1900s with little if anything to tax), no matter the reason—beauty and beaches aside—any savvy investor knows that Cayman is simply a good place to bet on.

And it's a thriving offshore financial center as well. Multinational companies do not pay corporate, income, payroll, or withholding taxes. Thousands have found it the perfect place to avoid taxation and establish an offshore subsidiary.

Especially popular among hedge fund managers, there's no taxation on interest or dividends earned on investments either. Offshore corporations are subject to an annual licensing fee, paid to the government, and, of course, doublecheck your home country's tax laws. (U.S. citizens can sometimes exempt a portion of their foreign income from their U.S. obligations, for example.) Lucky for investors, like all tax havens, privacy laws are taken very seriously.

V

WESTERN EUROPE

There's a common misconception that Europe is expensive and that a comfortable retirement there is beyond your reach...

I'm happy to report that's not the case.

My husband, Lief, and I divide our time between our homes in France and Panama, and it might surprise you to learn that our monthly costs are higher when we're in Panama City than they are when we're at our Paris base.

There are a number of reasons for this...

In Panama City, we need a car. That's not the case in Paris, where a walk to the store or to work is a joy rather than a chore. And, when the weather doesn't cooperate, the city's excellent public transport is cheap and easy to use.

Our utility bills are lower in Europe, too—air conditioning is neither the norm nor necessary here. Our phone plan is also cheaper in Paris and offers unlimited free calls to the United States and throughout Europe.

The fact is, across Europe, your cost of living can be hugely variable and highly controllable.

So, if you dream of a retirement in Old World Europe but fear your budget puts it out of reach, it's time to think again.

Of course, there are other huge benefits of living in Europe. For starters, there's the café culture. Outside Europe, the café society doesn't really exist anywhere else. What's better than walking for a while and stopping when you start to flag for a coffee... or a champagne... perhaps a snack... Even if you're not stopping for lunch or a drink, nothing beats being in a café city surrounded by the clatter of silverware and dishes, the toasting of glasses, the smells of the dish of the day, and the people-watching.

And then there's the food. French and Dutch cheeses, Italian prosecco, Spanish meats, Irish butter, Swiss chocolates... In Europe, you're not paying the price you are back home for these luxury goods. They're a trip to the grocery store down the block and cost no more than anything else on the shelves.

Whether expat or foreigner, people here are more interesting than you're likely to meet back home—either they're foreign or they're expats and have some story to share about how they came to be here. Most expats are serial—they have already been living in other countries, and they have so many experiences to share. And making local friends who have a whole new culture to open up to you is invaluable as well as interesting.

Europe is one of the best places in the world to explore. It's so easy and affordable to do when you're in the heart of the Continent already. Hop on the Eurostar and travel from Paris to London for the weekend. Book a cheap flight with a budget airline and fly from Dublin to Madrid for a couple days of exploring. It's all convenient and possible wherever you're based in Europe.

So many cultures, so many histories, and so many landscapes—you could spend your entire retirement exploring all of Europe's secrets.

One more great thing about living in Europe...

The American work ethic truly is a unique thing in the world. It's a cliché, but the rest of the world really does work to live. People here don't care if they can make overtime on a holiday or that there might be tourists to shop on a Sunday. Nothing can cut into a non-American's leisure time. In some parts of Europe, the daily siesta is still a time-honored tradition.

Society here doesn't push you to always go, go, go—it encourages you to slow down. In Europe you'll be forced to take a step back and appreciate what matters most.

So, can you really live in Europe... and within your means?

Let's dive in to the top destinations in Europe that are worth your consideration.

CHAPTER 9

FRANCE

Few countries combine lifestyle, culture, and convenience like France...

From the rolling vineyards of Bordeaux to the snow-capped Alps, from the lavender fields of Provence to the chic streets of Paris, France offers a remarkable diversity of landscapes, climates, and communities to choose from.

For 100 years or so, it's been a magnet for expats seeking a rich cultural life, excellent health care, and an enviable standard of living.

France balances history and modernity seamlessly. Imagine wandering cobbled streets in medieval villages, sipping coffee at a café overlooking the Seine, or enjoying a leisurely afternoon in one of the country's vast public gardens.

Regional cuisine changes from coast to coast, offering everything from buttery Normandy seafood to Provencal olive oil-infused dishes... And France's gastronomy isn't just for Michelin stars—it's daily life. From local markets overflowing with cheese, bread, olive oil and seasonal produce to prix-fixe bistro lunches that deliver three courses and a glass of wine at a modest cost, food culture is part of the social fabric here.

For many expats, farmers' markets become a weekly ritual, and regional specialties (from Provençal ratatouille to Normandy's seafood) offer endless culinary exploration. Wine regions like Bordeaux and Burgundy are practically in retirees' backyards if they choose them, making food a social experience rather than just sustenance.

France has a way of feeling timeless, even in its cities. Strolling through a city neighborhood, you'll pass weekly markets overflowing with fresh bread, cheeses, fruits, and vegetables, just as locals have done for generations. Small cafés spill onto cobblestone streets, and artisans' shops display handcrafted goods in wooden storefronts. In the countryside, life slows down even more—vineyards, orchards, and farmhouses dot the landscape, and neighbors greet each other by name.

Rural living in France can feel like stepping back to America a century ago, with a strong sense of community, local traditions, and a pace of life that celebrates simplicity, quality, and connection to the land.

France consistently ranks as safer than the United States in key measures of personal security and public services, contributing to a general sense of calm and predictability retired life can thrive in.

Modern transport networks (including high-speed trains), green spaces, cultural institutions, and well-maintained regional towns offer both convenience and charm. Whether you seek a lively city like Lyon or Nantes, a historic town like Aix-en-Provence, or a quiet village in the Dordogne, the country's infrastructure supports a wide variety of lifestyles.

France isn't just beautiful—it's structured to help you enjoy life. The French famously embrace a work-to-live mindset, not the reverse: a 35-hour workweek is standard, with generous vacation and protected lunch breaks. This isn't just a stereotype, it's part of the legal fabric of life here and you'll feel it as soon as you arrive.

Even for retirees or part-timers, this cultural approach makes daily life more relaxed: cafés, leisure walks, cultural festivals, and outdoor markets are not afterthoughts, they are woven into everyday routines.

France is home to nearly three million foreign residents, including tens of thousands of Americans who value the country's high quality of life, stability, and welcoming communities.

English is widely spoken in urban areas and tourist destinations, and the presence of active expat networks ensures newcomers can adapt quickly, whether they settle in a vibrant city, a quiet village, or a seaside town.

Top Picks For A New Life In France

Paris

Who doesn't dream of living in Paris—this is, after all, one of Europe's great cities. It's also the place that I'm lucky to call home for six months of every year.

Back in 2004, we moved from Waterford, Ireland to Paris. Back then, and still now, one of the greatest delights of Paris for me is sitting at a bistro table street side, sipping, reading, and watching. I'll choose a table with a view of the park across the way, and order a pot of tea and a tartine with jam, all while watching as this corner of Paris we call home goes about its day.

I was first drawn to living in Paris for her culture, with hundreds of museums and galleries and some of the most revered cuisine in the world; space to lounge in parks and on riversides... plus a superb and affordable public transportation system; and other modern amenities, including top-notch health care and good schools for my children.

The history, the art, the food, the fashion, the wine, the architecture, the language, the romance... the je ne sais quoi. For most, Paris doesn't disappoint.

This Grand Dame of cities really seems to have it all...

France has the best health care in the world, an enviable quality of life, and some of the best gastronomy the world has to offer.

The downsides are that taxes are high, everyone's always on strike, customer service is generally terrible, and the French invented bureaucracy, so getting anything administrative done is a nightmare.

And you'll pay a high price to live here. Paris is one of the most cosmopolitan cities in the world, but all that luxe comes at a cost. Property prices, both for owning and renting, are sky high for very little space. But Paris can be more affordable than most people imagine.

As a couple, your monthly budget will be about 3,350 euros to 4,200 euros a month. Rent for a small apartment costs 2,100 euros and up. Transport costs are about 50 euros a month (but this is a very walkable city so you may not need to spend so much); eating out twice a week will set you back about 675 euros a month; and your groceries will be about 500 euros.

A doctor's visit, if you pay out of pocket, costs 65 euros; a specialist is 90 euros. Living in Paris, you'll have access to the best medical care in the country and it's all within easy access—you won't have to go far to find any of the care you need.

Plus, doctors still make home visits in France, and you can expect even a basic consultation to last half an hour.

And, if you're a member of French Social Security (if you're paying taxes in France), most of the cost of this extraordinary health care is covered.

Even if you're not, the care is affordable.

In terms of safety, any big city can generally be dangerous in the same ways... densely populated spaces breed petty crime; this is true all over the world. You'll have to have your wits about you living in Paris. Take the same precautions as you would in any major city.

Paris gets a full four distinct seasons. Autumns are often gray and rainy; springs are usually brighter and rainy. Winter has just as much blue sky as gray, though coming off a long spell of gray, it can feel disproportionate. You might even get a few snow days in winter. It's rare to get snow in Paris, so it's exciting when it happens.

Summers are hot and August is sticky... which is par for the course in much of the world, the difference here is that air conditioning is scarcely to be found.

Temperatures range between about 48°F and 61°F (9°C to 16°C) with average humidity hovering at about 76%. You'll typically see about 25 inches of precipitation a year.

Weather extremes are a more recent phenomenon—in recent years Paris has seen some more snowfall in the winter and record-breaking heat waves in the summer. With weather patterns becoming more extreme worldwide, this is likely to continue.

If you're a city person at heart but still appreciate a more traditional, less streamlined way of life... If you want to go to the opera one night and a local produce market the next morning...

If you love being active and walking everyday... If you never tire of museums... If you live for a spontaneous café lunch... If you want to easily make expat friends after arriving... you can have all this and more living in Paris. Plus, if you want to hop around Europe, exploring every country on the Continent it's easy to do from your base in the city.

I personally love living here. Some of my best afternoons in Paris have been spent on a blanket in a little park with friends, a bottle of champagne, a loaf of baguette, a wheel of brie, and Notre-Dame just skips away.

Gascony

Rustic and slow-paced, Gascony is known for rolling vineyards, sunflower fields, and charming villages. Life here is pure traditional rural France, with weekly markets, farm-to-table dining, and a strong sense of community.

Located in the southwestern corner of France (about seven hours by car from Paris), between Bordeaux and the Pyrenees and close to the Spanish border, this safe and peaceful region is a true hidden gem.

This is a place to get back to a lifestyle that was once how everyone in the world lived, content with their lot...

Gascony tries hard not to change too much, and aside from improvements in agriculture or to raise awareness of its attributes to increase tourism, there's not much on the horizon here by way of innovation. You won't encounter any big development projects taking place—no large-scale construction, super-highways, or big shopping malls exist here now, nor are planned in the future. The only industry is farming, whether crops or livestock.

Gascogne people are often self-sufficient to some degree, with farms ranging from 150 hectares to a kitchen garden for herbs and vegetables. Co-ops are a mainstay of commerce here, so it's easy enough to bring raw materials to various co-op centers that can help you turn olives into oil, grapes into wine, or milk into cheese, etc.

This is a pastoral place, where the traffic on the roads is tractors and livestock… and where farmers run things and the weather or the harvest is the main topic on anyone's lips…

Where folks are up well before the sun and drinking red wine by 11 a.m...and where the food is hearty and fresh from the pasture…

Where the village markets are the main social affair of the week and people are in bed by 9 p.m.... This is a place to get back to a lifestyle that was once how everyone in the world lived... And they want to keep it that way.

Some of our favorite towns here include Fourcès, known for its weekly produce market and annual flower fair… Lupiac, hometown of the legendary d'Artagnan of the Musketeers… La Romieu, said to have been saved from the plague by a young girl's illegal cat, now reveres felines for this reason…

Lectoure, one of the larger towns offering shopping, restaurants, and art galleries… and Auch, the department's capital, more cosmopolitan and the closest thing to a city in the region…

Gascony has been a main stop on the Camino de Santiago, the pilgrimage route of Santiago de Compostela, for over 1,000 years.

When it comes to making a home here, you'll need to make a few adjustments to adapt to the local culture…

First, you'll need to make a serious effort at learning French, as few people here speak English.

You'll also need to get used to "country hours."

For example, you can only eat meals during certain hours of the day. Lunch won't be served past 2 p.m., and dinner won't be had before 7 p.m. or after 9 p.m.

With such a low population density, most restaurants only open on weekends... maybe only for dinner... and perhaps not at all on Sundays or Mondays.

Hiking and biking are great pastimes here, and the abundant countryside provides a wealth of opportunities for long walks.

The flat landscape also makes for ideal biking conditions. Picturesque trails running through oak forests and medieval villages are best explored on horseback and you'll find many stables in the area offering half-day rides with lunch included.

With no access to the sea, water sports are limited to swimming and pleasure boating on the rivers, lakes, and canals, of which there are plenty. Lac de l'Uby has sandy shores and is a popular spot for swimming, canoeing, and paddleboarding.

Gascony is yet another destination that proves that life in Europe is not financially out of reach for Americans...

You can rent a house for about 675 euros a month; a meal out will set you back only 25 euros (for two); go see a movie for 8 euros; and a GP visit is 35 euros. Overall, a monthly average of 1,760 euros will cover a couple's cost of living.

And this region of France offers excellent health care. For anything minor, there are doctor's surgeries in the villages. If larger-scale care or an ER visit is required, you'll likely be just a short drive from a small local hospital—each town has its own, so there are about a dozen in this small region.

For specialists or serious concerns, you'd head to one of the larger hospitals that can be found on the outskirts of the region.

Gascony gets four distinct seasons, including cool, wet winters and warm, relatively wet summers. Mild Atlantic winds have a nullifying effect on the temperature, so extremes are rare. That said, you may see a bit of snow here during winter—about three or four days per year.

While expats here are spread out among the many towns, villages, and countryside in between, they do exist, the largest communities being found in Condom, Auch, Fourcès, and Montréal-du-Gers.

Made up of mostly Brits and Northern Europeans, Americans and Canadians are just starting to find their way to this quiet little corner of France.

The international airport in this area is in Toulouse. It doesn't offer regular direct flights to the United States, but it offers one to Canada by way of Montreal.

To get to Gascony, you'll likely fly into Paris, which has a plethora of direct flights to the States and Canada, and take the train (four-and-a-half hours to Toulouse direct or six hours and 45 minutes to Auch with one change) or drive to Gascony—which takes around seven hours.

Gascony is a sprawling region encompassing several towns and villages of different sizes... You'd be perfectly safe in any of these. Simply put, Gascony is one of France's safest rural regions and it's highly unlikely that crime would affect your life living here.

The picturesque landscape and the secluded nature of the area draw people from elsewhere to Gascony... not the multitude of entertainment options or the raving nightlife.

The social life you'll have here will consist of gossiping with neighbors on market days, chats over coffee, and long, leisurely meals with friends.

During summer, the night markets amount to local parties for the whole family, with food, music, dancing, and lots of fun had by all. The lifestyle here is a quiet one...so if that is the life you're after in retirement, you should take a closer look at Gascony.

La Rochelle

The medieval port town of La Rochelle is located in southwestern France, just north of Bordeaux and about a three-hour train ride from Paris. It's a favorite holiday spot for the French, and becoming increasingly popular with European tourists.

A picturesque Atlantic port city, La Rochelle combines maritime charm with vibrant city life. Its historic harbor, seafood markets, cycling paths, and festivals make for a relaxed yet engaging lifestyle, perfect for retirees who love coastal living with cultural flair.

La Rochelle is known for seafood and sunny weather. Nicknamed La Ville Blanche for its dazzling sunshine, you'll want good sunglasses and a brimmed hat most of the year.

The day-to-day life here is vibrant and active. Most days see folks of all ages enjoying the salty sea air—grocery shopping at the historic market, playing cards or board games in the park, taking a bike ride, hitting the beach, or simply enjoying a crisp glass of local white wine next to the harbor. Oysters are the first (and often second and third) item on every menu.

The town is completely accessible by foot or bike, and much of the historical center is pedestrianized. Bike lanes and buses crisscross the city, and boats, buses, and trains take you to any place near or far, making a car unnecessary for most residents.

La Rochelle is home to about 175,000 people, making this the most populous city in the Charente-Maritime department. Aside from the permanent residents, the city sees the influx of students and tourists every year. This is the third most touristed town in France, with over 3 million visitors a year.

What are the top reasons why La Rochelle makes a great retirement haven? For many, it's the dream of a beach lifestyle—living in a city that's minutes from the sea.

Another big draw is for boaters. This has to be one of the most active boating cultures in France. Plus, the seasons are mild, allowing you to take advantage of the beaches and the sea for most of the year.

Outdoor recreation opportunities abound in La Rochelle. No matter the time of year, the beaches are in use. If it's too cold for a dip, the coast is the perfect spot for a stroll.

Green spaces are never far, with many small parks throughout the city and the nearly 100-acre Parc Charruyer running through the middle of town. Starting at Plage de la Concurrence, the park continues inland about a mile, providing a complete escape into nature in the heart of the city.

The city walls provide a lovely promenade route along the seaside. Biking is a major part of the culture here. Aside from being a means of transport, biking is a popular pastime among all ages, and the bike paths that wind through the city and surrounding areas are a pleasure to travel. You can even bike across the bridges to Île de Ré or Île d'Oléron, and the islands are bike havens.

Golf isn't a common pastime in France, yet there are several courses in the area. An 18-hole course is just 20 minutes from town, and there are several 9-hole courses, driving ranges, and academies within an hour.

The cost of living in La Rochelle is moderate at between 2,100 euros and 2,600 euros per month... but keep in mind, this is a top-tier city that was rated the third-best in France for quality of life. It's a coastal city with mild weather, meaning you'll always be close to the sea...

Rent, variable by location and property size, ranges from 720 euros to 1,350 euros per month. Dining out at French restaurants serving fresh seafood can run you 35 euros to 65 euros for two. Groceries, including fresh produce, are fantastically affordable.

Two things that will come cheaper in France than the U.S. or Canada are transportation and health care. Both are well-organized with solid infrastructure and come at almost negligible costs.

A general practitioner here charges 25 euros per consultation, and that's what you'd pay for a clinic visit, too. Specialist visits are about 50 euros.

La Rochelle is home to a small selection of hospitals and health centers, the primary being Le Centre Hospitalier Saint-Louis De La Rochelle, a large hospital complex that's among the best in France.

La Rochelle is perfect for people who want to live by the beach and enjoy temperate weather. You can get by without air conditioning here (air conditioning isn't easy to find anyway), although you might want heating at home.

Temperatures don't fluctuate much throughout the year. Summers don't get extremely hot, and winters don't get extremely cold, although they're a bit rainy.

You'll need to learn French to live here and integrate well, but because the city has been welcoming British, Irish, and Dutch tourists for so long, many in the service industry speak English.

If you move to La Rochelle, you won't be the only foreigner here... but there aren't big expat groups. This is the type of place where you'll need to make an effort to integrate into the local community.

La Rochelle has a small airport with seasonal flights to a few cities in Europe beyond France. To get here from North America, you have a couple of options...

The simplest is to fly to Paris and catch the three-hour train to La Rochelle. You could also fly to a European hub with a flight service to La Rochelle, although this option will only be available during certain seasons.

There's little to no concern about crime in La Rochelle. Crime rates are very low, and violent crime is practically non-existent.

This laid-back city offers a wealth of history, an active arts scene, and fabulous shopping prospects, and it's not an expensive place to live. This is a real city with plenty to see and do, but it's got the feel of a small town. If that sounds like the kind of place that could make you happy, come check out La Rochelle yourself.

Health Care In France

France's health care system is widely regarded as one of the best in the world. This distinction isn't just about good hospitals, it reflects affordable, accessible universal care, English-friendly services, and preventative health systems that give retirees peace of mind.

This is huge for Americans used to high out-of-pocket costs and unpredictable insurance. France's public system reimburses a significant portion of medical expenses (often about 70% or more), and with the addition of a Carte Vitale health card, routine appointments become both easy and inexpensive.

Legal residents, including most American retirees, are eligible for coverage under Sécurité Sociale, thanks to a reciprocal health care agreement with the United States. Public health care is high quality and affordable, and many expats choose supplementary private insurance for faster access to specialists.

A general practitioner here charges 25 euros per consultation, and that's what you'd pay for a clinic visit, too. Specialist visits are about 50 euros.

English-speaking doctors are easy to find in cities and expat-heavy areas, though you might have trouble finding one in more remote regions or villages.

Residency Requirements

France, like most European countries, will grant residency if you can prove you can support yourself without undertaking paid work. You need to prove income of between 1,270 euros to 1,700 euros per month for a single and between 1,950 euros to 2,500 euros for a couple, which gets you a one-year long-stay visa that you can renew.

Private health insurance with 30,000 euros cover is required for an initial period of at least three months after which you can apply to join France's national public health insurance system, Caisse Primaire d'Assurance Maladie.

France does not offer a golden visa, retirement specific visa, or digital nomad visa.

Real Estate Restrictions

You can buy real estate in France with no foreigner-specific restrictions.

Taxes

France is a high-tax country... but this doesn't really matter for U.S. retirees because of the U.S.-France tax treaty.

Basically, if you're not working, you're not taxed on anything that isn't earned in France. The tax treaty gives you a "deemed" tax credit for the total tax amount in France for any income taxable in the U.S. If all your income is passive, you're not taxed in France at all as an American.

The U.S.-France tax treaty is so advantageous that our tax specialist calls it "the bee's knees for American retirees."

Earned income is a different story, but there are still ways to reduce your taxes in France using the treaty.

If your tax domicile is in France, you're subject to income tax on your worldwide income. A surtax of 3% applies to income that exceeds 250,000 euros.

Social surcharges (on employment income, rental income, interest, dividends, and capital gains) of 7% to 9% also apply.

Different types of capital gains are taxed differently in France. For real estate sales, if the home sold is your principal residence, it's exempt from capital gains tax. Tax treatment on real estate sales varies depending on the situation, so it's important to consult a real estate tax specialist.

France imposes an inheritance tax of up to 60%, but it does not apply if the inheritance is between spouses or brothers and sisters living together under specific conditions. Between direct dependents, progressive rates apply after a rebate on 100,000 euros.

It also imposes a net wealth tax of 0.5% to 1.5% on worldwide real estate assets that exceed 1.3 million euros.

CHAPTER 10

MALTA AND GOZO

A string of small islands in the southern Mediterranean makes up Malta. One of the tiniest countries in Europe, it also has the tiniest capital: Valletta covers less than a square kilometer but is full of buildings that give evidence to Malta's colorful history. The country is home to some of the oldest human artefacts in the world, some of which predate the Egyptian pyramids and Stonehenge.

It's been occupied by various groups throughout its existence, from the Phoenicians to the Byzantines, the Ottomans to the Knights of Templar... All have left their mark on the place.

Malta's islands became a hub of Mediterranean artistic and architectural excellence, and artists such as Caravaggio, Mattia Preti, and Favray were commissioned by the knights to embellish churches, palaces, and auberges.

The era of the knights came to an end in 1798 when Napoleon Bonaparte swept into Malta en route to Egypt. The French didn't stay long—they were ousted by the English just two years later. The English remained in control until 1964, when Malta finally secured its independence.

Valletta is a modern European capital with great shopping by day and entertainment nearby at night. The city has been a UNESCO World Heritage City since 1980, and in 2018 it was chosen as that year's European Capital of Culture.

Its center fills up with tourists in high season, turning out to enjoy its mix of casual and fine-dining restaurants, as well as its Baroque churches and palaces.

Beyond the city, the gnarled, limestone islands of Malta, Comino, and Gozo conceal an impressive array of caves, scenic sunsets, and some of the most stunning harbors on the planet. Its rugged coastline boasts secluded bays, dramatic cliffs, and tiny coves dotted with ancient forts and quaint fishing harbors.

Malta is one of the sunniest places in the Mediterranean, enjoying about 3,000 hours of sunshine a year. Valletta has often been ranked among the best expat destinations in the world, and weather is one of the most cited reasons.

These waters are one of Europe's best sailing locales, and it's easy to see why. With a near-perfect climate and a long sailing season, Malta works well as a location both for experienced "salties" as well as those just starting out... not to mention all the other watersports to avail of here.

The Maltese waters also boast some of the best scuba diving in Europe, with plenty of marine life and interesting things to see below the surface...

Gozo's Blue Hole has a reputation as an iconic diving spot. Carved out by thousands of years of wave erosion, it's 15 meters wide and contains an underwater arch 10 meters below the surface.

Maltese cuisine, heavily influenced by Italian culinary traditions, is delicious, affordable, and easy to find. Many of the restaurants in popular resort areas like Sliema focus on drawing in British tourists and often offer pub grub like fish and chips and bangers and mash... But you don't need to go much farther beyond the tourist traps to get something genuinely Maltese.

Along with Maltese, English is one of Malta's official languages, making a transition into expat life easier. Living here, you'd never need to try to speak a word of Maltese. Business, banking, and legal affairs are all conducted in English. It has a long-standing, stable democracy in place, is a member of the EU, and the currency used is the euro.

During summer, towns and villages all over Malta have their own small festivals. Every town or village has at least one feast dedicated to a saint. In the summer months, you can catch one virtually every other week. The feasts usually run for a full week, coming to a climax on a Saturday.

Towns are decorated with statues, ornaments, and tapestries, and fireworks light up the night sky. Towns invariably attempt to outdo each other in the extravagance stakes, and there are some long-standing and well-known rivalries. Expect the locals to go all out in their bid to have the best party.

Along with Valletta, Sliema is a popular town for expats on Malta. Located in the northeast coast of the island, Sliema is a large residential and commercial area.

The Inner Harbour region, where Sliema is located, is the most popular location for foreigners (both tourists and expats). It's busy, culture rich, heavily populated, and close to the water. This area is where you will find the majority of expats because this is where many new turn-key developments are being built.

The Harbour has plenty of commercial activities such as shopping centers, commercial offices, restaurants, hotels, nightlife, and many other entertainment options.

The area is home to most of the island's high-rise buildings and major real estate projects. In the summer months, the Northern Harbour district is especially popular with tourists. Monthly rents for a two-bedroom apartment normally cost about 1,000 euros.

Gozo

Rumor has it that the island of Ogygia in Homer's "The Odyssey" is really Gozo—Malta's smaller, more scenic sister island. A bedraggled Odysseus washes up on its shores after surviving a horrible shipwreck...

He's in the middle of his epic struggle to return home to Ithaca and his wife, Penelope, but ends up spending seven long years on Gozo. Whether it's the island's stunning natural beauty or the sultry sea nymph, Calypso, that keeps him from his wife for so long is up for debate...

What is known beyond doubt is that Gozo is an extremely picturesque little rock in the middle of the Mediterranean where you can enjoy abundant sunshine, turquoise waters, and inexpensive property with historical charm, all set within a traditional village atmosphere...

People from Gozo are fiercely proud and distinguish themselves from mainland Malta. Their culture syncretizes many foreign influences, which probably has to do with the island's geographic position. For centuries, it served as steppingstone between Western Asia, North America, and Southern Europe since the days when the Mediterranean was the superhighway of trade and cultural exchange...

Inevitably, many conquering groups made pitstops on Gozo and exerted their influence over it and its people. Ruins and varying architectural styles across the island attest to this history... Some of the world's oldest religious structures are found here. Ggantija Temple, for instance, predates the pyramids of Egypt and Stonehenge... even the invention of the wheel.

Because, for hundreds of years, Gozo existed in a state of constant siege, it was impossible for its people to set up permanent establishments anywhere outside its heavily fortified Cittadella in capital city Victoria. In fact, the island's inhabitants were subjected to a nightly curfew for safety reasons until 1637...

This meant villages didn't develop on Gozo until relatively late in its history. Around the mid-1600s came a time of peace, and Gozo's first town—Xewkija—developed in 1678. Over time, more towns sprang up, and today, the island is home to 15 major villages.

All of them are traditional, featuring homes, restaurants, and businesses organized around a central church and town square... but at the same time, each offers something unique and has its own distinct flavor. For instance, Marsalforn, where there over 40 restaurants, stands out for its culinary scene...

Xlendi is a picturesque coastal town with great swimming and boating opportunities around a bay flanked by cliffs... Xaghra is a quiet, non-touristed village in northeast Gozo that sits at about 108 meters (354 feet) above sea level, affording it phenomenal views of the sea and rest of the island...

Other villages may have eye-catching architectural features or particularly lively festivals during the year... Spending time in each village and discovering its vibe, its microculture, its unique offerings is part of the joy of living in Gozo. It's also an important step in figuring out where on the island you want to settle.

What's on offer across the board is historical architecture in a traditional village setting, where church bells sound at the same time every day, you see the same faces over and over, and life moves at a relaxed pace. None of Gozo's villages has a population bigger than 7,000 people, so the small-town feeling is consistent across the island.

On top of that, the island itself is small. At only 67 square kms (26 square miles), where you settle isn't hugely important, as you can get from one side of the island to the other in under an hour anyway. The lifestyle is safe, peaceful, and quiet, and that's the way people like it. If you're after the party scene or enjoy spending time at the mall, Gozo isn't for you.

The landscape is famous for its cacti-spotted hills and peaceful, desert scenery... It's so distinctive, in fact, it's often featured in television and film. If you've ever seen "The Count of Monte Cristo," "Game of Thrones," or "By the Sea," then you've already laid eyes on Gozo's landscape.

Gozo is only 4.5 kms (3 miles) from mainland Malta, but this slight separation and the logistics of getting here on a ferry have been enough to preserve Gozo's small town appeal. If you're after a traditional village setting shared by expats and locals, as well as proximity to the sea, access to Europe, and a reasonable cost of living, you've got to go to Gozo.

The climate in Malta is typical Mediterranean, with hot summers and mild winters. Temperatures range between an average low of about 59°F and an average high of 72°F (15°C and 22°C) with humidity hovering around 76%. From June to September it's hot and super sunny; from December to March it's a little cooler.

Malta is a bargain compared to the rest of Europe, and Gozo is a bargain compared to Malta. Everything from groceries to utilities, eating out to transport is inexpensive here and will likely cost you less than it does at home.

Here's an overview of basic items to give you an idea of what you might spend living in Malta (in Gozo, you'd spend 10% to 20% less). This is per month based on a couple living in Valletta.

Rent for two-bed apartment will come in about 1,000 euros; transportation (if you're driving your own car) is 48 euros; utilities are about 77 euros; your monthly grocery bill will be 290 euros; and dinner for two, including drinks, will come in around 100 euros.

A local draft beer is 3.90 euros and you'll get a bottle of wine for 6 to 10 euros. Coffee costs 2.50 euros.

Malta is often cited as the world's safest country when it comes to natural disasters: earthquakes and floods are very unlikely, and infrastructure is well-prepared for rising sea levels.

There are a number of expats on both Malta and Gozo. Most hail from the U.K., but there are also many Italians, Germans, Bulgarians, Swedes, French, and citizens of other EU-member nations, as well as Americans. Gozo has a British Residents' Association that hosts coffee mornings every first Monday of the month as well as other events. Volunteering is one way to get involved and meet people.

Being an island doesn't have to mean isolation... Malta proves this with its well-connected international airport. Located in Gudja (on the mainland), Malta International Airport runs regular and seasonal flights to over thirty destinations in Europe, five destinations in Asia, and three destinations in Africa.

It doesn't offer direct flights to North America but services every major travel hub in Western Europe, including the heavyweights—Heathrow, Frankfurt, and Schiphol. Therefore, getting here from the

States or Canada will involve a layover.

Malta and Gozo are extremely safe. According to locals, the only people you see wandering the streets at 5 a.m. are grannies on their way to mass. You're unlikely to fall victim to even petty crime anywhere in Malta.

Whether you choose Malta or Gozo, you'll be living on a picturesque little rock in where you can enjoy beautiful beaches with turquoise waters, and an interesting local culture, all steeped in a rich historical ambiance.

Both islands offer the ideal Mediterranean lifestyle. Sipping an espresso outside a quaint café overlooking a cobblestoned courtyard in the early morning... taking countryside walks as the evening sun warms banks of olive groves... and eating freshly caught seafood with hunks of bread and washed down with local wine...

Because Malta ticks so many boxes—with its superb health care, low crime rate, fantastic climate, and friendly locals—it is a country with broad appeal... quintessential Mediterranean Europe.

Health Care In Malta And Gozo

Malta's health care system is one of the oldest in the world and a major source of pride for locals. The first hospital opened in 1372. The knights who ruled the country for 300 years were first to provide care to the often-ragged pilgrims turning up in Jerusalem. During World War I, the island acted as a vast hospital providing high-level care to injured and sick soldiers.

The country's health care system consistently ranks high by world standards and is home to a number of state-of-the-art public and private facilities staffed by highly trained staff who are all fluent in English. In recent years, Malta has also been building its reputation as a destination for medical tourism.

Built in 2007, the country's main hospital—just one of several high-standard health care facilities on the island—is Mater Dei Hospital, one of the largest medical facilities in Europe. It's located just 15 minutes from Valletta.

Gozo has just one hospital—Gozo General Hospital. Located in Victoria, it provides high-quality care. Gozo has a handful of clinics and plenty of pharmacies (also with English-speaking staff) with the same medications you'd get anywhere else in Europe... Be forewarned, though, that medicine isn't free here: You'll pay the full cost of the medication, not just the cost of the prescription.

While the standard of care is high and there are plenty of English-speaking doctors, the health care on mainland Malta is superior. The highest-rated hospitals on the mainland are DaVinci Health, Saint Thomas hospital, and Saint James Hospital. Gozo General Hospital offers air ambulance service to hospitals on Malta.

Public health care is free to Maltese citizens at its point of delivery. It's also free to citizens of EU member countries granted that you carry a European Health Insurance Card (EHIC).

If you aren't from the EU or aren't earning an income in Malta, you'll need to pay for private insurance... But you'll still pay considerably less than you do in the States. Standards for public health care are high, but standards for private facilities are even higher—a reason Malta has become a destination for medical tourism.

Residency Requirements

Tourists from the States, Canada, and many other nations don't need a visa for Malta for visits of up to 90 days. If you want to stay any longer than this, you'll need to apply for a visa. The good news is, you have several options to choose from, and the requirements are generally easy to meet.

Malta offers a visa option specifically for retirees, too, known as the Malta Retirement Programme. To qualify, you need to own or rent property, receive a pension, not be employed, and have health insurance. A benefit of living on Gozo instead of Malta is that the qualifying values for property ownership or rent are lower. The retirement visa is issued five years after you apply.

Malta also offers a residency by investment program, known as the Malta Permanent Residence Programme (MPRP), which is one of the most competitive in Europe. On top of Malta residency, it affords applicants visa-free access to the Schengen zone, the opportunity to apply for residency for four generations, and other benefits.

You need to be a third country national (non-EEA and non-Swiss) with a valid travel document and health insurance to be able to apply.

Applicants must demonstrate substantial net assets rather than a specific annual income, typically at least 500,000 euros in net worth (including financial assets), rent or purchase qualifying property, pay a government contribution, and maintain their property and residency status for a minimum of five years.

Real Estate Restrictions

Buying property in Malta is generally a pretty straightforward process, but non-EU/EEA citizens (and EU nationals who do not meet the five-year residency criteria) will need to acquire an Acquisition of Immovable Property (AIP) permit when buying a property.

This permit allows you to purchase one property which cannot be rented out.

The minimum purchase value for AIP properties as of 2026 is 174,274 euros for apartments and maisonettes and 300,619 euros for other immovable property.

However, if you look within Special Designated Areas (SDAs), you can buy multiple properties and rent them out without needing an AIP permit and without minimum investment thresholds.

In Malta a 5% stamp duty is applied to property purchases. Sales are subject to an 8% capital gains or final withholding tax.

For sellers, properties that have served as their primary residence for at least three years are exempt from the 8% tax, while properties sold after less than three or five years may qualify for a reduced rate of 2% or 5%, respectively.

Taxes on property transactions are calculated on the full sale price.

Taxes

Personal income taxes for resident Maltese citizens range from 0% to 35% on their worldwide income... By taking advantage of one of the country's residence schemes, however, you can pay far less.

Because Malta is a former British colony, it offers a remittance-based tax system. In other words, as a foreign resident of Malta, you'd only be subject to: 1. Malta-sourced income, and 2. Foreign-sourced income that's remitted to Malta.

In other words, if you don't earn your income in Malta and don't remit it to a Maltese bank account, you won't be subject to income tax here. That includes income from capital gains (even when they are remitted to a Maltese bank account).

Although Malta charges a stamp duty on transfers of Maltese real estate (5%) and on certain shares in Maltese companies (2%), it doesn't charge an inheritance tax, gift tax, or wealth tax... Being a foreign resident of Malta has major advantages from a tax point of view.

CHAPTER 11

GREECE

Greece is home to some of the world's most enchanting islands, each offering its own mix of history, culture, and natural beauty.

Whether you're seeking a quiet retreat, rich historical exploration, or an active lifestyle, Greece has a little something for everyone.

Living here, be it on the mainland or on one of the islands, you'll enjoy fantastic weather with year-round heat and sunshine, an affordable, high-end lifestyle, good residency options and health care, beaches and mountains, and even a tax incentive program for new residents.

As anywhere, there are also going to be some drawbacks to living here, including the language, which can be difficult to learn (with a new alphabet), infrastructure is not consistent, plus, it's far if you live on one of the islands. From North America, you'll have to fly into a major European airport, connect to Athens, then get another flight, ferry, and/or drive to your specific destination in Greece.

One major draw for expats to Greece is that it remains one of the more affordable European countries, especially compared with Western and Northern Europe.

Outside of the cities, rent can be as little as 420 euros per month; even in some of the more popular parts, you can still easily keep rent under 845 euros a month.

The Greek people have some of the longest life expectancies in Europe thanks to the Greek diet. It has one of the most studied and celebrated culinary heritages on the planet and emphasizes things like fresh fish, vegetables, and grains.

Greece is a culturally fascinating place—the cradle of Western civilization with foundational concepts, like democracy, western philosophy, political science, and literature, originating here. Sites of cultural and historical importance, some dating back thousands of years, are found all over the country.

UNESCO World Heritage Sites are scattered all over, with streets and buildings dating back hundreds of years. Find architectural remnants, castles, and ruins from the various cultures that influenced these islands over history, from Byzantine to Venetian, Greek to Roman, French to British.

Modern attractions like museums, galleries, shopping, restaurants, cafés, and more are also available.

Seasonal events and festivals take place throughout the year. In the summer, you can watch outdoor movies, attend cultural festivals, enjoy classic and modern music and theater performances, and more.

In more rural areas, life is quiet, and entertainment options are limited to the local taverna, where you can have a meal and chat with neighbors.

Local produce is cheap and of superb quality—olive oil, cheese, and vegetables often come from nearby farms. Dining out is a pleasure, with hearty meals at a taverna rarely exceeding 17 euros per person. A typical meal would include a small starter, a generous main, a glass of local wine, and a complimentary dessert—no fuss but plenty of flavor.

Two expenses you'll most likely have to take on are the cost of car ownership (fuel can be pricey) and electricity because you'll definitely want air conditioning at home.

All said, you can comfortably keep your monthly budget at around 1,700 euros.

Greece is an ocean and beach-lover's paradise. Islands are surrounded by the turquoise waters of the Mediterranean Sea, coves and protected pockets are found all over, and the sea is perfect for swimming and snorkeling.

There are downsides, of course. If you use a wheelchair, walker, or otherwise struggle with mobility, some of the Greek islands may not be the best places for you. As in many historical destinations, the buildings and streets of these islands were not designed with people with mobility issues in mind.

Accessibility is improving slowly, and newer infrastructure projects include ramps and wider sidewalks. Some beaches have wheelchair access as well. Old town lanes are often cobbled and uneven; modern neighborhoods and new developments are more practical day to day.

Life on a Greek island isn't without quirks. Bureaucracy can test your patience, drivers can be impulsive, and service culture is far from fast. Ferry delays and power cuts happen occasionally.

Yet most expats quickly learn to take these with a shrug. The payoff is a life that values a slow pace and conversation over schedules and simplicity over stress.

Life here suits those who crave authenticity, nature, and connection more than nightlife or luxury brands. Artists, retirees, remote workers, and families all find a sense of belonging here.

Greece is not just a place to move to, it's a lifestyle to grow into. Here, the sea glitters outside your window, neighbors wave as they pass, and every day feels just a little longer and fuller than the one before.

If those sound like the kind of lifestyle you're looking for, then Greece could well be your Shangri-la...

Top Picks For A New Life In Greece

Corfu

The island of Corfu is amazingly green, sheathed in the silvery-green leaves of olive trees as well as Mediterranean cypresses, pine trees, leafy shrubs, and flowering plants. With all the vegetation, the scenery looks more like Lake Tahoe than the dry and dusty scenery of your typical Greek island...

The island is flat and low-lying in the south, undulating in the center, and mountainous in the north. Despite its small size (only 40 miles and 20 miles wide at its thickest part), Corfu is home to a huge number of jaw-dropping land formations. Because it's made up of sedimentary rock, it's constantly being shaped by the elements, creating wind-sculpted cliffs, stalactite-laden caves, craggy bluffs that drop down into the ocean...

Serving as backdrop for all this dramatic scenery is the dazzling aquamarine of the Ionian Sea, arguably some of the most beautiful water on this planet. The island has 135 miles (217 kms) of coastline and 57 beaches—some sandy, others pebbly... some developed, others completely isolated. Living here, you can take advantage of proximity to the sea regardless of where you settle on the island. Glorious ocean vistas are around every corner, and enjoying the sea every day, whether boating around the island or simply going for a dip, is the way of life.

At its core, the island remains traditional. You get a sense of the authentically Corfiot way of life at its many charming villages, particularly the inland mountain ones, where life is still carried out the same way it was a couple generations ago.

In short, what people love about Corfu is its stunning natural environment, friendly locals and wholesome way of life, delicious cuisine, interesting history and culture, and low cost of living.

Corfu Town is the major metropolitan area on Corfu... if you can call a city of roughly 40,000 metropolitan. Much of Corfu Town is walkable, particularly in the pedestrianized historic zone. So, too, are Corfu's 22 villages: you can easily walk to most places you'd want to go—the beach, the grocery store, the bar...

But if you want to venture beyond your immediate village and have the most flexibility possible, you'll want to have your own means of transport. Having a car is the best way to get around, although lots of people drive mopeds and quads, too.

The condition of the roads that crisscross the island varies... The roads that connect towns and villages are wide, well-paved, with frequent roundabouts to control traffic flow. Within villages, roads are narrow and routes are circuitous, often diverting around trees and other obstacles that have been around long before anyone thought to put in a road.

While you can't count on accessibility infrastructure all over the island, Corfu's Old Town is now 80% accessible, and an app is being developed with maps showing different routes for wheelchair users. On 20 of the island's beaches, you'll find floating wheelchairs. One even has a Seatrac system—a mechanism that lets people with mobility issues get in and out of the water independently.

On summer afternoons, the only respite from the heat is going for a dip in the calm, cool ocean waters. Beaches range from totally isolated to resort-dominated, but there's no wrong place to go for a swim here. Even in the center of Corfu Town, the closest thing the island has to a city, you find people lounging in the water right next to the Old Harbour.

For the golf lovers, Corfu offers the Corfu Golf Club, an 18-hole, par-72 course with a high-quality club house. There's a waterpark called Aqualand for the kids, and organized sports for kids and adults alike. Corfu is also a great place to practice adventure sports, like mountain biking, quadding, and dirt biking.

For the highest concentration of things to see and do on the island, you need to go to Corfu Town, the capital and main city. This is where the airport, governmental buildings, and shopping centers are, as well as the Old Town. This is the historical center of Corfu, a UNESCO World Heritage Site with streets and buildings dating back hundreds of years. Here you find architectural remnants from the various cultures that influenced Corfu over history, from Byzantine to Venetian, Greek to Roman, French to British.

To get a dose of Corfu's modern culture, visit one of its 22 villages. If you venture outside the tourist zones, you can get a taste for the authentic Corfiot way of life, where people still gather in village squares ringed with tavernas after dark, kids play freely in the streets, everyone is friendly and familiar, and life moves at a slower pace. It's true that much of the island has been developed for tourism, but there are certain villages that retain their charm, like Liapades, one of the oldest villages in Corfu.

Some Greek islands have a reputation for being expensive, even over-priced for what they offer... Corfu isn't one of those islands. Here you can enjoy a high standard of living for a low cost, especially considering it's in Europe and a major beach destination. Your lifestyle will determine exactly how much you pay, but about 1,500 euros a month should be enough for a couple to live comfortably...

Renting a two-bedroom apartment costs about 500 euros a month; for a house, you'll pay between 510 euros and 560 euros a month, though you'll have to negotiate for a long-term contract. Most rental agents prefer to keep their rentals unoccupied during summer months so that they can make more money off of short-term rentals during the tourist season.

Your transportation costs will run about 100 euros a month. Utilities (gas, electricity, and water) will be about 150 euros with another 50 for an internet and cable package. Budget about 400 euros for entertainment for two and another 300 euros for your monthly grocery shop.

Greece's health care system is a combination of the National Healthcare Service, compulsory social insurance, and a voluntary private health care system. Corfu General Hospital is the island's main hospital, providing pulmonary, intensive care, gynecology, pediatric, pathology, cardiology, surgery, orthopedics, and neuroslogy clinics as well as external care medical units.

The hospital has mixed reviews from expats. Those who review it negatively cite lack of funding and low-quality attention from nurses and doctors as the main problems.

There are a few private clinics on Corfu. The Therapia Clinic has pathology and surgery departments, radiodiagnostic and microbiology laboratories, and a private ambulance service. Alexandros Mastoras General Clinic offers doctors from a range of specialties and modern technology. Both have English-speaking employees and deal with international insurance.

From ordering in restaurants to asking for directions to having conversations with locals, you'll have no problems communicating in English in Corfu. It's a well-established tourism destination with historical ties to the U.K., so there is a strong basis for speaking English here.

There are a few thousand expats living here—mostly from the U.K., though you'll also find Canadians and Americans. The expat community organizes itself through online resources like Corfu Forum, where you can find out about local news, upcoming events, volunteer opportunities, and more.

Corfu is a tiny, sickle-shaped island just off of Greece's northwest coast. It straddles the Greece and Albania border offshore and floats in the Ionian Sea.

To get here from abroad, you can fly into Corfu International Airport. There are no direct flights to the States or Canada, but there are options to fly into big European hubs, like London-Gatwick (in the U.K.) and Schiphol Airport (in Holland). Otherwise, your best option is to fly into Athens and catch a low-cost domestic flight onwards to Corfu.

Corfu's climate is classic Mediterranean, with hot summers and mild winters. Temperatures range between about 22°C and 12°C (71°F and 53°F), with humidity hovering around 71%. From June to September it's hot and stuffy; from October to May, it's a bit cooler.

The island is a safe place to live. Children still play in the streets... Nuns don their black habits and make their way to church in the early hours of the morning... People gather in the town square after dark to chat with their neighbors... It's a very safe, simple way of life—the type of place where you can leave your front door unlocked and not worry about a thing.

The lifestyle in Corfu is laid-back and simplistic, so if you're the type of person who needs to be constantly seeing new things, have convenience at your fingertips, and requires everything to work at maximum efficiency, this may not be the place for you.

On the other hand, this slowed-down pace of life might be just what you're looking for.

Crete

If your interests are basking in the sun, enjoying life by the sea, exploring ancient ruins, and indulging in the original Mediterranean diet, look no further than Crete.

The biggest island in Greece and the fifth biggest in the Mediterranean, Crete offers more lifestyle options than your typical island... from cities like Chania and Heraklion to untouched wilderness, beach towns to snow-capped mountains, and ancient olive groves to mountain villages.

Crete's historical roots go deep. It was home to Europe's first advanced civilization, the Minoans, and it has sat at the crossroads of Africa, Europe, and Asia Minor for millennia. Evidence of this rich history is found across the island.

Chania, a city on the island's northwest coast, is a microcosm of that history. In its Old Town alone, you find evidence of the Romans, the Byzantines, the Venetians, the Ottomans, and the Egyptians... every culture and civilization that shaped Crete's story.

Chania is one of the most popular choices for expats on Crete. Its Old Town, with its Venetian port and labyrinth of museums, boutiques, restaurants, and ancient churches, is encircled by city walls that seem to protect not only the architecture but the lifestyle within.

Here, daily life involves buying fresh bread in the morning and watching the sunset over the lighthouse with a glass of wine in the evening. Stone alleys wind between pastel-colored houses, and the scent of grilled octopus drifts from tavernas beside the Venetian harbor...

If you wander farther, the New Town of Nea Chora wraps around the Old Town with a sandy in-town beach, a small fishing harbor, and cafés where the day starts with strong coffee and ends with raki.

Western Crete is a haven for the estimated 18,000 expats that live here.

Sunshine and great weather plays a big role in this. The island gets some of the most hours of sunshine in all of Europe.

With its diverse landscapes and great weather, Crete is ideal for lovers of outdoor recreation.

The obvious attraction is the Mediterranean Sea. The beaches that surround Crete are outstanding. There are rugged outcrops, completely unspoiled beaches, sandy beaches, pebble beaches... there are even pink beaches on Crete.

Most water sports are available here, from swimming and kayaking to scuba diving and sailing. From the port at Kissamos, boats head to Gramvousa Island and the Balos Lagoon.

On land, Crete's sprawling and mountainous landscape provides more opportunities to get active than your average Greek island. You can cycle, hike, mountaineer, or go horseback riding or paragliding.

You can even ski in the Lefka Ori mountain range in winter and spring or enjoy total isolation on the remote islands off Crete's coast.

There are remarkable natural formations, like the Samariá Gorge, which offers hiking in otherworldly surroundings, and the Vai palm forest—the largest palm forest in Europe.

Crete remains one of the most affordable Mediterranean destinations. Outside major cities, a couple can live comfortably on around 2,400 euros a month.

Rent for a one-bedroom apartment starts near 420 euros in smaller towns, rising to 845 euros in central Chania.

Local produce is cheap and of superb quality—olive oil, cheese, and vegetables often come from nearby farms. Dining out is a pleasure, with hearty meals at a taverna rarely exceeding 20 euros per person.

Your monthly utilities will cost about 170 euros and add another 60 euros for an internet and cell phone package. For entertainment for two, add another 300 euros and you'll spend about 225 euros on a basic monthly grocery shop.

Crete is large enough to avoid island fever yet small enough to maintain a sense of community. Getting off the island is simple, with two international airports and daily ferries connecting it to Athens and other islands.

If you plan to explore beyond your immediate area (and why wouldn't you on an island as big and diverse as Crete), a car is essential. You'll find taxis in urban areas as well as intercity buses, but having your own car is always going to be the best, most comfortable way of getting around Crete. Transportation costs run about 76 euros a month.

Crete's main highway runs along the north coast, linking major towns, while scenic mountain roads wind through olive groves and villages where time seems frozen.

English is widely spoken in Crete—you won't need to pick up Greek to get by here.

Once here, many expats find they rarely leave. The island is self-sufficient, and with modern health care, international schools, and a thriving expat community, it's easy to settle in for the long term.

Crete has several microclimates, but it's generally warm and dry. Summers are long and bright, and winters are mild enough for outdoor lunches. The south coast gets more sunshine than anywhere else in Greece, averaging over 3,200 hours per year. Inland areas see cooler nights and occasional snow, while the mountains can have a full winter season. Air conditioning is essential in July and August, and a small heater might be needed in January, especially at higher elevations.

Both public (available through the National Health System; ESY) and private health care facilities are available on Crete. Most are centered around Chania and Heraklion. Rural areas have limited facilities. Standards of care are generally high, and you can have most health care needs taken care of here.

Bigger public hospitals are well-equipped and have English-speaking staff. With a residence permit, you'd gain access to Greek public health care. That said, many expats maintain international health insurance (affordable relative to insurance costs in the U.S.) to receive care faster and access private facilities. For routine needs, you'll find English-speaking doctors and dentists in the cities; for major procedures, you'll likely be referred to larger hospitals on the north coast.

Greece ranks among the world's safest countries, and Crete is safer still. Violent crime is rare, and petty theft is uncommon even in tourist areas.

In most towns, you'll find the same faces at the café every morning, and people look out for each other. For many expats, that sense of community safety is one of Crete's greatest comforts.

Despite its popularity, the island hasn't been overrun by mass development. Regulations limit building heights and density, preserving both landscape and charm.

Compared with other Mediterranean destinations, Crete still feels authentic, with family-owned businesses, small-scale farming, and a strong sense of local identity.

Rhodes

Rhodes is an island where history isn't confined to museums—it's woven into daily life. Medieval walls enclose neighborhoods where residents shop for groceries, walk their dogs, and stop for coffee. Ancient ruins sit beside modern cafés. Crusader castles, Ottoman mosques, Byzantine churches, and neoclassical buildings coexist within a few square miles, creating a sense that time here layers rather than replaces itself.

Located in the southeastern Aegean Sea, just a few miles from the Turkish coast, Rhodes has long been one of the most strategically important islands in the Mediterranean. Over centuries, it was shaped by the Knights of St. John, the Ottomans, the Italians, and the modern Greek state. Each left behind architecture, traditions, and infrastructure that still define the island today.

But Rhodes is not a living relic. It's a modern, functioning island with strong services, a sizable year-round population, and one of the most developed economies in the Greek islands. With more than 300 days of sunshine per year, a long swimming season, and a pace of life that encourages daily routines over constant novelty, Rhodes appeals strongly to retirees looking for beauty without impracticality.

Rhodes Town is the island's administrative, cultural, and commercial center. It's large enough to support full services—hospitals, private clinics, government offices, large supermarkets, and international schools—yet small enough to remain walkable in many areas. The medieval Old Town is pedestrianized, while surrounding neighborhoods offer more modern housing and conveniences.

Outside the capital, towns like Ialyssos, Kremasti, Faliraki, and Lindos provide different lifestyle options, from resort-adjacent living to quieter village life. Many expats choose to live just outside Rhodes Town, where rents are lower, streets are calmer, and daily errands remain easy.

The cultural heart of the island is the Medieval City of Rhodes, a UNESCO World Heritage Site and one of the best-preserved medieval towns in Europe. Walking its cobbled streets becomes part of daily life—passing through ancient gates, lingering in shaded squares, or enjoying coffee inside centuries-old stone buildings.

History lovers will never run out of places to explore. The Palace of the Grand Master, the Street of the Knights, ancient acropolises, Ottoman baths, Byzantine churches, and archaeological museums are scattered across the island. Lindos, with its whitewashed houses cascading toward an ancient acropolis, feels both dramatic and intimate.

For those who enjoy the outdoors, Rhodes offers a long swimming season and varied beaches. The east coast has calmer waters and sandy beaches ideal for relaxed swimming, while the west coast is windier and popular with surfers and kiteboarders. Many locals swim daily well into autumn.

Walking is one of the island's great pleasures. Coastal promenades, forest paths, and archaeological trails provide gentle exercise and scenic views. Cycling is popular along flatter routes, particularly near the coast.

Social life tends to revolve around food and conversation. Long lunches, late dinners, and casual coffee meet-ups are the rhythm of the day. Dining out is affordable and unpretentious—fresh fish, grilled meats, seasonal vegetables, and local wine enjoyed slowly and socially.

In terms of cost of living, Rhodes remains affordable; a couple can live comfortably on about 2,100 euros per month. Rent for a one-bedroom apartment typically starts around 420 euros to 600 euros outside the historic center, rising to 760 euros or more in prime locations or newer buildings. Utilities are reasonable (about 100 euros a month), though summer air conditioning will increase electricity costs.

Groceries, as on all the islands, are affordable and high-quality, with fresh local produce, cheese, bread, and olive oil keeping monthly costs for a couple around 300 euros. Add another 250 euros for entertainment.

Health care is among the best you'll find on a Greek island. Rhodes has a large public hospital, several private clinics, diagnostic centers, and many English-speaking doctors. Many expats use a mix of public care and private services, often supported by international health insurance for faster access.

In or near Rhodes Town, you can comfortably live without a car. Public buses are reliable, inexpensive, and frequent along the east coast and between major towns. Taxis are plentiful and affordable for occasional trips.

You'll probably want to invest in a car sooner or later, though. Having one gives you the freedom to explore quieter beaches, inland villages, archaeological sites, and mountain areas that buses don't reach easily. Roads are generally well maintained, signage is clear, and driving is less stressful than in larger Greek cities.

English is widely spoken, especially in Rhodes Town and coastal areas. Tourism has been central to the local economy for decades, and daily life is navigable without Greek. Still, learning basic phrases helps with integration and is appreciated by locals.

The expat community here is well established and diverse. You'll find retirees from the U.K., Germany, Scandinavia, and other parts of Europe, as well as a smaller but growing number of North Americans. Many expats live full-time on the island, while others split their year between Rhodes and their home country. For expats and locals, the island is a safe place to live. It has a low crime rate and violent crime is extremely rate.

Whether you're seeking a quiet retreat, rich historical exploration, or an active lifestyle, Rhodes has something for everyone.

Health Care In Greece

Both public (available through the National Health System, ESY) and private health care facilities are available throughout Greece, but the specific levels of care you can expect will vary. High population centers will have more and better care. Rural areas have limited facilities.

Standards of care are generally high, and you can have most health care needs taken care of on the mainland or any island. Bigger public hospitals are well-equipped and have English-speaking staff. With a residence permit and an AMKA number (the social security ID) you can gain access to Greek public health care.

That said, many expats maintain international health insurance (affordable relative to insurance costs in the U.S.) to receive care faster and access private facilities.

Private clinics and hospitals have English-speaking doctors, many of whom trained overseas. A private consultation can cost anywhere from 40 euros to 100 euros depending on the doctor and specialty.

Online booking platforms such as DoctorAnytime.gr allow you to filter by English-speaking doctors in different areas of the country (just search by name in the location field). If there isn't a local doctor, you can still book online video consultations from wherever you are. For less urgent issues, telemedicine services like Mobi Doctor offer video call consultations with English-speaking doctors.

Pharmacies are widespread, accessible, well-stocked, and staffed by well-trained pharmacists.

Residency Requirements

Greece offers several paths to residency, but it doesn't offer a retiree-specific visa. The residence permit that most retirees use to live here long-term is an independent means visa called the Financially Independent Person (FIP) Permit.

The basic requirement to qualify for the FIP visa is showing that you receive enough income to support yourself while living in Greece. You need to show that you receive 3,500 euros per month. This residency permit is available for two years and is renewable.

Greece also offers a digital nomad visa which as the same financial threshold as the FIP—this increases by 20% for a spouse and by 15% for each child included. When granted, it permits to live in Greece for up to 12 months, with the option to extend for an additional two years through a residence permit.

Finally, the Golden Visa program allows you to invest in the country in exchange for residency. The real estate amount option has increased significantly in 2024, now requiring 800,000 euros spent on a property in high demand areas (e.g., Athens, Thessaloniki, Mykonos, Santorini, and islands with larger populations) or 400,000 in other regions.

The start up Golden Visa offers non EU investors a renewable one-year residence permit by investing at least 250,000 euros in an eligible start up and helping create jobs.

Real Estate Restrictions

Non-EU citizens face a couple restrictions when it comes to buying property in Greece. These restrictions apply to agricultural land and areas that are close to international borders. You'll need to apply for a license to buy or sell property in one of these areas.

Taxes

Residents of Greece are taxed on their worldwide income, and income tax rates are relatively high... But Greece offers a tax abatement program called the Non-Dom Regime for retirees. It allows for a 7% flat tax on many types of passive income (including pensions) for 15 years.

Also, the tax treaties in place between Greece and the United States and Canada help residents avoid double taxation.

Inheritance tax applies to the current value of property in Greece. It kicks in on properties worth 150,000 euros or more.

CHAPTER 12

PORTUGAL

Portugal is one of the world's best-loved expat havens and it has surged in popularity with U.S. retirees in recent years...

A reported 20,000 Americans are currently living in Portugal. However, Portugal has long been a destination for foreigners seeking sunny retirement. In fact, Portugal has the largest population of Brits outside of the U.K., with the number estimated to be around 50,000.

Expats across the country tell us that even in small towns, populations are diverse and multi-cultural, including, in addition to Brits and North Americans, many Europeans, Brazilians, and others.

For nearly a decade, Portugal took top billing in our annual Overseas Retirement Index, because it offers everything would-be retirees could want, including near-perfect weather and sunshine year-round; an established and welcoming expat community; top-notch medical facilities; an affordable cost of living for a high quality of life; First-world infrastructure; and easy access to the United States and all of Europe.

If you're looking for a mild year-round climate, easy access to the rest of Europe, and want to connect easily with other expats overseas, Portugal is a great option.

Plus, English is widely spoken here among locals as well as foreign residents, so it's a good choice for those who are nervous about learning another language.

Top Picks For A New Life In Portugal

Lisbon

Four centuries older than Rome and the second-oldest European capital after Athens, Lisbon, Portugal's capital, is drenched in historical ambiance and holds its own against any other Continental haven in terms of Old-World charm.

Then again, it's a coastal city, found at the point where the River Tagus empties into the Atlantic Ocean, with a swimmable beach only 10 minutes away...

Where Lisbon stands out most, though, is in its uniquely cosmopolitan attributes...

This is a global city with an important role in finance, commerce, media, entertainment, arts, international trade, tourism, and education.

There is a population of about half-a-million people in its administrative limits, while in the Lisbon Metropolitan Area, the population is about 3 million—about a quarter of the country's total population.

It boasts incomparable museums, galleries, concerts, and theater and serves up world-class cuisine. It draws on thousands of years of history to provide gorgeous architecture that will have you tripping over yourself as you look ever skyward...

Lisbon also has some spectacular parks, like Parque Eduardo VII (26 hectares, with manicured gardens and walking paths) and Guerro Junqueiro Garden (another city park popular for walking and with kids).

With a good pair of walking shoes and some stamina (watch out for those hills!), Lisbon is a fantastic city to explore on foot. It's an incredibly scenic place, with varied elevation, the river, and architectural styles spanning many decades to gawk at.

When it comes to walking in Lisbon, you need to be aware that the pavement is often made up of ornate, hand-laid tiles. While beautiful, the tiles are also incredibly slippery and time-warped, making walking difficult for some.

Runners and cyclists will find trails across the city. A popular one with locals and expats is to follow the trail along the Tagus on a sunny day, venturing off-path here and there for a snack or to explore a new neighborhood.

At about 10:30 p.m., the city comes alive, and people spill onto the streets to enjoy themselves. The prime neighborhoods for going out are Bairro Alto and Cais do Sodré. Bairro Alto is said to have the most bars per square meter in the world.

Portugal is a top global golf destination. Most of the attention is focused on the Algarve, but Lisbon has some quality courses in close proximity.

In the capital's zone (and surrounding areas) a few highlights in the international golfing circuit include: Belas, Penha Longa, Quinta da Marinha, Troia, Oitavos Dunes, Aroeira I and Aroeira II, Praia del Rey, and many more...

Lisbon is one of Western Europe's most affordable capitals, with the average monthly cost of living estimated at about 2,800 euros for a couple. Plus, it's the one of the cheapest Western European capitals for real estate purchase.

A one bedroom apartment in central Lisbon typically rents for 1,000 euros to 1,420 euros per month. In less central or emerging neighborhoods, this can drop to 1,100 euros to 1,600 euros for a well-located one bedroom, or 450 euros to 750 euros for a room in a shared flat.

Utilities (gas, water, and electricity) will be about 170 euros per month. A cell phone and internet package will cost 50 euros. Expect to pay about 275 euros per month on groceries as a couple and budget 400 euros for entertainment.

Eating out is super affordable, though—about 10 to 12 euros for a main course at a Portuguese restaurant. Because of the proximity to the ocean, seafood is a specialty in Lisbon.

Local wine is high-quality and inexpensive. At a restaurant, a glass will cost you about 3 euros. You can get a decent bottle of wine for about the same prices or up to 5 euros at a grocery store.

Transportation and health care—the second and third biggest expenses for Americans in the United States over 65—are two areas where you'll save a fortune in Lisbon...

In the national health system, you'll pay a small surcharge on doctor's visits (about 4 euros) and tests (about 10 euros). A medical appointment in the private system is still affordable—between 50 and 80 euros.

With 34 hospitals and clinics throughout the city, you're never far from care is Lisbon. The top hospital in the country is Lisbon's Centro Hospitalar de Lisboa Central (Hospital Dona Estefania). Instituto Portugues de Oncologia de Lisboa ranks third. Hospital da Luz is the most expat recommended.

Living here, you can say goodbye to car insurance, maintenance fees, and concerns about gas prices. You definitely don't need a car in a city like this. In certain neighborhoods, you may not even need public transportation and can meet all your needs by walking.

Public transportation options in Lisbon include the metro, trams, trains, buses, and ferries.

The metro consists of four color-coded lines (blue, yellow, green, and red) that are served by 55 stations between 6:30 a.m. and 1 a.m. This is the fastest and most stress-free way to get across the city.

It's also much cheaper than a taxi—3.50 euros is the starting rate in a cab—and takes a lot less time. A one-way metro ticket is 1.50 euros; a monthly public transport pass is 20 euros for retirees.

Trams similar to the ones found in San Francisco run across the districts of Alfama, Bairro Alto, Bica, Baixa Chiado, and Princípe Real. They've been part of the city since 1901 and are cost-effective (each ticket under 3 euros).

The trams are so unique and charming, some with original 1930s features like wood interiors with brass dials, they've become tourist attractions. Tram 28 is particularly popular; riding it start to finish takes you on a scenic tour of Alfama, Baiza, Estrela, and Graca.

Greater Lisbon covers the north bank of the Tagus River. Areas of the Lisbon Metropolitan Area and Setúbal Peninsula are on the south bank. To cross the river, your options are bridge, train, or ferry...

Lisbon is well-connected to the rest of Portugal via train. Four train lines depart Lisbon from five major stations (Santa Apolónia, Rossio, Gare do Oriente, Entrecampos, and Cais do Sodré).

Portugal's trains are an efficient, inexpensive, and comfortable way to get around. You get better discounts by booking in advance. For anyone over 65, you can get a 50% discount on full-price domestic train tickets.

Living in Lisbon, you'll also benefit from being within two to three hours flying distance from all the major cities in Europe.

You can go out and feel safe pretty much anywhere at any time... another reason it's been historically popular with expats. Beware, though, that pickpockets target tourist areas. Pay particular attention when traveling on the trams. The cramped interiors make for an easy snag of your cell phone or wallet.

Portugal is not on the Mediterranean Sea but it enjoys a Mediterranean climate. Winters are mild and rainy, with the daily mean between December and March at 54°F or 12°C. You can expect about 15 days of rain per month during that period. Summers are hot; the daily mean is about 73°F or 23°C.

English is the second most spoken language in the country. A big reason for this is Portugal's long relationship with the U.K. and the fact that about 50,000 of the country's total expats are British.

More Americans and Canadians are moving to Portugal than ever before. With conditions in the United States pushing Americans to look outside the borders of their country for a better life, Portugal is becoming an ever-more attractive option...

Those who'd like the Californian lifestyle without the political issues, insane housing prices, crime, non-stop natural disasters, and so on can come to the California of Europe (sometimes even called "Eurifornia").

As an expat to Lisbon, you won't have any trouble meeting other expats. There are endless opportunities to socialize, and you'll hear

English spoken in every bar, café, or restaurant.

All sorts of interest-based groups are available if you want to get involved and socialize in a more structured setting. Resources and media specifically for English-speakers are available, too.

A major drawback of ancient, historical cities like Lisbon is that they're not friendly to people with mobility issues. It's difficult to make things accessible retroactively.

In newer construction (new museums, train stations, etc.), you'll find better accessibility... but there's a long way to go before the government is able to meet the basic needs of people with disabilities.

If you want to pick up some Portuguese in Lisbon, always recommended to enrich your new life overseas, there are a handful of schools where you can learn. Some of the most recommended are Lusa Language School, Portuguese Connection Language School, and Portuguese Et Cetera.

Living in Lisbon, you get the opportunity to live in a village atmosphere despite being in a major city, because each neighborhood is so ancient and well-established...

It's the chance to take a moment and enjoy a coffee on the terrace of your favorite kiosk... or sit in the sun and watch the meandering River Tagus from a secret *miradouro.*

It's the possibility of discovering something new, even surprising, every time you walk out your front door...

If those simple charms sound appealing to you, Lisbon should be at the top of your list.

Braga

Braga is the culturally vibrant capital of Portugal's northern Minho Province, famous for its lush, green landscapes that produce vinho verde wine.

It's an off-the-radar retirement choice in Portugal... especially compared to the Algarve, Lisbon, and Porto...

Portugal has long been popular with expats, but its popularity has skyrocketed in the last decade or so. Most of the attention is focused on those three areas (the Algarve, Lisbon, and Porto), and that attention has driven up property prices and costs of living.

Braga offers a more authentically Portuguese, tranquil, and affordable way of life relative to those places. It's appealing in its own right.

Braga is an attractive, well-loved city, with narrow lanes and lively plazas hemmed in by historic buildings and elegant baroque churches.

Its key appeal comes from its historic center, a dense, buzzy neighborhood that's full of cafés, restaurants, boutiques, churches, supermarkets, businesses, hotels, homes, and more...

Once surrounded by medieval walls, a stunning Renaissance gate announces the entrance to the city's pedestrianized historic heart today. It's a pleasant place to walk around, people-watch, and enjoy lunch on the sunny outdoor terrace of a café or restaurant.

Braga is a small city with a population of under 200,000 people. But because it's a university town, the ambiance is always lively, with people out enjoying its gastronomic offerings, parks, and plazas. It's also compact, so you can easily get by without a car and make your way from A to B on foot.

Dating back to 296 B.C., the city today features landmarks in a range of architectural styles. It's long been a religious center, and with magnificent churches and cathedrals, it continues to be a destination for religious pilgrims.

Braga also has a lively event calendar. Christmas, Easter, and Carnival are the "big three" in terms of festivals, attracting thousands of visitors to the city each year...

But Braga also has its own home-grown events, like Verde Cool, a month-long restaurant festival during which participating restaurants offer a small plate plus a wine pairing for 3 euros.

It's a gastronomic hub, and savory Portuguese dishes and drinks can be enjoyed on the cheap because they're priced for the biggest client base: university students.

Braga is the center of Portugal's Minho region, an area that's famous for outstanding natural beauty, with lush landscapes, mountains, river valleys, and a rugged Atlantic coastline.

Residents take advantage of all this natural beauty with walks, hikes, cycles, and drives in the countryside, plus excursions into the nearby national parks.

Within a 30-minute drive, you can be at the beaches of Portugal's northwest coast, including Esposende, Fao, Ofir, Geres, and Porto. There's also river access across the region, providing opportunities for kayaking and waterfall canyoning.

Sports are a part of life in Braga. Soccer is the most popular sport nation-wide, and Braga has a team (Sporting Clube de Braga) and stadium in Portugal's top division.

Motorsports are also a big deal here, with several race tracks nearby and the European Hillclimb Championship (a motorsport competition) hosted here every year.

Braga is well-situated, less than an hour from Portugal's second city, Porto, as well as the country's rugged Atlantic coastline. The sprawling landscape of Minho Province surrounds it, providing ample opportunities to commune with nature.

Above all, what Braga offers is tranquility in a well-appointed, well-maintained, and elegant city. It enchants visitors with its vibrant cultural offerings, blending ancient and youthful energies with its historical ambiance and modern-day university town buzz.

Braga is affordable not only relative to the costs of living in the United States and Canada, it's also affordable relative to other places in Portugal.

Property prices and costs of living haven't been inflated as much as in places like the Algarve, Lisbon, and Porto. For its rich lifestyle, Braga is a bargain.

The average cost of living per month for two is 2,500 euros.

Monthly rent for a two-bedroom apartment will be about 1,000 euros. If you decide to buy a car, your transportation costs will be around 270 a month; utilities (gas, water, electricity) 135 euros. Budget 350 euros for your monthly grocery shop for two and another 400 euros for entertainment.

Public health care is extremely affordable. Going to the family doctor or general practitioner, for example, will cost you 4.50 euros—a fee called *taxa moderadora*. Some health care services are completely free on the SNS.

In Braga, there are public hospitals and health centers, as well as private hospitals and clinics.

Hospital de Braga is one of the biggest hospitals in the region, offering a wide range of services. Braga Private Hospital provides quality care in the private system. Porto has several more hospitals for anything that can't be treated in Braga.

You should have no trouble meeting your health care needs here. In fact, you'll likely be upgrading the quality of care you receive by relocating to Braga.

English is the second-most spoken language in Portugal. It's taught from an early age in schools. Most people, especially the younger generation, speak it at a high conversational level.

You can get by with English alone in Braga and shouldn't have a problem finding English-speaking doctors, real estate agents, and lawyers, as well as English-language media.

The expat community here is smaller than the Algarve, Lisbon, and Porto.

That's part of its appeal—it's authentic, laid-back, uncrowded, and tranquil.

That said, you won't be isolated here as an expat; there's an active community of international folks who organize social activities, making it easy to make connections.

Braga has the Mediterranean climate that Portugal is famous for, despite not being on the Mediterranean. It gets a full four seasons, including warm to hot summers and mild winters. The average high is 69°F (20°C) and the average low is 49°F (10°C).

Because it's inland, summers are hotter and winters are cooler than in other places in Portugal. Minho Province is the wettest area of the country, so expect rainfall.

With buses, trains, taxis, and ride-hailing apps, you won't need a car to live in Braga. It's easy to get around this city and beyond using the well-appointed public transportation system. Plus, it's pedestrian-friendly.

It's also easy to get to Braga from North America, with a handful of direct flights to Porto. Porto is less than an hour from Braga on a train or in a car.

Portugal is extremely safe. Living in Braga, there's a good chance that crime will not affect your life at all.

Braga is an undeniably appealing place to live Portugal's lesser-known northern region. If you're looking to live in Portugal, but outside its more popular expat destinations, then Braga, with its historical buildings, monuments, gardens, and fountains should be on your list. It's culturally vibrant, with events, festivals, concerts, and exhibitions year-round... so you'll never be bored.

Algarve

Few places in the world could be called perfect, but Portugal's Algarve is about as close as it gets...

Picture a chain of historic and charming small towns strung together by a single-lane highway, people walking or biking along, passing roadside stands offering fresh fruit at unbeatable prices.

Stretching along Portugal's entire southern coastline from the Spanish border in the east to the Atlantic cliffs of Sagres in the west, the Algarve is home to close to 500,000 people—a number that more than triples in the summer months as vacationers flock here.

You can take your pick of bustling coastal cities, resort towns, and quiet inland villages. Faro—home to the international airport—is the regional capital, while other towns such as Portimão, Lagos, Albufeira, Tavira, Lagoa, and Silves are popular with expats. Smaller villages such as Carvoeiro, Ferragudo, and Moncarapacho offer a more traditional way of life.

The weather is warm... blossoming vines grow over the stucco walls that hide beautiful properties inside. Thanks to fantastic weather year-round, with more than 3,000 hours of sunshine per year, most every day is a perfect day to get out and enjoy your new home...

The best months can be September and October, when the summer crowds have gone but the weather and sea temperature are still ideal. January and February can be cold enough that you'll want a coat.

There are plenty of museums and archaeological sites throughout the Algarve, though art museums are still relatively few. You will, however, come across small galleries showcasing local and regional artists, and several contemporary spaces are to be found in towns like Faro, Lagos, and Tavira.

Thanks to the large expat community in the Algarve, there is nearly always a film or play available in English, and a wide array of interest groups, hobby clubs, and cultural associations are easy to join if you are looking for company or shared activities.

Music is ever-present on the Algarve. Outdoor festivals and concerts are staged throughout summer, many open-air and often free. Experience jazz at Lagoa's Sitio das Fontes and local youth concerts at the Lagoa Auditorium. The Arade Congress Centre (a former fish canning factory) often plays host to large scale events and exhibitions.

Carvoeiro offers a well-stocked book exchange where visitors can donate and borrow books in English, a favorite meeting spot for expats, and other towns like Lagos and Tavira have begun hosting English-language book clubs and literary evenings, reflecting the region's increasingly vibrant international community.

You could join fellow expats at the Carvoeiro Tennis and Padel Club which also has a clubhouse and wellness center. Pay and Play and yearly membership options are available with the cost being around 4 euros or 6 euros a game.

The Algarve is all about the great outdoors. Its more than 150 miles of Atlantic coastline is punctuated by jagged rock formations, lagoons, and extensive sandy beaches, 85 of which have earned coveted Blue Flag award from the European Blue Flag Association.

The Albufeira area leads the region with the most Blue Flag beaches (25), followed by Vila do Bispo and Loulé (both with 10). The water off these shores is azure, and the clifftop vistas are spectacular. Most beaches have lifeguards during the summer season.

In the western Algarve, the coast is known for its wild waves (making for world-class surfing) and jaw-dropping cliffside views.

In the eastern Algarve, the coast is no less beautiful... but gentler.

Algarve has more golf courses per capita than anywhere else in the world, and many rank as some of the best courses in Europe. Portugal is regularly named Europe's Best Golf Destination and 42 of its top courses are in the Algarve.

You'll find more than three-dozen 9-hole or 18-hole layouts around the region. Probably the most famous is the Quinta do Lago, close to Faro airport.

Also well-known is the course at the Penina Hotel to the west of Portimao. Formally opened by Antonio de Oliveira Salazar, Portugal's austere but golf-loving dictator from 1932 to 1968, the hotel bar today proudly displays the club, tee, and ball used on that ceremonious occasion by the former dictator.

Green fees at more affordable courses will be around 42 euros for 18 holes off-peak running to 250 euros at swankier spots. Memberships, often through golf societies rather than full club equity, start at around 130 euros a year for associations like 6 Golfe Algarve or Golf for Greys which can unlock decent green fee discounts. High-end resort memberships will start around 2,000 euros and go up from there.

This isn't the world's cheapest place to live, but it's a bargain compared with elsewhere in Europe and one of the best places in the world today to enjoy a safe and enjoyable retirement on the ocean.

For a couple, a monthly budget of around 2,600 euros is a good guide but of course this will depend on where in the Algarve you choose to call home and how you choose to live.

In the central Algarve, about 12 miles west of Faro Airport, lies "The Golden Triangle" an upscale enclave encompassing the ritzy resorts of Vale do Lobo and Quinta do Lago, along with the bustline town of Almancil. The resort town of Vilamoura, while not technically part of the Golden Triangle is often included due to its proximity and luxurious lifestyle offerings. Settle in this part of the Algarve and you'll both live and spend well. Monthly rentals start from around 2,000 euros in these parts.

For more budget-friendly options consider the lively coastal city of Portimão in central Algarve or head east to the fishing town of Olhão or the charming riverside town of Tavira. In each of these spots monthly rentals can still be found for under 800 euros.

If you're after city living, in Faro you can find monthly apartment rentals starting from around 930 euros. For a house you'll pay around 1,700 euros a month.

Your monthly utilities (water, electricity, and gas) will cost about 160 euros. Internet and cell phone will be around 68 euros. Budget 425 euros for entertainment and the same again for monthly groceries.

To shop for groceries, Pingo Doce, Continente, and Auchan are popular expat choices. You'll find a good range of international brands on offer and large produce sections. German chains Lidl and Aldi are also here and great for budget basics.

You'll also find specialist food stores stocking favorites from back home but you will pay a premium. Shop like a local at the markets for your fresh meat, fish, fruit, and veggies and you'll make big savings.

When it comes to dining out, you can enjoy a simple breakfast or lunch for around 10 euros. You'll find restaurants offering "*prato do dia*" (dish of the day) for around 15 euros. It's usually a main course and drink but can also include dessert and coffee.

In more upmarket spots or tourist areas you'll pay closer to 21 euros per person for a mid-range meal out and if you're after Michelin-level eats you can easily double that.

There are three main public hospitals in the Algarve: Hospital of Faro, Hospital of Portimão, and Hospital of Lagos. All three offer full emergency care (112 is the number for emergency services in Portugal), surgery, and specialized medical treatment, and have English-speaking staff.

The Algarve is also home to a number of private hospitals offering a high standard of care. Benefits can include a more personalized service, shorter waiting times, and more comfortable surroundings. You'll also find English-speaking staff working at these facilities. Options include Alvor Private Clinic, Hospital Particular do Algarve, and Clínica Particular de Faro. You'll pay about 40 euros for a basic consultation at a private clinic.

Faro's Hospital Particular do Algarve has insurance agreements with ADM, ADSE, Advance Care, Allianz, CGD, Future Healthcare, GNR, Médis, Médis - CTT, Multicare, PSP, PT ACS, RNA Medical and SAMS Quadros.

One of the many reasons so many Anglophones live here is that English is the second most spoken language in the country. Living here, you could get by without learning to speak Portuguese... though any effort to learn the local language is a show of respect and appreciated.

Portugal has been a haven for foreigners for decades. Over one-and-a-half million foreigners call it home and numbered among them are an estimated 100,000 expat retirees...

Newcomers can avail of *The Portugal News*, the only digital Portuguese newspaper that covers all the major news about Portugal, Algarve, and Lisbon in English and The Portuguese-American Journal (PAJ), an interactive blog dedicated to sharing news and giving insight into the Portuguese-American experience. In more expat-heavy areas you may see other handouts in English, from expat meetups to local offers.

Thanks to its fantastic weather, beaches, golf, friendly and English-speaking population, and the solid infrastructure, the Algarve is home to thousands of expats from around the world. Making friends is easy, both with the locals and the expats.

Almost every town across the Algarve has a strong expat community. Walk into any local café or restaurant, and you're likely to meet people from all nationalities. Friendships can be formed casually, or you can join a club that interests you. All sorts of groups and clubs meet across the region, and Facebook is an excellent place to look for them. There are sports clubs and activities for all ages and abilities, as well as art and photography classes and groups.

You could also consider volunteering. There are several pet-rescue centers that always require dog-walkers, or try Centre Algarve, which is a holiday center for children with special needs. Having a dog that requires a nice long walk every day is another excellent way to meet people, especially locals.

Temperatures in the Algarve generally range from the mid-40s°F at night in winter to the mid-80s°F in summer. Humidity averages around 70%, and while you won't see any snow, the region gets some rain—about 22 inches over the course of the year. Sunshine is plentiful, with many bright, clear days, especially in late spring and summer.

In the Algarve, violent crime is rare, and petty crime is limited to street crime during the busy tourist season. Beware of parking your car in busy lots by the beach. Theft of and from cars is not uncommon.

In all ways, Portugal is one of the most welcoming countries you'll ever experience, plus, in the Algarve English is spoken widely. You could land here tomorrow and slip right into everyday living without much struggle or hassle at all...

With an impressive list of things to do here, including both highbrow culture and an abundance of outdoor activities (including Europe's best selection of golf courses), you'll never be bored in retirement here.

Health Care In Portugal

Portugal's health care system has some problems with staff shortages, but still, it's one of the top worldwide, ranking 9th best in Europe and 12th in the world. While it used to be completely public, austerity measures forced a huge cut in the health services budget, resulting in part of the system being privatized.

Every citizen and legal foreign resident who has registered with their local health center benefits from the national health care system, which guarantees all basic health—accidents and illness—is covered.

The hospital network has modern, well-equipped units, and at least 90% of all doctors are English-speaking. Specialty consultations at a public hospital will cost you about 8 euros and emergencies about 20 euros.

Because of the long wait times in the public system, most expats supplement public care with insurance that allows them to visit private facilities. Locally, you could consider Multicare, Médis, or Liberty Seguros. Most private hospitals and clinics have agreements with these providers.

Health insurance isn't expensive in Portugal depending on the plan you choose. As one expat tells us they pay around 22 euros per month, flat rate. All specialty consultations are at least 50% covered by insurance, meaning you pay less than half the total cost of the appointment. For example, an average specialty consultation costs about 80 euros; with insurance you'd pay only 35 euros.

Residency Requirements

To come to Portugal as a tourist, you don't need a visa as an American or Canadian passport-holder. As a tourist, you can stay for a maximum of 90 days within any 180-day period.

Portugal is party to the Schengen agreement, which eliminates all internal border controls between the 29 participating countries.

To enter one Schengen country is to gain up to 90 days of continuous travel between the member states. This means that, once you are in a Schengen country, you do not show your passport when you cross borders.

It also means that the 90 days you are granted applies to all 29 countries of the area as a whole. If you spend the full 90 days in Portugal, you have to leave the Schengen area entirely after that. You can't cross the border to Spain (another Schengen area country) for an addition 90 days, for instance.

To stay for longer than the 90 days, you'll have to apply for a residency visa. Portugal offers several residency visa types, from student visas to investor visas. They're generally easy to qualify for and obtain.

The residency visa that most Portugal expats choose is the Passive Income Earner Residence Permit, or D7 visa. As the name suggests, this is an option for people who have income or capital that allows them to support themselves in Portugal.

To qualify for the D7, you have to meet a minimum income requirement, which is determined by the minimum wage.

The immigration officer that processes your application has discretionary power, however, so we recommend you have more than the minimum amount for the best chance of being accepted.

About 1,500 euros per month should do it. For a couple, you should be able to show one-and-a-half times this amount. The liquid assets you can use to qualify can be pensions, dividends, royalties, salary (as long as it's not Portugal-sourced), or capital.

Applications for residency must start in your country of residence. If approved, you'll get a residence visa that is valid for 120 days. During this window, you'll need to come to Portugal and apply for a residence permit.

Residence permits are valid for one year and can be renewed for periods of two years. After five years with a residence permit, you can apply for a permanent residence permit.

One downside of the D7 visa is that it's designed to make you tax-resident in Portugal. It requires you to spend at least 16 months in the country during the first two-year period.

By doing so, you will trigger tax residency. You will have to file taxes in Portugal, though this doesn't necessarily mean that you'll have a huge tax bill. In some cases, you may not owe any tax at all.

Portugal's Golden Visa Program is a residence by investment program, and it's aimed at non-EU citizens, including Americans and Canadians. It enables investors and their family members to enter and live in Portugal and to freely travel within the whole Schengen area.

It's a great alternative to the D7 visa option because it does not require you to become tax resident in Portugal in order to qualify. You only have to spend seven days in Portugal in the first year and a total of 14 days in each of the subsequent two-year periods to maintain your status.

That said, it's expensive...

- **Cultural Heritage Support:** Donating 250,000 euros or more to support arts or cultural heritage. If funding a qualifying initiative in a low-density region, this amount can be reduced to 200,000 euros.
- **Venture Capital/Private Equity Fund:** Transferring at least 500,000 euros to acquire units in venture capital funds, as long as they are not connected to real estate. This amount can be distributed among multiple funds.
- **Company Creation:** Creating a company or adding to the share capital of an already existing one, employing at least 10 locals (or 8, if done in a low-density area) alongside a capital transfer of 500,000 euros. If you are a business owner or entrepreneurs in your home country, this option will let you build a European operation.
- **Donation to Research Activities:** Transferring at least 500,000 euros for research done by either public or private scientific research institutions.

Venture capital/private equity funds are the most popular choice, as they offer a wide range of investment options and do not require active management or a donation to the government. Qualifying funds with incentives, such as fixed returns and upfront interest payments, are gaining quick interest.

Real Estate Restrictions

Portugal doesn't impose any restrictions on foreigners looking to purchase real estate. It has a centralized, reliable property registry system, and the law protects property, real estate rights, and the right to access and use one's own land.

Mortgage loans are not commonly available to foreigners but can be, particularly if you transfer sufficient savings to cover all of or the majority of the loan to their branch. This enables expats to bridge finance two properties until the sale of their property overseas is finalized without diminishing a nest egg.

Taxes

You become tax resident in Portugal if you spend more than 183 days in country in any 12-month period (it doesn't matter if these days are consecutive or not), and/or if you maintain a residence in Portugal at any point in the same time period.

Portugal has double taxation treaties in place with Canada and the United States, so you're at no risk of being taxed twice here.

CHAPTER 13

IRELAND

I began my own adventures overseas in Ireland.

Early one autumn morning what today seems like a lifetime ago, I packed my 8-year-old daughter Kaitlin, my laptop, and eight very oversized suitcases into an SUV. Then Kaitlin, my husband of one month Lief Simon, and I boarded a plane bound for Dublin.

From there, we three found our way south to Waterford, where we made our home for the next seven years.

When I undertook this move from Baltimore to Waterford some two-and-a-half decades ago, I'd already been covering this live and invest overseas beat for 13 years. I thought I knew what I was doing.

Lief and I arrived with our little family and our business, expecting to plug into the kind of infrastructure we were used to back in the States. We thought things like opening a bank account, finding office space, and placing ads for staff would be simple, everyday tasks, to be accomplished in short order.

They weren't... and getting them accomplished at all, we came to realize, depended not only on how you approached things, but also, in great part, on who you knew.

At first, we couldn't even decipher the Property For Rent ads in the local papers. Some places were advertised as having "All Mod Cons." Finally, our first landlord explained, with pride, that houses and apartments with all mod cons were those boasting all modern conveniences... things like central heating.

We were surprised, as well, to find that banks closed for lunch and that the entire city shut down at 5 p.m. We needed to buy a car, but dealerships were open only weekdays and, again, only until 5 p.m.

When were we supposed to go car shopping? We had a business to run.

We felt like we were continually banging our heads against a collective Irish wall. Employment contracts had to allow for tea breaks...

The plumbers and electricians we hired to help with the renovation of the house we finally purchased would go missing for days at a time then return to continue their work as though nothing unusual had happened...

Staff not only got four weeks' vacation each year by law, but they also took it!

These things were impossible for us hard-charging, Type-A Americans to process. How did anyone get anything done in this place, we found ourselves asking ourselves every day.

Finally, frustrated and confused, we had to admit that we weren't going to change how the Irish lived and did business. We'd have to go along.

And we did. Begrudgingly.

We bought a 200-year-old Georgian farmhouse and restored it. We bought another 200-year-old house in the city and renovated it into office space. We hired dozens of employees. We did, eventually, succeed in opening bank accounts and buying cars. We created infrastructure for things like paying bills, shopping for furniture, complying with local tax codes...

I gave birth to our son at Waterford Regional Hospital. He and his sister attended school, made friends, went to birthday parties...

Lief and I made friends, too. Some of our dearest friends today are Waterfordians. They write regularly to keep us in touch with life in this part of the world.

As the years have passed, I've found that my perspective on Ireland has shifted.

When Lief and I took our leave of the Emerald Isle so many years ago, we'd had it with life among the Irish. They'd frustrated and confounded us at every turn as we'd tried to start a business and build a life.

They didn't value efficiency or deadlines or any of the other building-a-business things that for us, at the time, were sacrosanct.

A bit of craic over a pint in the pub... a lively discussion around a peat fire on a chilly evening... merry sessions of traditional music...

These were the things that the Irish valued... the ways they most enjoyed spending their time.

Lief and I would shake our heads. Look at these folks... wasting so much time that they could be spending on something more productive!

Today we realize that we were the ones with our priorities upside-down.

One day, after we'd been living in Waterford for three years, a couple of readers stopped by the office. The pair of New Yorkers were in the country to investigate the possibilities for relocating their company from the States to Ireland... just as I had done.

Did I have any advice, they wanted to know...

This was the contradiction of the day. The Celtic Tiger was roaring loud, attracting investors (like us) from far and wide, entrepreneurs and businesspeople looking for opportunity.

But, as I only years later came to realize, we were all misguided.

Ireland was holding out great opportunity, but not of the kind we were in the market for at the time.

That young couple from New York was confused when I warned them away.

"Don't come to Ireland to run a business," I told them. "You'll be driven mad."

I'd stand by that advice today. But I'd add something.

If your agenda is business, you have better options...

But if your agenda is something else, you might want to take a close look at this little emerald isle.

We lived in Ireland during the apex of the Celtic Tiger, which generated great amounts of wealth, more money than this island had ever known. As a result, the Irish then, like us, were distracted from was right in front of them.

They were busy covering their ancient green land with suburban track homes, shopping malls, and fast-food franchises. We watched as pubs were replaced by nightclubs and as, yes, eventually, car dealerships kept Saturday business hours and banks remained open through lunch.

Ireland wanted so badly to compete on the global business that it lost sight of how it was already head and shoulders above the rest.

Today, when I think of our time in Ireland, I think of the owner of the corner shop across the street from our office...

How he and his wife sent us a small gift when Jack was born and how they inquired after both Jack and his older sister Kaitlin every time we saw them...

I remember the cabinet-maker who helped to restore our big old Georgian house to its original glories, shutter by shutter, wood plank by wood plank...

I think of the castles and the gardens we explored on weekends with Kaitlin and Jackson. I think of the times we braved the beaches at Tramore, sitting on the sand in sweaters, huddled together and shivering, while, out in the cold Irish Sea, the locals swam and surfed...

I think of cows in the roads and sheep in the fields. Of Kaitlin learning to ride a horse in our front paddock and of Jack learning to walk in our forever muddy back garden...

I think of these things more often as time passes, remember them and appreciate them. And, as a result, appreciate Ireland in ways I wasn't able to when we called her home.

Ireland has long been a top retirement choice, a beautiful, welcoming, peaceful nation of friendly, hospitable folks who speak English and who have a long-standing affinity with the United States. For decades, the retirement daydream of many Americans has been a white-washed, thatched-roof cottage on the Emerald Isle.

Over recent decades, Ireland has seen unprecedented boom and dramatic bust. Through the wild ups and downs, though, she has retained her heart. Irish retirement living is as appealing and charming an idea as it ever was...

Top Picks For A New Life In Ireland

Copper Coast, County Waterford

It's this quirky mix of dramatic coast, quiet beaches, immaculate countryside, sleepy villages, and rich heritage, that draws us back to this special part of County Waterford time and time again.

Most visitors that make it as far as Waterford, in Ireland's southeast, head for the beaches of Tramore or Dunmore East in the eastern part of the county. But the largely overlooked beaches and coves to the west are special. Even UNESCO has recognized the fact and awarded a stretch of this coast, known as the "Copper Coast," geopark status.

When you first set eyes on this curious stretch of coastline, you might think its name derives from the color of the sand or some of the rocks along its craggy shoreline. In fact, the area gets its name from the copper mining that took place here in the mid to late 19th century. The title only came into use since its European Geopark award in 2001.

Today, the Copper Coast covers the area from Fenor in the east of County Waterford to Stradbally at its western extremity, taking in the villages of Annestown, Boatstrand/Dunabrattin, Dunhill, and Bonmahon, and includes over 15 miles of beaches and coves.

Driving from Tramore on the R675 (in the direction of Dungarvan), you'll see the welcome signs to the Copper Coast just before arriving in Fenor (*An Fionnuir*), a blink-and-you'll-miss-it spot that ticks all the checkboxes of a traditional Irish village: café, church, school, pub.

While Fenor—the gateway to the Copper Coast—lies farther from the coast than its neighbors, its surrounding area is perfect for a country home. Kilfarrasy beach, a popular fishing spot, is about a mile from the village. Kids will also love the Copper Coast Mini Farm and playground just outside the village proper.

A few miles farther along the coast road is Annestown (*Bun Abha*).

On the River Anne, this little place holds the honor of being the only village in Ireland without a pub. It's also shop-less. But there's something truly special about this little non-village. You'll first come to the beach, a mix of stone and sand, with lots of rock pools. Just to the left, as you enter the beach, are the fort-like ruins of a former lime kiln. Continuing toward the village, stop at the foot of the hill to take in the view. From the small bridge here, you'll see the remains of 13th-century Dunhill Castle upstream. Finally, pass through the little clutter of dormer cottages that make Annestown.

For its dramatic scenery, the stretch of road between Annestown and Bonmahon is a spectacular drive. You'll wind around Kilmurrin Cove on the left (lovely for swimming, though beware of currents) and, shortly after, come to the restored remains of the Tankardstown engine houses on the right—a surreal presence among the fields of cattle. Dunabrattin Head is a prime fishing spot along this route and the little harbor at Boatstrand is worth a stop.

Next stop is Bonmahon (*Bun Machan*), the Copper Coast's greatest anomaly. With its two-mile stretch of golden beach, Bonmahon attracts more visitors than anywhere else on the Copper Coast.

Bonmahon has more amenities than Annestown. There isn't a shop, but there's a pub that serves good food and there's a café with outdoor tables for warmer days. And, despite the forgotten feel to the village, these gathering places have a certain charm.

There are some nice properties for sale around Bonmahon, where you'd be in a picturesque setting not too far from the beach. Bonmahon beach is a popular spot for walking, swimming, surfing, and kayaking.

Five miles from Bonmahon is the village of Stradbally (*An tSráid Baile*). No surprise that this village has reaped many awards in Ireland's National Tidy Towns competition—with its neat village square and colored cottages.

According to a plaque in the village, much of the Stradbally that exists today was built in the late 18th and early 19th century. Church ruins are all that remains of the original 13th-century village. Thousands of trees were planted around the cove in the middle of the 18th century.

Shaded by trees and with its own well-preserved lime kiln, it's as spotless as the village streets, with soft, white sand, clean water, and towering cliffs with hidden caves.

If you love city bustle—and need to be surrounded by crowds of people, shopping malls, restaurants, late bars, and other amenities—you would probably go insane living here. On the Copper Coast, you won't find big-name retail stores or supermarkets, fast food chains, public transport, leisure centers, theaters, or five-star restaurants. But that's where, for the right person, the attraction lies.

No morning or evening rush hour here. A herd of cattle changing fields, or a leisurely cyclist taking in the surrounding views, will occasionally cause you to slow or halt.

No bright lights here after dark, either. Apart from the activities at Harney's pub in Dunhill, most other pubs are quiet, with the occasional traditional music session.

All that said, though it feels a world apart here, it's only a 15- to 20-minute drive to either Waterford City (east) or Dungarvan Town (west), depending on where you choose to set up home. Both towns offer good shopping and entertainment choices (including cinemas, theatres, and gyms). Tramore has the advantage of being a little closer and is well equipped with amenities like supermarkets, pubs, cafés, bakeries, and restaurants.

For overseas travelers, the Dublin-Waterford motorway helps to make the area more easily accessible without impacting on the Copper Coast landscape (the journey from Dublin to Waterford is two hours).

Surrounded by glorious countryside, the Atlantic Ocean at your feet, and the Comeragh and Monavullagh mountain ranges in sight, there are few activities you can't arrange around the Copper Coast.

Starting with the sea, there's nothing more refreshing than a dip in these clear, cold waters. Yes, as attractive as it looks under blue skies, water temperatures don't normally rise above 59°F (warmest during the months of August and September). In the coldest months of January through March, it averages around 46°F.

But you wouldn't be alone if you went for a dip in October or March. Sea swimming year-round has become a fad in Ireland over the past few years and these days many brave the water for a dip even in the coldest months. Mobile saunas (another fad) dot the beaches along the Copper Coast throughout the year, too.

The Copper Coast geopark has a number of recommended and mapped out walking trails. You can do it yourself, get in with a local walking club, or take a guided tour. As part of the initiative to promote geotourism, guides have been trained in the local history and geology to take groups or individuals on guided walks. (Opportunities also exist to train as a guide.)

The mountain ranges provide good hiking ground, too, with popular trails around Mahon Falls and Coumshingaun (a corrie lake). Cycling and triathlon are both popular in the region.

Artists or writers will find lots of inspiration here. The little beaches, coves, and fishing boats beg to have their likenesses captured on canvas. And, photographers beware: you'll want a big memory card to survive a day here.

Ireland is internationally recognized as a top golfing destination, and, here in the southeast, golfers won't be disappointed. Dungarvan, Tramore, and Waterford City offer a good selection of clubs.

In Ireland, English is the first language, so you can forego hours of study before you hop on a plane. Gaelic, or "Irish" to the natives, is still compulsory at Primary and Secondary level education and lives on in the "Gaeltacht" areas (districts recognized by the government where Irish is the vernacular).

The closest Gaeltacht to the Copper Coast is "An Rinn" ("Ring" in its anglicized version); you'll see the signposts from the main N25 as you head toward Dungarvan. Ring is used to welcoming tourists, and locals will converse with you in English. But, as the *seanfhocail* (old Irish saying) goes: *Is fearr Gaeilge briste, ná Bearla clíste* ("Broken Irish is better than clever English").

It's no secret that Ireland is one of the most expensive places in the world to live. Certainly, it will cost you dearly to live in Dublin, paying the highest levels of rent in the country and lapping up the high-life in the capital.

But, here on the Copper Coast, where life is more laid-back, you could enjoy a good standard of living at an affordable cost. As with anywhere in the world, much hangs on your lifestyle and what qualifies as "the good life" to you. For a start, if you have a sizeable plot of land around your home, you could economize by growing your own vegetables and keeping a few hens.

Otherwise, for grocery staples, the best advice is to shop around. While it's convenient to buy everything in the big supermarket chains, local butchers and fruit and vegetable vendors offer cheaper prices—and the quality is superior. Expect to pay from 450 euros to 600 euros per month for a couple on your shopping basket.

If this is an area you decide you'd like to spend time in, start by looking for a rental property. This will serve as a good base while you get familiar with the area, scout out the local real estate opportunities, and decide where you'd like to ultimately settle. For a small cottage that would suit an individual, couple, or small family, expect to pay in the region of 1,000 to 1,200 euros a month. For a larger, four-bed-plus, modern-built home, this could rise to 1,500 to 2,000 euros a month or more.

Whether you're buying or building in Ireland, the biggest dilemma for buyers in the market right now is that prices are high. The median price for a house (as of early 2026) is around 390,000 euros.

Eating out is getting more expensive by the day. A meal for two—three courses and a bottle of wine in a good restaurant costs about 140 euros. Even pub grub for two can come to 50 euros, without drinks.

Utilities will cost about 60 euros per month—though you will need heating in the winter months, so your utility bills will be more expensive. And an internet and cell phone package is about 60 euros, too. You'll need a car if you live here, so budget about 70 euros per month to run it. All up, a couple would need about 3,500 euros a month to live comfortably here.

For health care, University Hospital Waterford is the main hospital for the southeast, and from the Copper Coast you're between 20 to 40 minutes away. Private health system standards are high. Whitfield Clinic in Waterford is excellent for care.

Family doctors (GPs) are widely available. These days, appointments are required. To avoid long waits, request the first appointment in the morning. GPs charge 70 euros per visit.

Pharmacists are knowledgeable in a wide range of conditions, so for minor ailments (and free advice), your local pharmacy is a good starting point.

Dental care is also of a high standard. You'll find a good selection of dentists in both Dungarvan and Waterford City.

Most overseas retirees who divide their time between countries try to set it up so they're avoiding harsh winters or intensely hot summers back home or in another foreign country. With Ireland, there's no real "best time" to be in the country.

Winters are generally mild and can have some of the most beautiful, crisp days of the year (perfect for exploring one of the geopark trails). And, there's nothing like gathering around an open fire on a cold, dark evening.

Summers in Ireland have some of the most unpredictable weather. This year, for example, one day with a high of 79°F was followed by another of 55°F. You need a wardrobe that caters for all seasons.

Living on the Copper Coast you'll enjoy a laidback lifestyle with stunning views of sea and mountains. Plus, it's safe. There's little petty crime and neighbors look out for one another. But gone are the days of leaving your front door unlocked when you pop out to do an errand or go for a stroll.

If you want to escape the busy city life and enjoy a bit of serenity, surrounded by a stunning coastline and fields dotted with sheep and cows, then the Copper Coast is an area worth your consideration.

Tralee, County Kerry

Most visitors to County Kerry head for Dingle, Killarney, or the famous "Ring of Kerry."

Meanwhile, the county town of Tralee—and the surrounding Tralee Bay area—is largely bypassed. Here, you're surrounded by some of Ireland's most dramatic landscapes and seascapes, while remaining close to the conveniences of town... a welcoming town that preserves its past culture and history like no other...

The great thing about Tralee is its rural location near the sea. You only have to drive five minutes out of town and you're surrounded by rolling farmland and open sea views. If you're looking for a slice of traditional Irish life, you should look to one of the villages on the outskirts of town.

The capital town of Kerry, modern Tralee is the administrative center for the county and, including its suburbs, has a population of 26,000. Its name comes from the Gaelic "Trá Lí," meaning "beach of the Lee." (The River Lee runs through the town.)

Almost 800 years old, the Norman town was founded in the 13th century where it became the home of the Earls of Desmond. The town was destroyed in 1580 as revenge for the Desmond Rebellions against Elizabeth I. It was then granted to Sir Edward Denny and the Dennys held their estate up to and beyond the Great Famine of 1845 to 1852.

The present design of the town took shape in the 19th century. Modern Denny Street is where the castle (home of the Desmonds and later the Dennys) once stood. It was constructed in 1826 and, despite the destruction of the castle, the street retains much of its former elegance, thanks to its period property.

West coast counties, including Kerry, were hit the worst by the Great Famine. During the years of 1845 to 1852, more than a million starving Irishmen, women, and children started out on the journey to America—on tall ships that became known as "coffin ships"—in the hope of a better life on the other side of the Atlantic.

Some 100,000 never saw the other side. Interestingly, those who traveled on the Jeanie Johnston from Tralee—"the luckiest ship in the world"—all got a second chance. The ship never lost a single passenger. (In recent years, a replica of the Jeanie Johnston was constructed and is a source of pride for the town.)

From those famine years, and for the next 100-plus years, the county suffered high emigration. Those that remained behind depended heavily on money being sent home from relatives in America. Conditions in rural Kerry lagged behind the rest of the country and can be appreciated by a remarkable photo exhibition in the Kerry County Museum.

Today's town is thriving, largely supported by agriculture and tourism, and it certainly makes the most of its resources.

To get up to speed on the town's ancestry, be sure to make the museum at the bottom of Denny Street one of your first stops in town. Housed in the Ashe Memorial Hall, completed in 1928, it takes the visitor through pre-historic times, medieval Tralee, the Great Famine, Civil War, and right up to more recent times that are movingly depicted by "Kerry Lives 1950-1973" in the Special Exhibition Gallery. This is a portrait of County Kerry as captured by husband-and-wife photographers Padraig and Joan Kennelly—it's worth the museum entrance fee alone.

So, what makes this area special? Looking at the big picture, you have the opportunity to live in a stunning rural setting, with mountains, sea, and sand—and with the amenities of Tralee town nearby.

The town has managed to preserve itself and so much of the Irish culture. Other cities and towns in Ireland, Dublin in particular, continue to move in a more European direction. You see the same brands, franchises, and shopfronts as any European city... with little of the town's own heritage and character shining through.

Although Tralee has its fair share of shopping streets, they blend in with, rather than take over from, the overall feel of the place. The town's architecture is well preserved. This is particularly visible on Denny Street, which is lined with Victorian and Georgian buildings, the beautiful Grand Hotel and Imperial Hotel (both of which hold up to their names), and runs right up past Tralee Town Park to the Kerry County Museum.

As well as preserving its architecture, the town has concentrated efforts to protect local flora and fauna, as evidenced by the Wetlands nature reserve and eco-tourism park. On the cultural front, the national folk theatre in Tralee—"Siamsa Tire"—has done a remarkable job of safeguarding traditional folk music, dance, and song.

To get here Cork Airport is under two hours. That services a host of European destinations—Barcelona, Malaga, the Algarve, and Paris to name a few. And, Shannon Airport, with flights to New York, is 130 kms (again, just under two hours) from Tralee by good roadway (including a stretch of motorway).

Roads in this part of the country are good by Irish standard. You won't find motorways in Kerry, which, it must be argued, helps retain its natural beauty... and forces you to slow down and enjoy the drive.

If you want to keep close to town and have everything within walking distance, there are opportunities to purchase character homes in Tralee proper.

Stepping outside the town center, you don't have to go far to find yourself surrounded by those lush green fields and dramatic sea views. Fenit, Ardfert, and Ballyheigue are villages all within easy distance of Tralee and have their own beaches, as well as shops and services.

On the Ballyheigue/Ardfert Road, roughly five kms outside Tralee, is Ballyroe, with enviable views over Tralee Bay and the Dingle Peninsula. All around the Kerry coastline, you'll pay more for ocean views. And, in this beautiful setting, you might say those prices are justified.

Ardfert is a charming little village with a few pubs, a couple of shops, an off license (liquor store), butcher, hairdresser, school playground... and most importantly, the ruins of the monastery originally founded by St. Brendan which was added to over the centuries, along with Ardfert Cathedral.

Best of all, you're right on the doorstep of Banna Beach, an unspoiled, blue flag beach, seven kms long. It's a favorite with local runners, dog-walkers, and surfers. The Banna Beach Resort and Leisure Club is open to members and, besides its 20-meter swimming pool and fully-equipped fitness center, it runs classes throughout the week.

Ballyheigue also has a blue flag beach, though it's stony. Since it's on the doorstep of the village, it attracts more of a crowd. You could find a lovely property away from the village and still be within easy reach of the sand. The beach is long enough that once you get beyond the main promenade, there's more unspoiled beach to enjoy.

The village of Fenit with its pretty harbor and landmark sculpture of St. Brendan, is a popular spot for vacationers. You'll find some elevated properties around here with breathtaking views and prices are typically higher than its more northerly neighbors mentioned above.

Rentals in Tralee town and the surrounds range from 950 euros per month and go all the way up to 2,000 euros per month (2,000 euros would get you a four-bed, three-bath house). It's best to shop around for groceries but there are plenty of supermarkets and grocery stores in Tralee. A couple's monthly shopping budget would come in around 450 to 600 euros.

Utilities will cost about 60 euros per month—you won't ever need air conditioning, but your heating cost will run up in the winter months. And an internet and cell phone package is about 60 euros, too. You'll need a car if you live here, so budget about 70 euros per month to run it. All in, a couple would need about 3,500 to 4,000 euros a month to live comfortably here.

You can't appreciate the unpredictability of the Irish weather until you spend any length in the country. And, nobody, of course, chooses Ireland as a destination—either vacation or longer-term—for its weather. But if you really can't stand the rain, County Kerry—or anywhere along the west coast—would not be the place to go. Because of its western and coastal position, it does tend to get more rain and stronger winds than elsewhere in the country. Annual rainfall in the west averages 39 to 49 inches.

Of course, Ireland gets its share of sunshine. Temperatures in July, August, and early September can reach the mid-20s. And, on the plus side, winters are mild. Snow is mostly seen only on high ground. Crisp winter days when the sun shines are fantastic for getting out on long country walks.

Bottom line, you just need to roll with the unpredictable nature of it. When you make plans for outdoor activities, be sure to pack your wet gear—or have a backup plan.

The closest public hospital in Tralee is Kerry General Hospital, close to the town center, which serves the county of Kerry as well as parts of Cork and Limerick. Its departments include Emergency; Ear, Nose & Throat; General Medicine; General Surgery; Gynaecology; Obstetrics; Orthopaedics; Paediatric; Pathology; Psychiatry; Radiography; Oncology.

Health insurance is highly recommended. With your health insurance, you will be covered (at least in part) at most private hospitals. Private health care is offered at the Bon Secour Hospital in Tralee. It treats for ailments that include angiography, cardiology, diagnostic imaging, dietetics, general medicine, intensive care, opthalmology, orthopaedics, paediatrics, pharmacy, physiotherapy, respiratory, urology.

Doctors, or General Practitioners (GPs) as they are called in Ireland, are of course English-speaking, too, and there are a number of clinics around town. You'll also find doctors in most of the outpost villages, if you'd prefer a local service to save you a full trip into town. Out of surgery hours and over weekends, there's the "SouthDoc" service to deal with cases requiring immediate attention.

Though you will have challenges in some places in Ireland, things are certainly improving for wheelchair-users. Supermarkets, retail outlets, theaters, and other attractions have designated disabled parking spaces. And most modern buildings are designed with disabled access in mind. The Irish Wheelchair Association has a branch in Tralee for further information.

And, wherever you go, you will find that most people will do whatever they can to help you access and enjoy your surroundings.

If you're looking at Ireland as a potential retirement haven, either part- or full-time, then you're probably looking for a lifestyle that encompasses the best of Irish country living... residing in a safe environment, surrounded by postcard-style images of green fields, stony walls, grazing cows, and country cottages.

All of these exist here in abundance.

County Clare

County Clare is one of the best kept secrets in Ireland. It's found in the Mid-West Region along the country's west coast and bordered by dramatic cliffs that look out broodingly at the Atlantic Ocean.

Here, among the small coastal towns and lively villages, the true Irish spirit runs strong. West Clare natives are a comically outrageous people with a bizarre sense of humor, always up for "the craic" and a bit of adventure.

Aside from its people, culture, and history, Clare entices people with its natural beauty: long white-sand beaches with surfable waves, rolling sand dunes, and patchwork green fields. The world-famous Burren National Park, a special region of glaciated karst landscape, is found here as well.

To go along with all this natural abundance, there's world class golfing, surfing, endless breath-taking hill walks, and even deep-sea fishing off towering cliffs. County Clare holds a near-mythical reputation among those who know it... It's where the Irish themselves go when they need a vacation.

The villages of Clare are strung together by narrow hedgerows that burst with wildflowers during the summer. As you travel the winding roads between villages steeped in character, you'll see bungalows, thatched cottages, donkey sanctuaries, and wild sheep wandering the roads.

Perhaps it's the postcard-worthy scenery, but there's something about this region that attracts those of a creative spirit. This is the only place in Ireland with more art galleries than pubs.

Of course, there are pubs, too... but you'll find that live music dominates, and that every second or third person is a musician or singer.

Only gaining her freedom from the English Empire a hundred years ago, Ireland is a relatively young nation built on millennia of ancient history. The old Ireland that people yearn to see is most evident in County Clare.

There are plenty of wonderful small coastal towns and villages to choose from in County Clare. Here are a few of the best...

Lahinch is only 4 kms from the art town of Ennistymon, which has galleries and Aldi and SuperValu supermarkets. It has a main street, a central car park along the promenade, shops, restaurants, pubs, and five different surf schools.

Lahinch boasts two 18-hole golf clubs, and Lahinch Golf course abuts the promenade itself. Experience Seaworld and Leisure Centre, game rooms, cinema, restaurants like Vaughan's, superior bars, and live music on season.

You can get everything you need from bakeries and delis, and there are Spar and Centra Supermarkets in Lahinch, too.

Liscannor... An enchanting little village a few miles north of Lahinch... Liscannor is home of the distinctive thick quartz-sandstone paving slabs made famous by their unique texture. They are composed of the fossilized sediment tracks of ancient marine creatures.

Stop by Joseph McHugh's pub for delicious food and fun. You can fish off the pier or the beach or take the four-kilometer walk to the Cliffs of Moher.

Doolin is a picture-perfect Irish village with a lot happening. One of the reasons Doolin is so successful is because two different ferry operators run tours to the iconic Aran Islands (a group of rocky isles off the coast of Galway Bay) and sea tours to the base of the Cliffs of Moher to offer a different viewing perspective and marvel at their size.

Doolin Pier is the gateway to the Aran Islands. Six ferries run to the islands of Inishmore, Inishmaan, and Inisheer in season, and only two ferries operate off season.

Winding steeply down the coast from Doolin is a cliff walk like no other, offering views of the entire seascape. Though not for the faint of heart or the unfit, this hike is well worth the effort if you're up for it.

Kilkee is centered around a small well-sheltered bay and beach. Its sheltered nature precludes any real surfing.

Kilkee is popular among residents of County Limerick during the summer months. It's only one hour from Shannon Airport and 1 hour and 15 minutes from Limerick.

There are excellent restaurants and guesthouses, including Hickie's Bar, Myles Creek, and Scott's. The Diamond Rocks Café at the top of the town is also a popular brunch spot among people returning from their invigorating cliff walks.

Kilkee has seen extensive development over recent decades, and prices for the prime locations are high. Significantly better value can be found just a little further out of town.

Fanore is home to misty mountain tops, stone and pebble beaches, and yellow sand beaches further out...

Look for postcard-worthy thatched cottages, stone walls, and karst limestone area. You'll be met with lovely views of ocean, horses on the hillside, and a scattering of holiday homes.

Fanore is as laid-back and quiet as you could ever hope a place to be, with only a couple lively pubs.

There are remarkable beaches with lifeguards on duty, farms all around, farmhouse accommodation, rustic cottages available for rent, a small shop, and much more.

Remains of famine roads still abound here...

West Clare has become a mecca for artists, and there are art galleries, studios, and displays in every nook and cranny in every town and village.

Ennistymon seems to have nearly as many art galleries as residents, and the local landscape and legends offer inspiration to artists from across the globe.

Bord Failte, the Irish Tourism Board, is actively promoting West Clare as part of their "Wild Atlantic Way" tour of the west coast of Ireland. There are supports and grants available for many types of sustainable tourism activities in the area.

Clare isn't being ruined by sprawling resort hotels and plastic paddy pubs. Developments are closely monitored by the local council for any negative environmental, social, or cultural impacts.

West Clare is home to many expats. It's a great option for those who understand the value of a slower pace of life, who love the wild outdoors but also want to remain close to people who like to laugh, love, and celebrate life.

You'll meet expats and locals at the golf clubs, pubs, restaurants, on the street, and on the beaches, but you won't have to band together as foreigners for protection or advice like you need to in other destinations.

You don't need expat support groups because you become part of the local community nearly as soon as you arrive.

Living in Ireland is not cheap by any consideration, but living in Clare can be cheaper than many areas in Ireland. The cost of real estate is high but many of the best amenities in Clare are free.

A couple could get by on 2,500 euros per month if you own your home, but to have a comfortable lifestyle, including rent, you would need at least 3,500 euros to 4,000 euros per month.

A deli sandwich is about 6 euros. A budget meal is about 10 euros. Midrange meals run about 14 to 24 euros, and fine dining or meals in award-winning restaurants will cost you more than 25 euros for the main course alone. A pint or glass of wine will cost you about 6 or 8 euros and a cocktail could cost you 10 to 12 euros.

Electricity costs in Ireland are significantly higher than older estimates — around 0.35 to 0.36 cents per kWh with typical household bills of roughly 1,700 euros to 1,800 euros per year.

Internet and cable are reasonably priced—about 35 euros per month for 150 Mbps internet. An internet and cable bundle costs about 55 euros.

A TV license costs 160 euros per year if you own a television. Water is free, but waste disposal is managed privately at about 20 euros to 40 euros per month, depending on service levels.

Holiday homes and retirement locations are being snapped up quickly, so you need to be financially prepared before you start house hunting in earnest. House prices continue to rise in Clare, as her secrets become more widely known.

The closest hospital is in Ennis, 40 kms away from most popular areas. The closest regional hospital is in Limerick City, about 70 kms from Lahinch. There are doctors' surgeries and dental practices in every town and village.

Anti-social and drunk and disorderly behavior sometimes occurs on the streets after closing time, but the Gardai (police) are well-used to handling it.

I can't imagine what crime might befall you in County Clare other than some sheep rustling or someone stealing your golf tee time.

The weather, as with the rest of Ireland, is subject to change. Sometimes with every form of weather occurring in the same day. There are plenty of overcast and rainy days in Clare... This might be what influenced the indoor pub culture. West Clare in particular is breezy so wind protection is a must.

The closest airport to County Clare is Shannon Airport—less than 30 miles from most places of interest. Unfortunately, recent cutbacks mean that there are no direct flights from the States to Shannon, necessitating a connection through a European airport.

Cork Airport and Dublin Airport offer a wider selection of flight paths, with more direct flights to the States as well as connections to Europe, Asia, and beyond. Cork Airport is about two hours away from Clare by car; Dublin Airport is a two-and-a-half-hour drive away.

County Clare is experiencing a surge in interest from people young and old who want to move here to live a better life. The wildness of the Atlantic coastline inspires those of an artistic spirit and those who feel a connection with the ocean.

Living in Clare allows you to connect with a deep feeling of Irishness—that mischievous, eternally young, and slightly irreverent side to ourselves that we all carry in our hearts.

Health Care In Ireland

Ireland has both a public and private health care system. Both services are often administered out of the same hospital.

The standard of medical care in Ireland is high, ranked 19th by the World Health Organization... but emergency rooms are often overcrowded. Should you require non-emergency treatment over a weekend, bring a book because you will be waiting a long time.

Outside the main cities, access to emergency and medical services can be a challenge. Apart from local clinics and community hospitals with limited services, your closest general hospital can be hours away if you plan to retire in a remote area.

There are doctors' surgeries in every town and village. If you have a health issue, it's recommended you go to your general practitioner first unless it's an emergency. If you require further care they will send you to a hospital for tests or onwards to a specialist.

Private health insurance is recommended, but it's expensive. Historically, part of the reason for this was the lack of competition in the market. That started to improve in recent years, when VHI, which once dominated the market, began to fight competition from Quinn-Healthcare (formerly BUPA Ireland), Laya, and Hibernian Aviva. However, over the last year, prices have started to climb again. The cost is about 180 euros per month per person.

Another option is to purchase an international health care policy that will cover you anywhere in the world. Depending on your circumstances, this may be more cost-effective than buying a local policy. BUPA International provides international coverage and comes recommended.

To give you an idea of costs, a doctor's visit is typically 70 euros; a visit to the Emergency Room 100 euros; an overnight stay in hospital averages around 1,000 euros.

Residency Requirements

Most Western citizens can stay in Ireland for 90 days without a visa. After 90 days you need to get a visa or work permit to remain in Ireland. Note that while Ireland is a member of the EU, it is not part of the Schengen Area. This means you're required to go through immigration if traveling to the Schengen Area from Ireland.

Ireland offers several routes to residency, including the Stamp 0 Visa and the Irish Immigrant Investor Program. It doesn't score well for residency, however, because the income requirements are prohibitive for many people, as is the cash lump sum requirement...

To get the Stamp 0 Visa, you must show 50,000 euros in income per person.

This amount is reflective of the high standard of living in Ireland and below the average Irish income.

The onerous income requirement is also compounded by the additional requirements of a lump sum sufficient to cover the down payment of a property in Ireland. You don't have to buy property, you just need to show the financial means. You'll also need sufficient health insurance.

The Irish Immigrant Investor Program (IIP) is a residency-through-investment program offering several paths to residency for defined periods subject to ongoing renewal. Investments you can choose from in order to qualify include:

1. Investing 1 million euros in an Irish enterprise. This is the best seller, with 81% of applications made through this route.
2. Invest 1 million euros in an Irish investment fund.
3. Invest 2 million euros in a real estate investment trust (REIT) that is listed on the Irish Stock Exchange.

4. Make a 500,000 euros philanthropic donation that benefits the arts, sports, health, cultural, or educational fields. This is the lowest amount available to invest in Ireland's IIP but doesn't provide any return on investment.

It initially grants you a two-year residency status, which can be renewed for three and five years. After their initial five-year period, if you have not withdrawn your Ireland investment and continue to be law-abiding and self-sufficient, you will be eligible to apply for residence in five-year tranches.

Funds invested in Ireland must be legally acquired and owned, not borrowed, by the investor. If you're investing in Ireland, you must also be found to be of good character and have a net worth of at least 2 million euros.

If these entry points to apply for residency in Ireland seem unreachable, there is a silver bullet solution that may apply to you... Ireland recognizes its far-flung sons and daughters with one of the best ancestral citizenship programs in the world.

If one of your parents or grandparents were born in Ireland, you're entitled to Irish citizenship and an EU passport. All you have to do is enter your birth into the Register of Foreign Births and apply for a passport. You may also be eligible through your great-grandparents, but only if your parent became an Irish citizen-by-descent before your birth.

Real Estate Restrictions

Foreigners and non-residents can buy property in Ireland without restrictions.

If you're looking to build a home in this country, you will face challenges getting planning permission. Planning laws in Ireland are strict, even for locals. You will only be given permission to build in rural areas if you can prove a familial connection to the area or have lived in the area for a long time (five to 15 years).

Planning permission is also required when renovating an historic property and when adding on to an existing house.

Taxes

In Ireland, you're considered a resident for tax purposes if you spend 183 days or more in the country in a single year, or 280 days over a period of two years. In the second scenario, you'll be considered a taxable "resident" in the second year.

Property tax was officially introduced 13 years ago. All eligible property owners must pay a property tax annually. The amount you'll pay depends on the value range your property falls within. It's up to each citizen to determine the correct assessed value.

When you buy a property in Ireland, it's subject to "stamp duty." Though, as its name suggests, it's charged on the documents necessary in the transfer of property, the amount you'll pay depends on the assessed value of your property.

If you make a profit from the sale of your Irish property, it will be subject to capital gains tax.

The Irish "Capital Acquisitions Tax" covers gift tax, inheritance tax, and discretionary trust tax. How much you pay depends on your relationship to the deceased, as well as the amount of the benefit. For full details, refer to the Irish Revenue website.

CHAPTER 14

SPAIN

It's been some 35,000 years since the first modern humans settled in what we today call Spain. The intervening period has seen empires rise and fall, kingdoms created, dynasties divided, golden ages, bloody wars, and even a 36-year fascist dictatorship in this Old World great.

Spain's geography is as varied as her history. Filling most of the Iberian Peninsula—the closest U.S. state in terms of size is Texas—Spain boasts a dual-coastline. To the north is the Atlantic Ocean's Bay of Biscay, to the south and east lies the Mediterranean Sea.

Home to more UNESCO Biosphere Reserves than any other country in the world, here you'll find towering mountains, fertile lowlands, lush forests, rocky cliffs, and over 3,000 beaches, the longest of which is Andalusia's Doñana Beach which runs for over 17 miles.

It's even got a desert—Tabernas, the only true desert in Europe. If you've never been, I'm still willing to bet you've spent time here... Tabernas has provided the backdrop for hundreds of films, including *The Good, The Bad, And The Ugly*, *Lawrence Of Arabia*, and *Indiana Jones And The Last Crusade*, earning it the moniker "The Hollywood of Europe."

Then there's the islands... 48 of which are inhabited. The two main archipelagos are the Balearics and the Canaries. The Balearic Islands are in the Mediterranean, off Spain's eastern coast, while the Canary Islands sit off the coast of northwestern Africa—just 62 miles from Morocco at their closest point.

Its history, geography, language, and climate are varied as are its culture, cuisine, architecture, and costs.

Indeed, the trickiest thing about expat life in Spain is choosing one spot to call home from the wealth of great options on offer.

If you like city life, Valencia, Barcelona, Málaga, and Madrid all have much to recommend them.

If you want to kick back on a palm-fringed island then Mallorca, Tenerife, or Ibiza would fit the bill.

For sunseekers, the Costa Blanca and Costa del Sol offer more than 300 days of sunshine each year.

Spain offers incredible value, but there's far more to love about this country than just low-cost living... There's first-class infrastructure and one of the world's best health care systems... A huge expat community and warm and welcoming locals... Laid-back living, year-round sunshine, and world-class beaches...

Top Picks For A New Life In Spain

Valencia

Valencia is Spain's third-largest city and the capital of the Valencia region, but with a mere 700,000 or so residents, it's a small, manageable city that doesn't feel crowded or overwhelming. The feeling here is laid back.

Located on Spain's eastern coast, on the floodplain of the Turia River as it empties into the Mediterranean Sea, the earth here is famously fertile. The surrounding countryside is abundant with crops—mainly, its world-famous citrus.

This sun-soaked city on Spain's Mediterranean coast offers an unparalleled quality of life surrounded by beauty, cultural richness, and community.

It's a vibrant, exciting city with endless things to see and do...

It has golden-sand beaches with bright Mediterranean waters and warm, sunny weather year-round. Its infrastructure is excellent, including its public transportation system and health care facilities...

It's safe, affordable, and friendly, with a welcoming community of locals and expats from around the world...

Americans are somewhat new to the scene in Valencia, though, with the city practically unknown to many on the other side of the Atlantic... unless you're familiar with the oranges of course...

Indeed, Valencia feels nothing like some other Spanish cities that have a high foreigner population. It feels authentically itself.

That's not to say there aren't foreigners here—more are discovering it every year. But Valencia is a small city and doesn't attract near as many expats or tourists as Barcelona, Madrid, or the southern Costas.

Valencia offers everything an expat could want, but it's not just us at Live And Invest Overseas who recognize its incredible value.

It took the top spot in InterNations' 2024 Quality of Life index, as well as its Personal Finance and Best Cities rankings. The European Commission named it the European Green Capital for 2024. And it came out as Europe's Best City in Condé Nast Traveler's 2024 Readers' Choice Awards.

Valencia has gained significant attention for its sustainability, innovation, and overall quality of life, and the list of accolades and honors awarded to it is endless.

It's ideal for active, outdoor-oriented lifestyles, whether you explore Turia Gardens, the riverbed-turned-urban park that snakes its way through the city, go for leisurely strolls on Malvarrosa Beach, or play rounds of golf at the many nearby courses.

Valencia has long been famous for its architecture, and to walk its streets is to take in 2,000 years of history, from the medieval Islamic era to futuristic structures that look straight off the screens of science fiction films. The City of Arts and Sciences, a geometric architectural marvel, is perhaps Valencia's most iconic building.

Valencia dates back to 138 B.C., so it's rich in history and sites of significance. The heart and soul of ancient Valencia is the Ciutat Vella, one of the biggest historic centers in Spain. It's home to iconic buildings like the Valencia Cathedral, the Lonja de Seda (the UNESCO-listed silk-exchange building), and other architectural wonders.

The Ciutat Vella is also an incredibly atmospheric neighborhood that's full of restaurants, bars, and shops... a romantic and charming place to spend time.

It's no surprise that many expats choose to base themselves here.

Another of Valencia's claims to fame is the City of Arts and Sciences, a complex with otherworldly architecture that contains a science museum, an IMAX theater, and Europe's biggest aquarium.

Life in Valencia is never dull, with lively annual events like Las Fallas, when the streets come alive with music, parades, and larger-than-life sculptures, as well as live opera and theater performances, concerts, sporting events, and a rich culinary scene. You could spend your days sampling traditional dishes and fine wines at charming local restaurants.

Valencia is walkable and well-connected with public transportation, so you can easily free yourself of car ownership and all its associated expenses.

Valencia is so rich in cultural entertainment, it's easy to forget that this city is on the Mediterranean Sea, with golden sand beaches accessible from the city center. These sandy stretches are perfect for walking, sunbathing, swimming, and water sports.

One of its top draws is its affordability. Valencia is a shining example of how Europe—even an amenity-rich, old-world regional capital with an exceptional standard of living—can be more affordable than most North Americans would think. Everything from housing to health care to a bottle of wine costs less here.

Rent is low compared to other Spanish cities, at between 600 euros and 1,300 euros a month. A couple will pay about 450 euros for a monthly grocery shop. Eating out is likewise affordable—at a good restaurant you can get a hearty meal for about 15 to 20 euros. Drinks cost 2 to 5 euros. Transportation is cheap and efficient—for an unlimited monthly metro and bus pass plus biking subscription you'll pay 20 euros. And electricity for a month is about 75 euros.

Overall, for a couple, you could live comfortably on about 2,500 euros a month. Even the best lifestyle in Valencia comes at a fraction of the cost of a life in North America...

Spain is among the world's top-ranked countries for medical care, and expats across the country speak highly of its health care system... And Valencia is also highly rated for health care, with modern facilities and highly trained professionals.

Excellent public facilities are available through Spain's National System (the SNS) as well as private hospitals and clinics. Hospital La Fe (one of the top-ranked hospitals in Spain) and Hospital Clínico Universitario are among the most highly regarded facilities.

As an expat, you'll need to take out private health insurance, at least initially, to access the Spanish health system. Costs are extremely affordable.

One expat we know, who moved with his wife and two sons from Georgia, got Spanish health insurance after moving to Valencia and pays 2,500 euros a year for the entire family. He said that would have covered them for about two months back home. A visit to the doctor costs 30 euros.

If you decide to settle here, you should feel confident about having all of your medical needs taken care of to a high standard.

The climate is another undeniable draw. Valencia gets about 2,700 hours of sunshine—300-plus sunny days—per year, with mild winters.

Valencia enjoys a Mediterranean climate, so it's a great choice if you want hot, sunny weather all the time. You'll want air conditioning in your home to live comfortably here.

A local weather phenomenon, called *ponentà*, brings dry, warm winds and shields the city from rain, making it warmer than it would be otherwise.

While it experiences some seasonal change, with summers that are dry and hot and winters that are mild, it never gets truly cold here.

You should pick up the basics of Spanish to live well in Valencia.

English levels are decent among locals, and there are plenty of international expats, so you could get by without Spanish. Things like ordering at restaurants or buying groceries shouldn't be a problem.

However, learning Spanish will come in handy when it comes to more obscure tasks like calling an electrician or hiring household help. It will also help you establish connections with locals.

Note that the traditional language in the Valencian Community is Valencian, which holds official status alongside Spanish. You won't be expected to or need to learn Valencian, though.

It's easy to make connections with expats in Valencia. You'll find fellow foreigners from the U.K., Germany, France, Belgium, the States, Canada, and beyond.

The best way to get connected, even before you arrive, is to get online. Join the Facebook groups and whatever other groups you can find for foreigners living in Valencia.

Public transportation is comprehensive. You don't need a car living in Valencia with the metro, buses, trams, and bike-sharing services, all of which are affordable and efficient.

Valencia's international airport doesn't offer any direct flights to North America, but it connects to many European hubs, making travel here fairly straightforward. Flying directly to Madrid and then taking the train to Valencia (about two-and-a-half hours) is another option.

On top of all of this, Valencia is safe, the type of place where you can breathe easy and let worries of crime and violence that may have affected you back home fade away. It has a welcoming community of expats and locals that makes it easy for newcomers to feel at home quickly.

Despite it being the third-biggest city in the country, Valencia does not have the same reputation for crime as other big cities like Madrid and Barcelona. Expats report feeling completely at ease at all times of the day and night. Chances are that crime will not affect your life here.

When it comes to launching a fulfilling new life overseas, one that's rich in adventure but at the same time comfortable and well-appointed, we can think of no better place than Valencia.

Costa De La Luz

Directly across Spain's southern tip lies the Costa de la Luz, the Coast of Light, and going from northwest to southeast, it stretches from Spain's border with Portugal down to Tarifa, the southernmost point in Europe, almost touching Morocco across the Strait of Gibraltar, along the Atlantic Coast.

This region is famous for the very thing it's named for: dazzling, always abundant sunshine.

The Costa de la Luz's centerpiece is Cádiz. It's often called "Little Havana" or compared to Old San Juan, Puerto Rico, because of its long boardwalked beachfront backed by colorful ancient buildings...

But Cádiz is the prototype that those New World cities were based on. It's touted as the oldest city in Western Europe, dating to 1104 BC.

But there's more to the Costa de la Luz than just Cádiz...

Cádiz Province (one of the two provinces that the Costa de la Luz covers; the other is Huelva) offers everything from well-appointed beachfront towns to ancient hilltop villages that can be seen for miles because of their brilliant white-washed buildings.

Across these towns, you find pockets of expats that love the region for its low cost of living, beautiful beaches and pristine nature, and authentic culture.

The Costa de la Luz covers Spain's Atlantic Coast, from its border with Portugal at its northwestern limit (it abuts the far eastern Algarve region specifically), to Tarifa at its southeastern limit. Tarifa is the most southern part of Spain and all of Europe. It's part of Spain's southern autonomous Andalucía region.

Heading south from Cádiz, our favorite towns include Chiclana de la Frontera, Conil de la Frontera, and Vejer de la Frontera.

To the north, El Puerto de Santa Maria, Rota, Chipiona, and Sanlúcar de Barrameda are towns to check out.

And to the northeast, Jerez de la Frontera is worth a look.

This region is proud, traditional, and culturally vibrant. Unique events based in ancient folklore are hosted throughout the year. Cádiz's claim to fame is Carnival, which takes place over 10 days every February. Expect colorful processions, live music, dancing, and revelry and entertainment for all. Cádiz's version of carnival incorporates *gaditano* humor, for which people from Cádiz are famous.

Across Andalucía, Semana Santa (Holy Week) is a big, important event, and though it also features floats and processions, it's a far more somber and serious event than carnival. Members of local parish churches parade their statues of Jesus and Mary to the cathedral and back accompanied by brass bands.

Don't try to get anything done during Carnival or Semana Santa.

Jerez de la Frontera is most famous for sherry wine. The area between Jerez, El Puerto de Santa María, and Sanlúcar de Barrameda is known as the Sherry Triangle, and it's the only place in the world with the conditions to produce sherry.

The closest thing to city-like amenities you find along the Costa de la Luz—things like shopping at malls and boutiques, dining at a wide selection of restaurants and bars, going to museums, shows, or live music, or taking in a generally lively, social atmosphere—is in Cádiz.

That said, this is a small city. If you're used to an action-packed, cosmopolitan environment with endless entertainment options at your fingertips, this may not be the right place for you. If you're after a low-key lifestyle, Cádiz or one of the even quieter small towns could be perfect for you.

Plus, a proper city—Sevilla—is only an hour-and-a-half train ride away when you need a dose of city action. Jerez offers bigger-city ambiance, too.

The Costa de la Luz is a place for nature lovers, and thanks to a number of natural parks in the area, the nature you find here is pristine... It's a different story to the Costa del Sol, just a few miles east, which is built up with all-inclusive resorts and beach clubs.

The countryside is Tuscany-like along the Costa de la Luz, featuring wildflower-dotted rolling green hills that are perfect for hiking or horseback-riding. Spain's southern Atlantic coastline is long and mostly undeveloped, with uncrowded beaches of golden sand.

Anywhere you settle along this coast, a stretch of soft sand will be within arm's reach. Even Cádiz, the city option, has a handful of attractive beaches right in the Old Town.

Some of the top beach towns in the area are Conil, Sanlúcar, and Chipiona. Note that the further south you go towards the Strait of Gibraltar, the windier the beaches become because the Strait acts as a natural wind tunnel.

Of course, with so much access to the waterfront, anything you could want to do on the water, you can do here, from boating, sailing, watersports, kitesurfing, kayaking, dolphin-watching, fishing, and more.

In the sprawling Doñada National Park, you can see endangered species like the Iberian lynx and Spanish imperial eagle.

For golf-lovers, the Costa de la Luz is a great choice. Some of the best golf courses in the area are Benalup Golf & Country Club, Barceló Montecastillo Golf, and Vista Hermosa Golf Club. Other outdoor activities you can do here are cycling, rock climbing, horseback riding, paragliding, and more.

You'll probably want a car in this area, and the roads are in excellent condition, well signposted, and well lit, though in the compact city centers cars won't be of much use. Within towns, walking is a good way to get around, but it's hot here and these old streets aren't mobility friendly...

If you live in a city center and decide to forego a car, the train system connects the region's towns and villages, and it's cheap, comfortable, and efficient. Just outside Cádiz Old Town is the railway station. From there, you can connect as far as Santander and Gijón, in the extreme north of Spain, or Madrid.

A couple's basic monthly budget here should come to about 1,700 euros. Rent on the Costa de la Luz is likely to be your biggest outlay, with a well-appointed two-bedroom apartment by the beach costing around 600 euros per month at the upper end of the spectrum.

Groceries cost an average of 260 euros per month. You'll often hear that in Andalucía (the region where the Costa de la Luz is located), "wine is cheaper than water," and it's true. You can get a decent bottle of wine for about 1 euro while a liter of water can be closer to 2 euros.

Dinner for two, including drinks, appetizers, mains, and dessert, could come to about 35 euro. A fancy coffee will be less than 2 euros; a beer, which is served in small glasses called *cañas* in Spain, will be about a euro.

Utilities (gas, water, and electricity) will cost about 110 euro per month. And you'll spend about 400 euros per couple per month on entertainment.

Transportation costs depend on whether you have a car. It's possible to get by without one thanks to the train, for which the basic fare is negligible.

In Cádiz, there is one public hospital (Hospital Universitario Puerta del Mar) and three private ones. You'll also find public and private hospitals in Jerez (five), El Puerto de Santa María (one), and Sanlúcar (one). Pharmacies are abundant in every town.

The Costa de la Luz is not the most popular destination in Spain for expats... but its authenticity and low-key local vibe is part of its appeal. That said, in certain towns around the region, you'll find some decent-sized expat communities that you can join, if you want to.

In Cádiz, despite being the biggest city on the coast, is not home to a huge number of expats. The Old Town is home to no more than a couple dozen expats, and most are here only here on a seasonal basis.

El Puerto de Santa Maria, Chipiona, Vejer de la Frontera, and Conil de la Frontera are home to sizable expat communities. And Rota, with its naval station that employees U.S. Navy and Marine Corps personnel, stands out for its big American expat numbers.

You'll find plenty of organizations, clubs, activities, and opportunities to socialize along the Costa de la Luz. Golf is a great way to meet people, and there are plenty of courses here. That said, Spanish skills are key to a well-rounded social life.

The trains are cheap, comfortable, and efficient. Just outside Cádiz Old Town is the railway station. From there, you can travel as far north as Santander and Gijón in Spain, or as far south as Madri in Portugal.

Cercanías Cádiz is the regional company that connects Cádiz to Jerez de la Frontera, with 13 stops between the two. Alvia is the company that provides long-distance trips on high-speed services.

The towns to the south of Cádiz (Chiclana de la Frontera, Conil de la Frontera, Vejer de la Frontera) are less accessible by train. Living in one of those towns, you'd probably want your own car to make the most of what the region has to offer.

The nearest international airport is Jerez Airport, a 30-minute drive to the Costa. Jerez Airport is tiny and only serves a handful of international destinations. It doesn't have any direct flights to North America, so it gets a slightly lower grade than Tavira.

The best way to get here from the States or Canada would be to connect through one of the major travel hubs in the U.K. or Germany, or fly into Madrid and catch a domestic flight to Jerez.

The weather in this part of the world is hot. Winters are mild and summers are scorching. A potential downside of the Costa de la Luz relative to Spain's more famous counterparts is that it's on the Atlantic Ocean, not the Mediterranean. Sea temperatures can be colder than expected: about 61°F in winter and 72°F in summer.

But the Costa de la Luz is a very safe area. Even in Cádiz, the most city-like environment along the coast, you can feel completely safe walking around at any time of the day or night.

In fact, you'll even see kids playing in the town squares, unaccompanied, well after dark. That should be a good indicator of the level of concern locals have about safety.

With a low cost of living, beautiful beaches and pristine nature, and authentic culture, the Costa de la Luz could be just what you're looking for in retirement.

Tarragona

Located in Spain's Catalonia region and sitting on the country's Costa Daurada (Golden Coast) 60 miles southwest of Barcelona, Tarragona offers a more relaxed pace of life than hotspots like Madrid or Valencia.

Once the Roman capital of the Iberian Peninsula, this beachside city is a wonderland of wide boulevards, golden-sand beaches, biscuit-colored-brick buildings, and lush parks.

This is authentic Spanish life with the same big city conveniences, great weather, rich history, beaches, and sunshine... but without the hustle, bustle, high prices, or tourist hordes.

Catalonia shares a border with France and Andorra and, in addition to a Mediterranean coast, has its own distinct language, history, and flag.

By turns a Roman colony, a Visogoth capital, and mighty maritime power, throughout history Catalans have held fast to their regional identity, culture, and language. In large part, people here consider Catalonia a nation without a state—not part of a region—and many want it to be recognized as a country separate from Spain.

It's an issue which has flared up in recent times, most notably back in 2017 when the Catalan government reported a 90% vote in favor of independence in a referendum with a 43% turnout. Spain's constitutional court declared the referendum illegal and dissolved the Catalan Parliament pending new elections in which Catalonia's separatists won a narrow victory.

Back in 2024 and for the first time in decades, Catalonia's pro-independence parties lost their parliamentary majority to the Socialists' Party of Catalonia. Many wonder if this defeat means the Catalan independence movement has reached an end. While that remains to be seen, it's not an issue that should impact anyone looking to make a move to this part of Spain.

One of the oldest cities in Spain, Tarragona is best explored on foot. You'll be stopping a lot, there's historic gems around every corner, from the breath-taking amphitheater on the shores of the Mediterranean Sea to the impressive cathedral, a blend of Romanesque and Gothic styles.

Tarragona's central market is a feast for the senses and unlike its Barcelona counterpart you can afford to shop here. It has a more local, laidback vibe...

Given its location, you won't be surprised to hear that seafood is a specialty in Tarragona. Check out El Pòsit Del Serrallo to sample some of the best of it. It's a good idea to make a reservation. If you have a four-legged friend in tow, request a table on the pet-friendly terrace.

For a mid-sized coastal city Tarragona punches above its weight in terms of cultural offerings. In the historic center, Roman heritage, medieval architecture, and lively plazas greet you at every turn.

For history buffs, highlights will be the Roman Ampitheater—built in the second century AD and named a UNESCO World Heritage Site in 2000—and Tarragona Cathedral and Diocesan Museum which houses an impressive collection of medieval art and stands as a grand example of the transitional architectural style linking Romanesque and Gothic periods.

The city's National Archaeological Museum and Casa Canals (a stately home) are well worth a visit and play host to exhibitions, workshops, and events showcasing the city's history and region's art.

Music lovers will find plenty to enjoy as well—there are frequent classical concerts, seasonal festivals, and live music gigs in bars throughout the city, particularly in the Part Alta and El Serrallo neighborhoods.

The city's theaters—including the 700-seat Teatre Tarragona—host a varied program of plays, dance performances, and concerts year-round.

You're spoiled for choice when dining out, too, from hole-in-the-wall tapas joints and family-run bistros to stylish seafood restaurants overlooking the Mediterranean and most everything in between.

Then there's the festivals... Saints, food, flowers, wine, flamenco...

there's always a reason to party.

In September at the Santa Tecla festival, the city's streets are transformed into a vibrant stage for castells, where teams (*colles castelleres*) compete to form the most complex human towers, demonstrating extraordinary feats of strength, balance, agility, and bravery.

Tarragona has a decent selection of shops and malls as well as a six-screen multiplex. During the summer, the city hosts free outdoor cinema screenings on the beaches at La Móra and L'Arrabassada.

Given its Mediterranean coastal location, many recreational opportunities here are in and on the water. The coastline and beaches are ideal for sailing, windsurfing, kitesurfing, and swimming, while the city's historic marina and the Royal Tarragona Yacht Club—one of the oldest in Spain—provide top-notch facilities for boating enthusiasts.

Platja del Miracle—the city beach—is just a short walk from the downtown area. Platja de la Arrabassada is about a 10-minute drive or 25-minute bus ride.

Both beaches have impressive facilities including showers, bars, restaurants, floating wheelchairs, and lifeguards. Platja de la Arrabassada is a Blue Flag beach.

Venture farther along the coast and you'll find at least a half a dozen more options ranging from long, sandy stretches to secluded coves enveloped by nature. The waters are generally warm and calm and ideal for swimming and paddling. Many of the beaches also offer water sport (such as kayaks and paddleboards) and sun lounger rentals as well as paved promenades lined with local eateries.

The Tarragona Tennis Club offers tennis, padel, a gym, wellness center, and restaurant. Adult membership will run you around 70 euros a month and they also have a "Vintage" membership option for those over 65 for around 65 euros a month.

For a more budget-friendly option, the *Patronat Municipal d'Esports de Tarragona* (Municipal Sports Board of Tarragona) operates public pools, gyms, and athletics facilities. A single-entry pool visit costs around 4 euros and a monthly pass covering gym, pool, and athletics track access is about 40 euros.

The surrounding hills and countryside are perfect for hiking and cycling, while numerous expat and social clubs organize guided walks and outdoor excursions.

For golf enthusiasts, the Costa Daurada region has several courses within an easy drive, providing opportunities for casual or competitive play in Mediterranean scenery.

Golf Costa Daurada offers an 18 hole, par 72 course, a clubhouse, driving range, practice area, and cart and trolley rentals. Standard green fees for 18 holes (with electric cart) is around 60 euros. Mid day offers, senior discounts, and 9 hole and off peak play will cut that cost.

One of Tarragona's big draws is the low cost of living. You'll pay less for housing, groceries, transport, eating out, and utilities here than in Spain's big cities. Overall, your monthly cost of living will come in around 1,700 euros.

Furnished studio apartments can be rented for under 550 euros a month. Two-bedroom, furnished apartments can be found for under 765 euros a month. For 1,500 euros a month, you could rent a centrally-located three-bedroom sea-view penthouse.

You can buy apartments here in need of refurbishment for under 65,000 euros. Renovated properties start around 100,000 euros.

You can get a coffee or beer for 2 euros and a movie ticket is 6.50 euros. When you're eating out, you can choose from casual tapas bars, relaxed bistros, and upscale restaurants. Prices are just as varied. A simple meal at a local spot will cost around 10 euros.

A lunchtime *menú del día* which generally includes a starter, main course, dessert, and/or drink, can be had for around 12 euros. Opt for a fancier restaurant and add wine and dinner will be around 30 euros.

For groceries, you'll find plenty of well-stocked supermarkets including Mercadona, Carrefour, Bon Preu, and Lidl.

It's also worth heading to the Central Market (*Mercat Central*) or smaller neighborhood markets for fresh produce, seafood, and local specialties, which are often cheaper and fresher than what you'll find in the big chains.

Convenience stores and small corner shops (*tiendas de barrio*) are also easy to find and handy for quick purchases or late-evening essentials. Your monthly grocery bill for two will come to 330 euros.

Monthly utilities will cost 152 euros; transportation will be 72 euros; budget 340 euros for entertainment.

Tarragona is a compact and very walkable city, which helps keep transport costs low. Most errands, the beaches, and historic areas can be reached on foot. Local buses are inexpensive, and a single ride typically costs just a couple of euros. If you'll be relying on public transport to get around there are a number of multi-trip passes you can buy which will lower your fares further.

Tarragona offers a well established mix of public and private health care services. The main public hospital is Hospital Universitari Joan XXIII—the largest hospital in the province, offering a full range of services from general medicine and surgery to intensive care, cardiology, diagnostics, and more. Tarragona also has a second public hospital, Hospital Sant Pau i Santa Tecla.

As with most locations, private clinics offer shorter wait times and more personalized care. Opened in 2025, the 96-bed Viamed Tarragona Hospital offers state-of-the-art facilities, 24 hour emergency services, an intensive care unit, multiple operating rooms, outpatient clinics, and advanced diagnostic imaging. Private clinics also tend to have more multilingual staff.

A visit to the doctor will cost you about 40 euros and there are a number of clinics as well as dental surgeries and pharmacies in town.

Tarragona has a Mediterranean climate, with hot, dry summers and mild, wet winters. It's a good choice if you enjoy mostly warm weather with some seasonal variation.

Winter temperatures can drop to around 41-43°F (5-6°C). Snow is extremely rare in the city itself, although the nearby inland hills may see occasional frost or a light dusting of snow. Winters also bring moderate rainfall which helps to maintain the region's verdant landscapes.

To stay comfortable year-round, you'll likely want air conditioning for the hot summer months and heating for cooler winter evenings.

You can get by in English reasonably well in Tarragona, especially in tourist areas, restaurants, and shops. While the locals primarily speak Spanish and Catalan, many understand English well enough for basic everyday interactions.

To really make the most of life here though you will want to learn some of the local language.

If you learn Catalan, you'll be on the same page as the locals. If you speak Spanish, you'll do fine, but be prepared to get answers back from some people in Catalan.

The city is home to around 140,000 people, around 33,000 of whom are foreign-born. While the expat community here is smaller than in hotspots likes Barcelona or Valencia, it is growing. Tarragona Expats Facebook group hosts regular social events and informal meetups across the city.

Local expat association, Tarragona Internacional boasts 1,000 members representing more than 40 nationalities. They host around a dozen meet-ups each month and represent interests in everything from sport to cultural activities and work opportunities.

Language exchanges are a great way to make new friends and local connections. Tarragona English Exchange (TEE) is a public meet-up group for people to practice English and Spanish language skills. It's open to everyone and meets regularly around the city. BlaBla Language Exchange Tarragona organize a mix of language practice and social get-togethers like board game nights and walks.

Tarragona's closest international airport is Barcelona–El Prat Airport (BCN) which is around 60 miles or a one-hour drive away. You can also take the train.

There are two train stations, a central one in the city and a second one, Camp de Tarragona, about a 20-minute drive away. Camp de Tarragona is where you'll catch the high-speed services from—you can get to Barcelona in 49 minutes or head in the opposite direction and pull into Valencia two hours later.

Flight time from Atlanta to Barcelona is eight hours and 40 minutes, it's seven-and-a-half hours from New York, and 11-and-a-half hours from LAX. Direct flights from Toronto take a little under eight hours.

Tarragona is a safe destination. Violent incidents are rare and overall crime rates are low, with petty theft mostly limited to crowded tourist spots, especially near the old town and beaches.

If you'd like the best of all worlds... big city conveniences, a small-town vibe, Mediterranean beaches, sunny days, and low costs, then consider the beachside haven of Tarragona.

Health Care In Spain

Across Spain, hospitals are of a high standard, with highly-trained medical staff and high-tech equipment.

Spain has both a private and public health care system. The public system, La Sistema Nacional de Salud (SNS), is taxpayer-funded and relied upon by around 90% of the population.

Established in 1986, the SNS is administered under the country's Ministry of Health, ensuring that Spain's health care services are decentralized and comprehensive.

Services covered by the program include emergency hospital visits (the emergency number in Spain is 112), doctor consultations, and inpatient and outpatient care but, notably, not dental.

Under European-wide reciprocity agreements, expats from EU countries have the right to medical treatment in Spain but different rules apply for those coming from non-EU countries including the U.S. and Canada.

Those working (legally) in Spain will automatically be paying into the SNS system through monthly social security contributions and so gain access to public health care as do their dependents.

Retired expats meanwhile will need to take out private health insurance—proof of which is a requirement for a residence visa—at least initially, to access the public system.

Monthly premiums for expats typically range from 100 euros to 300 euros but will depend upon factors including pre-existing conditions and your age.

It can be difficult to obtain private health insurance beyond age 74, but if you take out a policy prior to turning 74 and keep paying your premiums, your coverage should continue. Spain also offers a special government pay-in plan— the *Convenio Especial*—under which, after a year as a resident in Spain, you can pay a monthly fee (60 euros for under-65s rising to 157 euros for those 65 and over) to gain access to the national health system.

Many expats and locals opt to make use of both public and private health care depending on the issue. It is acceptable and commonplace to use both systems in tandem.

For minor ailments, take advantage of *farmàcias* (pharmacies) where knowledgeable staff will provide advice and recommend remedies—some of which would require prescriptions back home.

With the exception of children under 15 and adults in need of emergency treatment, dental care in Spain is not covered under the national health care system.

The good news is that private dental care in Spain is relatively inexpensive and the standard of care is high. Prices vary but as a guide figure on around 46 euros for a consultation, 68 euros for a check-up and cleaning, 50 euros for a filling, and 68 euros for an extraction.

Residency Requirements

As a tourist visiting Spain from the U.S. or Canada you can stay in the country for 90 days, no paperwork required.

For stays longer than 90 days, you'll need to get a residence visa.

Spain doesn't have a retiree-specific visa per se, but its Non-Lucrative Visa (NLV) is aimed at retirees and other people with passive incomes who can support themselves financially.

To qualify for the NLV, you need to show that you receive about 2,400 euros per month in income. This gets you a one-year residence permit, which you can extend for four years.

There's also the digital nomad visa, launched in January 2023, which allows those self-employed or employed by a foreign company to gain residency for a year. A self-employed person can work for Spanish companies as long it doesn't exceed 20% of their activity.

Real Estate Restrictions

No restrictions are imposed on foreigners when it comes to buying property in Spain. You'll need a local tax ID number to make a purchase.

Taxes

Spain taxes residents on their worldwide income. There are two types of taxable income: savings taxable income (including dividends, interest, capital gains from transfers of assets, and more) and general taxable income (including all other income that is not savings taxable income).

Savings taxable income is taxed at progressive rates between 19% and 28%. This includes capital gains arising from the transfer of assets. General taxable income is taxed at progressive rates between 19% and 47%.

Spain imposes gift and inheritance tax, although there are exemptions depending on the relationship between donor and benefactor. General rates range from 7.65% to 34%.

Spain also imposes a wealth tax on residents' worldwide assets. Several tax reliefs are available for this. Again, exact rates vary by autonomous community (otherwise a scale from 0.2% to 3.5% applies).

Spain has a taxation agreement with the United States, Canada, and the U.K. that prevents double taxation.

The Spanish tax system is complicated, and you should always get proper tax advice from a registered attorney.

CHAPTER 15

ITALY

If you're looking for quintessential Old-World lifestyle, Italy deserves your attention. The old towns are charming, and the countryside between is stunning. Not to mention the coastline, which stretches more than 4,000 miles—one of the most extensive in Europe. Even excluding the big cities like Rome, there is enough here to keep your interest and to support a fully appointed life on the Continent. What's more, life here can be much more affordable than back home.

Stitching together seascapes with lush mountain valleys, there are many parts of Italy that are truly secret treasures. Living here, you could be surrounded by castles, vineyards, and villages made of stone and memory. There are lots of places in Italy that haven't changed that much over the years, and it's like wandering into a gentler, kinder yesterday… a yesterday with little or no crime and neighbors who watch out for each other.

If you have ever thought about living in Italy, you are on your way to making a great decision. Italy is an incredible country with an abundance of culture, friendly people, stunning seascapes, and interesting architecture. It is an undoubtedly interesting place to live if you are thinking about moving abroad.

To help you better understand what to expect from Italy living, where the best places to live in Italy are, and what's it like to live in Italy as an expat, read on. It's little wonder that Italy has hit the headlines recently as a highly-coveted destination for retirement.

Top Picks For A New Life In Italy

Città Sant'Angelo, Abruzzo

Abruzzo is one of Italy's 20 regions, divided into four provinces: L'Aquila, Teramo, Pescara, and Chieti. While it's located more or less in Central Italy—directly east of Rome—it's administratively a southern region.

Known as one of the greenest areas in all of Europe, Abruzzo stretches from the Apennines to the Adriatic and is home to about 1,474 square miles of protected national parkland. The mountains here are the country's most important and most visited after the Dolomites.

Nestled within the verdant hills of Abruzzo, the little hamlet of Città Sant'Angelo, with a population of about 15,000, is one of the most culturally rich the region has to offer. Walking the stone streets here truly feels like being in a world removed from time...

This 9th century medieval town nestled between two rivers is home to magnificent palazzi, piazzas, churches, and monasteries... Quaint storefronts are home to butchers, bakers, pasta makers, and pharmacists, locals popping in from one to the next to get their daily shopping done...

The way of life here hearkens back hundreds of years... nothing here has changed much in that time, and that's the way folks like it.

It's a designated "Città Slow" city, a designation for cities that are dedicated to improving quality of life, protecting the environment, and resisting homogenization and globalization of towns. The movement started in Italy, though it now includes cities all over the world.

It was inspired by the slow food movement: the promotion of local, traditional cooking over replacement by global fast-food franchises. (Think a family-run restaurant on your street corner, where the recipes have been passed down across generations, rather than a McDonalds or Burger King.)

The mayor is serious about resisting development and keeping the town as authentic. Each year, one of the town's most popular festivals is devoted to traditional health care to illustrate how old remedies can be as or more effective than modern medicine.

Thanks to its architecture, Città Sant'Angelo earned the title "Borgo" a few years ago, joining the ranks of "I Borghi più belli d'Italia," Italy's association of towns of historical interest.

It's also called Città del Vino and Città dell'Olio: City of Wine and City of Oil. Surrounded by flourishing crops, the city produces so much excellent wine and oil it's now known for them. It's also a serious art town, having hosted works from the Venice and Istanbul Biennales and the Godart project.

While small, Città Sant'Angelo is a gem that packs a punch. It's as ideally located within the Abruzzo region as it could be.

Centrally positioned just 15 minutes from the coast and an hour to the nearest mountain slope, this town is ideal for whatever kind of outdoor fun you like to have.

This is one of the few places in the world that allows you to ski and hit the beach in the same day...

If you lived here, you would need a car to leave the city limits to enjoy the nature that this part of the world has to offer.

There are equestrian stables and a riding school just minutes outside of town, and golf courses are reachable within 40 minutes.

At about 45 minutes from Sant'Angelo, several locations are renowned for their excellent wind quality, making them highly sought out venues for paragliding and hangliding.

Sailing is popular all along the coastline, as well as windsurfing. Power water sports are also well represented here, with plenty of opportunities for jet-skiing, water-skiing, and motor boating. The fishing is good off the coast here, and the region is renowned for its therapeutic volcanic waters.

The most popular of Abruzzo's seaside towns Silvi Marina, is just under 20 minutes from town, and Pescara, at about the same distance, is home to one of the region's premier marina facilities.

Città Sant'Angelo is a bustling, active little city, with jazz concerts, theater, and an old church that draws worshippers from around the region. There is an outlet shopping center nearby (the biggest in the region that offers free shipping) that also draws visitors who stay in Sant'Angelo. Thanks to the highway passing right by the city, access is easy without spoiling the atmosphere.

There are plenty of empty houses available in the historical center, and the mayor has been working to streamline buying processes to increase sales. He's managed to reduce the bureaucracy involved, lifting certain restrictions and making partnerships with business groups like the bed and breakfast association and tour operators to bring in some fresh blood and innovation.

For rent, you can find a small apartment for about 600 euros a month.

Or you could choose to live outside the historical center and settle in one of the modern, suburban-style homes just minutes outside the city walls. Opting for this route gives you a multi-story townhome, a garage, a small garden, and generally a little more breathing room...

A couple's basic monthly budget here should come to about 1,950 euros. In general, this region of Italy is fantastically affordable. So much food (and pasta and wine and oil... etc.) is produced locally, it's like getting everything at a huge discount. Most locals shop markets and small shops to buy local.

Many locals even produce some of their own food, drastically cutting food costs.

In Sant'Angelo, you'll have to head out of town to find the nearest supermarket. Within the city walls, you can hop from one mom-and-pop to another—one for your meat, another for your bread, your produce, pasta, etc. Your monthly grocery shop will cost about 300 euros.

Entertainment options are mostly free ones—it costs nothing to enter the national parks or hit the beach. Movie tickets cost between 4 and 7 euros, depending on discounts. If you dine out often during the month, you'll need to budget about 200 euros for two people.

You'll spend about 60 euro for your cell phone, internet, and cable TV.

Gas is expensive in Italy, about 80 euros to fill a tank, so driving is a not insignificant cost. For utilities—electricity, water, and gas—you'll pay about 120 euros a month.

Città Sant'Angelo has a renowned hospital that draws visitors from all over the country and several assisted living facilities, mental health institution that specializes in Alzheimer's, and a rehabilitation center, Sant'Angelo is perfect for someone looking to age in place while surrounded by history, culture, and fine cuisine.

There are a dozen public and private health care facilities in its vicinity. Across the wider Abruzzo region, there are 18 public and 28 private facilities total and 11 government-certified nursing homes.

The climate is mild enough to go without heating or cooling, but there are four seasons, so you'll likely use air conditioning or heating for at least a few weeks a year. One upside is that most homes come with one or more fireplaces that help heat the house—and many even have wood burning ovens built into the kitchens.

Temperatures range between an average high of 19°F (66°C) and an average low of 9°F (48°C), with humidity hovering around 73%. The best weather months are May, September, October, when temperatures are between 68°F (20°C) and 77°F (25°C). The coldest month is January, when the average high is 50°F (10°C).

Time to start boning up on your Italian. Expats coming to Sant'Angelo will need to learn Italian. While those working in tourism in the big cities speak some English, it's rare to find it much known in the small hillside towns and medieval villages of Abruzzo.

Just as there are few English speakers in Sant'Angelo, there are likewise few expats. A few, mostly from Northern Europe, have found their way to the Abruzzo region in general, but none that we know of have yet settled permanently in Sant'Angelo.

It can be tough to crack into the Italian community—especially in a small, rural town. The stereotype of close-knit Italian families comes from a kernel of truth... small, clannish communities are hard to get a foothold in.

Full-time Abruzzo expats Karen and Dave say that they were the first expats to come to the small town of Palmoli in Chieti Province about 12 years ago, and the adjustment was hard.

For the first couple of years, they were almost ignored as residents, treated like a passing tourist might be. After more than a decade there, they have been accepted as part of the community, but it was an uphill road.

Community events tend to revolve around religion—feast days, saint's days, processions, and festivals. If you don't make an effort to join your local parish, community acceptance will be even harder to attain.

The rest of the expat population is scattered among the Abruzzo regions' cities, medieval villages, and verdant hillsides. The best way to keep in touch with the community is through the Abruzzolutely online forum.

The streets and sidewalks are in good condition, but they were not designed for the modern world. They can be narrow and uneven in places. And this town is located on a hill, so steep climbs are a given. It may not be a good choice for someone with limited mobility.

The closest airport to Sant'Angelo is Abruzzo Airport, about a 30-minute drive away. This is the only international airport in the region and an important transportation hub… That said, if offers no direct flights to North America.

To get here from the States or Canada, your best option is to fly to Rome's international airport, which offers a multitude of choices for direct flights. Rome is just under three hours driving from Abruzzo.

Sant'Angelo is extremely safe. It's highly unlikely that you'd fall victim to even petty crime here… This area consistently has one of the lowest crime rates in Italy. Most residents say they don't even lock their doors, especially if they live in the countryside.

Offering tranquility, a close-knit community, and small-town living in a well-preserved historical center, but with continued access to modern conveniences, Città Sant'Angelo is the best of all worlds.

Pisa

Pisa is so much more than just a tourist trap or an architectural project gone wrong. It's a vibrant city nestled in the heart of Tuscany that offers history and culture combined with the conveniences of modern living. If you're considering a move to Italy, you should put this highly liveable, underrated city on your radar.

Pisa is rich in historical and architectural heritage, a delight for leisurely strolls with landmarks around every corner. It is of course most famous for its Leaning Tower, but the Piazza dei Miracoli, the UNESCO World Heritage Site where the tower is located, is also home to other iconic buildings like the Pisa Cathedral and Baptistery.

There's a timelessness to Pisa... Narrow medieval streets spill out onto vibrant piazzas where people gather to socialize, enjoy meals, or chat over coffee. Pisa also has a youthful buzz thanks to the high proportion of students who come here to study.

Education is deeply ingrained in Pisa's identity. The University of Pisa is one of Italy's most prestigious schools. Scholars from around the world make their way here and broaden the range of cultural offerings, from live music to art exhibitions to theater performances.

Pisa is a small city of about 90,000 people, but it strikes the ideal balance between a village atmosphere and an urban one. The pace of life is slow, and there's a community feel, yet there are also excellent medical facilities, diverse shopping options, and a well-connected public transportation network.

This includes an international airport that makes trips around Europe easy and a train system that can connect you to Florence, Rome, and beyond in hours.

Pisa provides a connection to nature. The Arno River wends gracefully through town, providing scenic walking and cycling paths. It's surrounded by the best of Tuscany—soft hills and valleys covered by rows of grapevines, olive groves, and centuries-old cypress trees. And when you need a dose of sunshine, Mediterranean beaches are only a 20-minute drive away.

Pisa is steeped in Old World historical charm and full of historical landmarks. Again, it's not all about the Leaning Tower. There are 20-plus historic churches, bridges across the Arno, and several medieval palaces.

In town, there are several museums where you can take in the region's history and culture. You can view classical works of art at the Museo Nazionale di San Matteo or contemporary ones at the SMS Centro Espositivo.

There's a lively performing arts scene hosted at famous venues like Teatro Verdi, an opera house that hosts opera, ballet, and classical music performances, as well as small theaters and cultural centers.

The city hosts festivals throughout the year, such as Luminara di San Ranieri in June, which lights up the Arno River with thousands of candles. It also hosts regattas, book festivals, and other unique events.

And you can't talk about life in Italy without mentioning the fabulous cuisine and wine. Food is central to Italy's culture, and dining is an experience to savor. You'll find a wide selection of restaurants, bars, and cafés in Pisa that serve Tuscan classics—panzanella salad, wild boar pappardelle, and more.

The city offers a fairly wide selection of outdoor recreation opportunities. It's mostly flat, making it ideal for cycling, and trails slice through the surrounding countryside.

In town, there are gyms, parks, and facilities for tennis, soccer, and other sports. Nearby in Tirrenia, there's an 18-hole golf course set against picturesque Tuscan scenery.

The Arno River provides opportunities for boat rides and laid-back water sports like kayaking and canoeing.

Just outside the city are several nature reserves, such as San Rossore Regional Park, where you can walk or cycle through wetlands, forests, and coastal dunes. The Monti Pisani mountains are perfect for hiking and taking in panoramic views.

A couple can live comfortably in Pisa on a budget of about 1,688 euros per month. Remember that this is a university city, so prices for many things—accommodation, restaurant meals, entrance fees, etc.—are aimed at that demographic. Retirees should find Pisa easy on their pockets.

You can rent a one-bedroom apartment for as little as 500 euros per month. For as little as 900 euro, you could get a two-bed apartment in the city center. Prices start from 700 for a two-bedroom apartment outside the center.

One budget item that stands out as more expensive is the cost of utilities, which can run from 85 euros to 250 euros per month. There are a few reasons for this—limited local energy generation, taxation and fees (Italy tacks extras like TV tax onto your electric bill), and seasonal demand. Electricity costs go up significantly during winter months.

Pisa has four seasons, with cool winters (around 38°F or 3°C from December to February) and hot summers (around 85°F or 29°C from June to August). It gets most of its rainfall in summer and autumn. Snow is rare.

You'll likely want both heating and cooling systems in your home, however, Europe is notoriously bad when it comes to providing air conditioning. This can make summer temperatures feel much hotter than they are.

Cisanello Hospital and Santa Chiara Hospital are public hospitals that provide specialized care and emergency care. You can also find private facilities in Pisa if you need faster appointments. Facilities in Pisa are modern and well-equipped, and medical professionals are highly trained.

Italians are friendly, welcoming people, and they'll do their best to accommodate you in English... but you should plan to learn Italian to better integrate into the community and make day-to-day life easier.

Pisa isn't home to a massive expat community. Making friends and settling in socially will take some work. You'll need to seek out other expats by reaching out on forums and being active. To make friends with locals, you'll need to learn a bit of Italian.

This is a place for someone who's looking for a challenging yet culturally authentic relocation experience. Beyond the city, in the other towns and cities of Tuscany, you'll find scattered pockets of expats. The town of Lucca, about a 30-minute drive from Pisa, has a big expat presence.

Public transportation is well-developed, with buses, taxis, and a rail network that can connect you to the rest of Italy and Europe. You may want your own car to make the most of Tuscany, but it's not a requirement.

There are no direct flights from North America to Pisa International Airport, but there are plenty of options to connect through a European hub. You could also connect through Milan and Rome.

Pisa is a safe place to live. Concerns about violent crime are very low. Petty crime is more of a possibility because so many tourists make their way here. You should be mindful of your possessions if you're on public transport, for instance, but overall, crime shouldn't factor much into your day-to-day life.

With its cultural richness, historical charm, and modern amenities, Pisa is far more than just a place to visit—it's a great place to put down roots and enjoy a well-rounded lifestyle.

Sardinia

About 120 miles west of mainland Italy, in the Mediterranean Sea lies the Italian island of Sardinia.

Nestled underneath Corsica (a region of France), Sardinia is Italy's second largest island (Sicily being the biggest) and home to over 1.5 million people.

Covering some 9,300 square miles it's around the same size as New Hampshire and boasts over 1,100 miles of coastline featuring rocky coves, pebble bays, white-sand beaches, and crystal-clear waters.

In the late 1940s investment in tourism infrastructure began on the island and its future was secured when, in the late 1950s, English financier, John Duncan Miller paid a visit. He was there in his role as vice president of the World Bank to check on the progress of a mosquito-eradication program but the island captured his heart and he set about establishing a consortium of investors who purchased a picture-perfect stretch of land along the island's northeast coast.

Keen to preserve the natural beauty of the area, the group established strict architectural and zoning standards and went on to create one of the world's best-known tourist destinations: Costa Smeralda (Emerald Coast).

At its heart is Porto Cervo which became a playground for the rich and famous.

Here you'll find a 700-berth marina, luxury hotels, a yacht club, and an airport. Over the years this ritzy resort has attracted everyone from Grace Kelly and Jackie Kennedy to Brigitte Bardot and Kirk Douglas.

Once Costa Esmerelda put Sardinia on the map, a wave of tourism development washed over the island and today there's something to appeal to all tastes and budgets for visitors and expats alike. Whether you want designer boutiques or wellness resorts, golf or fine dining, boating adventures or wine tasting afternoons, you'll find it all here.

Solid choices for expats to call home include the capital, Cagliari. It offers a rich cultural scene, lively social scene, and good health care. It's also close to beautiful beaches and where you'll find a larger English-speaking community than in most other parts of the island.

Also popular is Alghero, a city on the northwest coast of Sardinia. Here you'll find all the usual amenities (plus an airport) and a welcoming expat community. It's more laidback than the capital and boasts a distinct Catalan heritage, medieval architecture, and a charming old town. It's also a great spot for foodies—the seafood is incredible—and shopaholics who can pick from upscale boutiques and markets heaving with local craftmanship and vintage finds.

Also in the north is the coastal city of Olbia, gateway to the Costa Smeralda. Of course, with that connection comes a higher price tag but also museums, medieval treasures, shops, parks, pubs, and with its own port and airport it's an ideal jumping off point for nearby beaches and further travel in the region.

Sardinia has a surprisingly rich cultural scene with a decent offering of galleries, museums, and theaters. In Cagliari the National Archaeological Museum showcases Sardinia's Nuragic history while the *Cittadella dei Musei* complex hosts rotating art and history exhibits.

Sassari and Alghero have a number of contemporary art galleries and Cagliari's Teatro Lirico is the go-to spot for opera, ballet, and classical music performances.

One of the oldest folk festivals celebrated is the Carnival of Mamoiada. Every year, in the small town of Mamoiada in the province of Nuoro in the central-interior of the island, this pagan festival sees participants clad in unnerving masks take to the streets clanging cowbells and lassoing unsuspecting spectators.

Sagra di Sant'Efisio is one of the most important religious festivals on the calendar. This four-day event pays homage to Saint Ephysius, a Roman Commander sent to Sardinia to suppress Christianity he instead converted and ended up being beheaded by the Romans and made a martyr. Locals clad in traditional dress escort a statue of the saint from Cagliari to Nora (where he was killed on the beach) and back again.

In fall, Autunno in Barbagia is a craft and food festival in the Barbagia region in the heart of Sardinia. The festival is a three-month long extravaganza of food and wine tastings, artisan demonstrations, traditional music and dance, and historical exhibitions. Each weekend it relocates to a new village in the region with different folklore, events, and local crafts and cuisine on offer.

One of Sardinia's key attractions is of course its beaches—49 of which have been awarded Blue Flag status. This international award recognizes a high level of environmental and quality standards.

Perhaps the best-known corner of Sardinia is Costa Smeralda (the Emerald Coast), a glittering stretch of coastline frequented by the jet-set. Here you'll find white-sand beaches and mega-yachts anchored in crystal clear waters. Piccolo and Grande Pevero beaches are great for watersports, sunbathing, and star spotting.

Spiaggia del Principe has been named one of the world's most beautiful beaches with white-sands and waters of ever-changing shades of turquoise. Its calm, shallow waters make it a great spot for snorkeling.

La Cinta in San Teodoro, on the north-eastern coast of Sardinia, offers miles of dazzling white sand, shallow, clear waters, and an array of facilities including boat, sun bed, and umbrella rental. It's a hotspot for kite-surfers and you can even spot pink flamingos in the large lagoon behind the beach.

On the Tyrrhenian coast of Nuoro, famed for its unspoiled scenery, you'll find a great choice of wide, sandy beaches with clean, clear waters. Lido di Orrì, Riviera di Ponente, Bucca e Strumpu, and San Gemiliano are all worth a visit.

Most every watersport is catered to on the island from swimming to kayaking, scuba diving, jet-skiing, stand-up paddleboarding, canyoning, surfing, and more.

If you're into sailing, yachting or fishing, you can charter boats or take lessons from the marinas in Porto Cervo, Alghero, and Cagliari.

Beaches aside, Sardinia's mountains are a gift for hikers, bikers, climbers, and skiers. Gennargentu National Park and the Parco di Porto Conte offer scenic viewpoints, wildlife, and challenging trails.

Gennargentu is also where you'll find Bruncu Spina ski resort. Ski season here runs from December to March, depending on snowfall, and this resort has two ski-lifts and around two miles of slopes.

Sardinia's Selvaggio Blu trek is a near 28-mile route on cliffs along the Mediterranean coastline. It's known as Italy's toughest with some routes involving abseiling and graded climbs.

The cities and larger towns have well-equipped gyms and sports centers, and padel and tennis clubs are easy to find. Sardinia has around a dozen golf clubs ranging from pitch and putt to the impressive 27 holes at Is Molas Resort, which look out over the Sea of Sardinia.

Living in Sardinia can be relatively affordable when compared to

North America and other parts of Italy. As with most anywhere, life in the capital city will cost more and the same applies to the tourist hotspots. A budget of around 1,700 euros a month will see a couple living well here and that will include rent in a popular spot like Alghero.

If you're happy to get off the beaten track and live among the locals you can find homes renting for as little as 340 euros a month, which would reduce your overall budget considerably.

Generally, though, budget about 800 euros for a two-bedroom apartment. Your utilities (water, gas, and electricity) will be about 174 euros. Internet and cell phone will be around 70 euros. If you own a car, it will be about 100 per month.

For groceries, you'll find chain stores like Conad, SuperPan, and Eurospin in most of island's bigger towns and cities. Costa Smerelda has a large, well-stocked Carrefour in the Le Vele shopping center and there's a Dettorimarket in Olbia which is popular with expats. Olbia also has a Lidl (a German discount chain). Your monthly grocery shop for two will come in at about 340 euros.

The chain stores carry a wide range of essentials, from fresh produce and bakery items to household goods. Of course, the markets are the star of the show here and the best place for the freshest seasonal produce at great prices. Imported products from back home will cost more but high-quality local meats and cheeses will be more affordable.

When dining out, lunch at a low-key local spot can be as little as 8 euros and dinner around 20 euros. In touristy areas or upscale resorts, the sky is the limit. A budget of 360 a month would cover your entertainment costs.

Sardinia residents enjoy a classic Mediterranean climate with long, hot, dry summers. Winters are wet but generally pretty mild.

In the summer, temperatures along the coast peak around 86 to 90°F (30 to 32°C) with warm sea breezes. In winter, daytime temperatures hover between 50 to 59°F (10 to 15 °C). Inland, in mountainous areas temperatures can drop below freezing and winters can be harsh. The mountains of Gennargentu—home to Bruncu Spina ski resort—frequently see snowfall.

Spring and fall experience some rainfall, generally confined to the occasional short showers.

Italy's health care system is one of the world's best, so you should feel confident having your medical needs taken care of here although health care on Sardinia isn't as impressive as what you'll find on the mainland.

Cagliari is home to Ospedale Universitario di Cagliari which serves as a major teaching and research hospital in the region. It's a public facility comprising the San Giovanni di Dio hospital and Duilio Casula hospital and provides a wide range of medical and surgical care.

In Olbia, the Mater Olbia Hospital is a private facility offering state of the art facilities in a modern and luxurious premises. Highly-trained staff provide expertise in cardiology, neuroslogy, orthopedics, and general surgery. It's a popular choice for expats.

Sardinia has two CDS (*Casa della Salute*) facilities—one in Cagliari and one in Sassari. These are community-based primary care centers which offer medical examinations, diagnostic imaging, and dental services.

Italian is the main language spoken on Sardinia and after that it's Sardinian (also known as Sard, Sardo, Sardu, and Limba Sarda). English is more widely spoken in the capital, Cagliari, larger cities like Olbia and Sassari, and in tourist areas such as Alghero and Costa Smeralda.

Outside of these areas, the level of English spoken can be quite limited so if you're planning a move here you'll need to know or be ready to learn Italian.

The expat community on the island is relatively small—around 50,000 of the 1.5 million residents are from overseas—so making friends and settling in socially will require some effort. You'll need to seek out other expats by reaching out on forums, joining Facebook groups, sport and social clubs, and volunteering.

Sardinia has three commercial airports, two in the north— Olbia

Costa Smeralda Airport and Alghero Airport (also known as Fertilia Airport)—and one in the south—Cagliari Elmas Airport.

Delta Air Lines launched a new non-stop route from New York-JFK to Olbia (OLB). The flight operates four times a week during the summer season.

Sardinia stands out as one of Italy's safest regions, with official figures ranking its crime rates as the third lowest among Italy's 20 regions. It ranks far below the national average for serious offenses like theft, robbery, and violence.

Sardinia offers a sun-soaked escape in the heart of the Mediterranean, surrounded by natural beauty and also offering a rich cultural scene. If island-living in the Mediterranean is part of your retirement dream, you could live in style on this Italian gem for far less than you probably thought possible.

Health Care In Italy

Public health care facilities are available through the national health care system—Servizio Sanitario Nazionale (SSN)—which provides affordable and comprehensive care to residents. Denial for enrollment for any reason—even pre-existing conditions—is extremely rare.

Family doctors are entirely paid by the SSN, must offer visiting time at least five days a week, and have a limit of 1,500 patients. Patients are assigned a doctor but are free to change doctors if they want.

Private medical insurance is mandatory if you are a non-EU citizen applying for residency, once applied, you can enroll in the SSN. For EU citizens not employed in Italy, national care is available after five years.

Enrollment is open to non-EU citizens after paying the minimal annual fee (determined in proportion to income). The minimum yearly fee is 388 euros per person. Enrollment takes place at the Azienda Sanitaria Locale (ASL) in the region you decide to settle in.

While most services in the public system are free, co-payments can apply for certain services. This will depend on the region and individual circumstances.

For non-urgent issues, wait times in the public system can be long and as a result many expats opt for private care which offers quicker access and more comfortable facilities.

Residency Requirements

As a U.S. or Canadian citizen, you're entitled to stay in Italy (or any other Schengen country) for 90 days on your tourist visa, and you may be asked to show proof of return or onward travel before you depart.

If you come to Italy planning to stay beyond 90 days, you need to apply to do so before setting out. Apply for a residence visa (*visto per ragioni di dimora*) at an Italian consulate before leaving home. This acts as your temporary residency once you arrive, which is renewable for up to five years, when you can seek permanent residency.

If you don't apply before coming, you'll have to obtain a permit of stay (*permesso di soggiorno*) within eight days of arriving in Italy—this is the only document that legalizes your stay in Italy beyond your tourist visa.

Italy offers an independent means visa known as the Elective Residency Visa that many retirees use to live in the country long-term.

The basic requirement to qualify is proof of passive income (pensions, dividends, royalties, rents, etc.) of 32,000 euros per year. This grants you a one-year residence permit that is renewable.

Permanent residency can be requested after living in Italy for five years on *permesso de soggiorno* and is then valid for an indefinite period of time. You must go to the local town hall and submit your stay permit, original birth certificate (must first be translated and authenticated in your home country), a copy of your passport, and a copy of a deed showing adequate housing in Italy.

Real Estate Restrictions

No restrictions are imposed on foreigners when it comes to buying property in Italy. In fact, there are special programs with low-cost properties that are designed to attract and incentivize foreign buyers.

Taxes

Tax residents of Italy are subject to income tax on their worldwide income.

There are three types of income tax in Italy: national income tax, regional income tax, and municipal income tax.

Regional income tax ranges from 1.23% to 3.33% depending on which region you live in. Municipal income ranges from 0% to 0.9% (according to municipality).

Italy made changes to its property tax laws with the Italian Budget Law 2020. Now, the basic rate for a principal residence is 0.5%, but the municipality may increase or decrease this.

Capital gains taxes vary depending on the type of gain. For the sale of real estate, the gain is taxed at progressive rates or at a flat tax of 26%. If the home is a principal residence or was owned for more than five years, its sale is exempt from capital gains tax.

Inheritance tax rates vary depending on the relationship between the donor and beneficiary. For spouses or relatives in a direct line, it's 4% on the value of assets exceeding 1 million euros; for siblings, it's 6% on the value of assets exceeding 100,000 euros.

Italy imposes a wealth tax of 1.06% on real estate owned outside of Italy. Different rules about the tax base apply, so this is something to discuss with a real estate tax specialist.

Italy also imposes a wealth tax of 0.2% to 0.4% on financial investments owned outside of Italy.

Italy has a flat tax regime intended for individuals receiving a pension from abroad—and Sardinia is one of the areas covered under this system.

For those that establish their tax residence in one of the designated municipalities in Southern Italy—Abruzzo, Calabria, Campania, Molise, Apulia, Sardinia, and Sicily—a flat tax of 7% on all income will apply.

Naturally it's popular with foreign retirees but you must meet the following requirements:

- Be in receipt of a pension from a private or public institution outside of Italy.
- You must not have lived in Italy for the five years prior to your application.
- You must establish legal residency in an Italian municipality in Southern Italy, (Abruzzo, Calabria, Campania, Molise, Apulia, Sardinia and Sicily regions), that has less than 30,000 inhabitants.
- The flat tax can be applied for 10 consecutive years and can't be extended.

Italy also has a flat tax regime to attract high-net-worth individuals—there is no set amount but applicants typically have financial assets in excess of 1 million euros.

VI

CENTRAL & EASTERN EUROPE

When most people think about living in Europe, it's the hot spots along the Spanish Costas and the French Riviera that spring to mind. Places where the good life comes at a hefty cost... and property prices start in the multi-million range.

But there's a lesser-known corner of Europe—one that includes all the trappings of this good life—but where you can own property for a fraction of that.

In parts of Central and Eastern Europe, you can have all the perks of a Mediterranean lifestyle but for a much more attractive price. This part of the world has all the right ingredients for a dream retirement and fantastic investment and lifestyle opportunities.

Where the climate is blessed with year-round warm weather, clear blue waters, and thousands of miles of coastline. Summers are long, beginning in March and lasting until October, even November, with over 300 days of sunshine a year...

The food is light and fresh; fish and salad are served with every meal, and the coffee is strong and aromatic. Where you can enjoy a healthy meal and a cold glass of wine for just $15 per person...

Below we highlight four countries in this part of the world we think should get your attention. Two that are off the radar for a lot of Americans and Canadians...for now. Where a couple can enjoy the Mediterranean lifestyle for as little as $1,600 a month, all in. And another, which may very well be the oldest retirement haven in the world.

CHAPTER 16

MONTENEGRO

Montenegro is a Balkan country in Eastern Europe, sandwiched between Serbia, Bosnia and Herzegovina, Kosovo, Albania, and Croatia

Most people haven't heard of it, and that's OK. It's a tiny country of about 5,300 square miles (13,800 square kms), making it about the size of Connecticut.

It's also tiny in terms of population, with about 620,000 people.

The scenery in this little country is stunning. Picture towering mountains that plunge down into crystalline Adriatic waters and white-stone historical villages. Jaw-dropping vistas are available from almost every vantage point.

The Adriatic is the same body of water that laps the shores of southeastern Italy. It's a part of the Mediterranean. The waters are clear and warm, perfect for swimming, boating, any water-based recreation... or just for providing a beautiful backdrop for daily life.

There are charming historical villages dotted around the country, and in particular around Kotor Bay and Perast, where you'll find old neighborhoods as well as modern luxury developments where everything is new, high-end, and flashy—particularly in Porto Montenegro.

Montenegro is small but geographically diverse. You can ski the slopes in the morning and swim in the Mediterranean in the afternoon. Everyone points out how underrated it is for natural attractions.

You can feel completely comfortable walking around at any time of day or night, without any fear of crime. Locals tell us this is thanks to the small population. Everyone knows everyone, so it's hard to get away with bad behavior.

Montenegro became part of Socialist Federal Republic of Yugoslavia in 1945. When that dissolved in 1992, it became part of the Federal Republic of Yugoslavia along with Serbia. In 1996, Montenegro began severing ties with Serbia.

In 2006, Montenegro gained independence. That same year it joined the UN and then NATO in 2017.

Today, Montenegro is well-known among investors... but it has big, yet undiscovered potential when it comes to lifestyle, specifically as a retirement haven and digital nomad hub.

There are great reasons to live here: it has a mild climate, a Mediterranean coastline, a low cost of living, access to nature, diverse recreation opportunities, stunning scenery, and places to sit back and enjoy yourself (outdoor cafés overlooking the sea, rooftop bars, and so on).

Montenegro's government values foreign investment and wants to attract more foreign residents. It makes it easy for expats to set up life here with its turn-key residency policies.

It continues to invest in tourism and construction... more hotel chains are establishing themselves here... cruise ships sail up to Kotor's harbor on the daily... It's only a matter of time before word about Montenegro spreads as far as North America, and Canadian and American tourists and expats start to arrive.

The biggest objective on Montenegro's agenda right now is joining the European Union, which it's poised to do in the next few of years (some say by 2028; some say by 2030). It became an EU candidate in 2010 and adopted the euro as its currency in 2002.

It seeks to attract more foreign hotel chains, and all around the Bay of Kotor, luxury tourism and lifestyle complexes are in various stages of development, including many high-end ones with superyacht marinas.

You can tap into Montenegro's investment potential or just enjoy a comfortable, low-cost lifestyle here as a retiree or a digital nomad. As of right now, it offers easy paths to residency and citizenship... which puts your foot inside the door of the EU when it eventually joins.

With its stunning scenery, low cost of living, easy residency and citizenship policies, diverse expat community, interesting culture, and endless recreation opportunities, it also offers huge lifestyle potential.

Top Picks For A New Life In Montenegro

Kotor Bay

Kotor Bay, also known as the Bay of Kotor or Boka Bay, is a deep, craggy inlet of the Adriatic Sea found in southwestern Montenegro.

It boasts 57 miles (107 kms) of sparkling coastline backed by towering mountains and dotted with a charming mix of medieval towns and luxe modern developments equipped with glossy superyacht marinas.

It has a unique geography, full of nooks and crannies that together make up one of the most indented areas of the Adriatic Sea. Gorgeous views of the sea and mountains are a given regardless of where you are in the bay.

Kotor Bay is made up of three main towns: Kotor, Tivat, and Hercig Novi.

Kotor is in the southeastern corner of the bay. The jewel in its crown is Kotor Old Town, a three-sided walled city of great historical significance that's widely regarded as the best-preserved medieval town in the Mediterranean.

Kotor is not just Kotor Old Town. It stretches for a few miles to the north and northwest, with little towns and villages lumped in with it.

One of these small towns is Perast, about 12 kms (7 miles) north of Kotor Old Town. It's tiny but has charming historical buildings and a quiet, relaxed, village feel.

Kotor could be an option for you if you want to be near the historical center of this region or right inside it. You could live right in Kotor Old Town, although it'd be a niche choice...

It's a tiny area. You could walk from one end to the other in about five minutes. A couple times a day, tourists unload from massive cruise ships and overwhelm its narrow streets... something you'd have to accept if you chose to live here.

Kotor is shaped like a V and surrounded by tall mountains. The downside to living here is that, for half the day, one side of the V gets sunshine while the other side is in the shadows...

This pattern reverses as the sun makes its way across the sky. No matter where you choose to be in Kotor, you're going to be in relative darkness for half the day.

If you want old-world, European charm, you'll find it in Kotor Old Town or Perast.

The combination of medieval architecture backed by sharp gray mountains with old stone walls climbing up, all overlooking dazzling sea views, is something out of a fairy tale.

Saint Tryphon Cathedral, built in the 11th century and one of the country's two Roman Catholic cathedrals, is a notable structure in the Old Town. Its church bells ring out often and reverberate around the mountain walls.

A couple of small museums are found in the Old Town, like the Maritime Museum, where you can learn about Kotor's famous seamen, and the off-beat Cats of Kotor Museum, with an impressive collection of engravings, antique books, coins, medals, and more, mostly from Venice.

Modern amenities, like restaurants, cafés, and plenty of artisanal gelato shops, are available, too. Local cuisine is heavily Italian-inspired... but for a taste of something local, try *rakija*, a grape brandy. Montenegro also has its own wine and beer industries.

A 15-minute drive north of Kotor Old Town is Perast, a small, historic stone village. Off of Perast's shore are two islands that are steeped in local folklore: Saint George and Our Lady of the Rocks, both of which you can visit.

The former features a church, which, according to legend, was built in 1603 after fishermen came across an icon of the Holy Mother of God at the site. The latter is also steeped in legend... Supposedly, a French soldier was once stationed there and fired a canon at the house where his beloved lived. (The island's other name is "island of the dead captains.")

There's lots to do in Kotor Bay and many ways to be entertained, including the occasional opera, symphony orchestra, and events related to local culture... But this is not Paris or London... The main appeal of the area is what's available in terms of nature.

Tivat

Just a 15-minute drive from Kotor is Tivat. The two towns are bisected by a mountain and connected by a highway tunnel. Tivat has more wide-open valley views compared to Kotor's steep mountain views... The scenery isn't quite as dramatic, but it gets blasted by sunshine all day.

Tivat has a more modern, lively feel than Kotor. The main town has businesses, restaurants, cafés, shops, housing of all kinds, and a couple of small parks.

Tivat has a long boardwalk on the water, which leads to Porto Montenegro.

Porto Montenegro is one of the bay's luxury modern developments, where the rich and famous like to hang out. The boardwalk transforms into something much more manicured, and you start to pass bigger and more expensive-looking boats as you walk along it.

It has high-end restaurants and shopping, including brands such as Balenciaga, Louis Vuitton, and so on. It boasts a sleek marina with massive yachts tethered up just off the boardwalk. It also has residences—all brand-new and designed to look like Tuscany aesthetically, but modern.

Porto Montenegro is a place to see and be seen. You pick up on that based on the way people who live and hang out here dress and carry themselves. It's one of several such luxury developments scattered around the bay.

There's also Portonovi in Hercig Novi and Lustica Bay, just outside the bay. They offer yet another niche lifestyle type, one that is steeped in luxury and a high level of comfort, though not necessarily authentic.

In Tivat, the attractions are less history-based compared with Kotor... This is where you go when you want a flashy night out on the town, whether you want to indulge in a gastronomic experience at one of the chic restaurants, sip craft cocktails while watching the sunset, or break the bank at Louis Vuitton or Balenciaga.

In the Bay of Kotor, it's all about the sea. You can do any type of water-based sport you like. The boating lifestyle specifically is a major draw, and it's not just for Saudi princes and Russian oligarchs, who are known to moor their mega-yachts here.

Marinas are available in the following places:

- **Kotor:** Marina Prcanj and Marina Kotor
- **Tivat:** Porto Montenegro and Marina Bonici
- **Hercig Novi:** Portonovi Marina
- **Just outside Kotor Bay:** Lustica Bay

Land-based attractions include hiking in the hills that surround Kotor Bay. An easy afternoon hike starts in Kotor Old Town and takes you up the mountain slope behind it, passing the old crumbling city walls and other ruins as you ascend.

Austro-Hungarian fortresses lie scattered in the hills and forests surrounding Kotor. Visiting them combines a hike and a little historical education... Fort Vrmac is worth a visit. It dates to 1860 and saw action in WWI, when it was bombarded by Montenegro.

Within a couple hours' drive there are several national parks. Lovcen National Park has peaks of 1,749 meters (5,738 feet), which you can hike up. Durmitor

National Park is UNESCO-recognized and contains Europe's deepest gorges.

There are two main ski resorts: Ski Resort Kolasin 1450 and Ski Resort Savin Kuk, with smaller ski centers nearby. Facilities, like equipment rentals, ski-lifts, ski schools, and more, are all set up here. Montenegro has big potential as Europe's next ski destination.

Because of this country's extreme landscape, it's naturally an extreme sport destination... Paragliding, rafting down the Tara River Canyon, rock climbing... Whatever adrenaline-spiking activity you're into, you can probably do it here.

Considering all that's on offer, and unlike comparable destinations like Croatia, the cost of living in Montenegro is low. A couple can live comfortably here on a budget of 2,000 euros to 2,500 euros per month.

Prices vary from town to town, with Kotor Old Town and Tivat's seafront drag costing the most compared to the villages scattered around the bay. You can rent a small, one- or two-bed apartment in Kotor Old Town for about 800 euros per month.

Property prices are on the rise... but most American and Canadian retirees would probably consider Kotor Bay property a steal, especially considering the proximity to the sea and deep historical significance.

You can buy a modest, two-bedroom home, albeit one likely in need of some TLC, for as little as 100,000 euros. Inland, this price can go even lower.

For high-end property, i.e., property in a private development like Porto Montenegro, the average two-bed costs 700,000 euros to 1,000,000 euros.

Other expenses, like utilities, are low, too... One expat quoted 40 euros per month for electric and water... He pointed out that if you're moving to an older property, make sure that the meters were read recently so that you're not stuck with the previous tenant's unpaid bill.

If you're taking taxis to get around, expect to spend 18 euros to 20 euros on the journey between Kotor Old Town and Tivat.

A meal for two at a nice place will cost 50 euros to 60 euros, including drinks, mains, and dessert. You can have hearty meals at local spots for much less than this: 20 euros to 40 euros for two.

Public buses and taxis operate in Kotor Bay. Taxis are plentiful and easy to find, with taxi ranks in popular areas (like outside Kotor Old Town and just off Tivat's boardwalk). Drivers speak English, and rates are reasonable; most drivers use the meter to determine the fare.

The roads are generally good quality, but Montenegro is extremely mountainous, which translates to hairy roads and a lot of driving through tunnels. All the more reason to have your own car—to put safety in your own hands when you're traveling around the country.

There are no direct flights between Montenegro and North America. The best way to get to Kotor Bay is to fly into Tivat or the capital, Podgorica, by connecting in one of Europe's major hubs. Note that both airports serve only a few destinations year-round. The selection expands during summer.

Podgorica is a two-hour drive from Kotor Bay.

There's a large, diverse, and active expat community in Kotor Bay.

The best way to meet people is by joining the expat Facebook groups, like Expat Living Montenegro, Foreigners in Montenegro, and Montenegro Digital Nomads & Remote Workers.

Expatwoman.com's Montenegro page is a wealth of information for the new arrival in Kotor Bay (or anywhere else in the country) and is where much expat organization takes place. In addition to the practical information, you can join clubs like Internationals in Montenegro, International Women's Club of Montenegro, and so on.

You'll have no trouble finding English-speaking waiters, real estate agents, taxi drivers, shop attendants, and so on.

Some expats have picked up a conversational level of Montenegrin—not an easy language to grasp, but seemingly possible. The language is similar to Croatian and Serbian and uses the Latin alphabet (in addition to the Cyrillic).

Kotor Bay and Tivat have a Mediterranean climate. Year-round, temperatures average between 36°F (2°C) and 88°F (31°C), with humidity hovering between 50% and 74%.

From June to September, it's hot and stuffy, with temperatures reaching into the high 80s; in July and August, you might see mercury in the 90s on occasion. From December to February, it cools off considerably, with lows regularly reaching the mid-30s regularly but rarely dropping to freezing.

It's rare to see snow here, although you'll probably be able to see it at the tops of the mountains and, of course, at the ski resorts. You'll get a bit of rain—about 55 inches over the year.

Access for people with mobility issues varies across the bay...

Tivat is the most accessible option for people who are wheelchair-bound because it's the most modern. Buildings that have multiple floors are likely to have elevators, and restaurants and shops are level with the town's long, flat boardwalk.

More modern areas of Kotor may be slightly more mobility-friendly...

Kotor Old Town is not very accessible. Most shops make you go up at least one step to enter, and there aren't many ramps. Old buildings in this area do not have elevators, and the UNESCO status likely means that they can't be retrofitted for them.

It's best to stick to the areas with more modern development, like Tivat and parts of Kotor, if you have a mobility issue.

Montenegro is extremely safe. You can feel comfortable walking around by yourself at any time of day or night without fear of crime. Locals say this is because everyone knows each other (the country's population is only 620,000), so it's not possible to get away with random crime.

Expats love this area for its safety, its access to nature, the diverse recreation opportunities, and the diverse and interesting community. The downside is the lack of international-standard health care... although they say for basic treatment, they're happy with Montenegro's care.

Health Care In Montenegro

The health care in Kotor Bay is decent. Expats tell us it's fine for basic care, but for serious procedures, they prefer to go abroad. Health care is free to Montenegro residents, but many expats prefer to keep a private insurance plan in place for access to private clinics and quicker treatment.

One expat we spoke to (who had a medical background) told us of the caring and attentive treatment her husband received during the pandemic when he was diagnosed with cancer and they were unable to return to their home country to start treatment.

There are two main medical centers in this area of Montenegro...

Kotor General Hospital is a public facility offering emergency treatment for adults and children. It specializes in internal medicine, anesthesia, resuscitation, gynecology and obstetrics, and has a surgical department.

Tivat Health Centre is also a public facility with emergency medical service, as well as dental services, pediatrics, gynecology, internal medicine, diagnostics, neuropsychiatry, and ambulance service.

Residency Requirements

Americans and Canadians can come to Montenegro visa-free and stay for 90 days within a 180-day period. For longer stays, you'll need to apply for a temporary residence permit.

Up until this year, Montenegro offered a unique residency program, whereby you could buy real estate worth any value and be granted temporary residency.

As per the new rules, those seeking residency through real estate ownership must now show that their property has a taxable value of at least 150,000 euros as determined by the Tax Authority's transfer tax assessment.

Applicants will need to prove ownership and use of the property and all related tax obligations must be settled.

Aside from the real estate purchase, the basic requirements to qualify this way are that you have a clean criminal record, receive an income of about 10 euros per day (or you can deposit 3,650 euros in a Montenegrin bank), provide a birth and marriage certificate if you're applying with your partner, and provide proof of accommodation and health insurance.

The temporary residence permit this gets you is valid for one year and can be renewed. You can leave the country for more than a month in a year, but you have to let your local immigration inspector know. After five years of temporary residency, you can apply for permanent residency.

After five years as a temporary resident, you can apply for permanent permission, valid for five years and extendable. This gives you the same rights as a Montenegrin, except for the right to vote.

Real Estate Restrictions

Montenegro imposes some restrictions on foreign buyers when it comes to property ownership. These restrictions apply to agricultural and forested land. It's more difficult, although not impossible, to buy this type of land.

Taxes

You become a tax resident if you spend 183 days in a tax year in Montenegro, have a domicile here, or use the country as a center of personal or economic activities.

Income is taxed at progressive rates...

- €0 to €700: 0%

- €701 to €1,000: 9%
- €1,001 and up: 15%

A local surtax is due to your municipality in Montenegro, which is 13% unless you base yourself in Podgorica or Cetinje, in which case it's 15%.

Capital gains tax applies to real estate sales and sales of shares in a legal entity and securities. You can avoid paying capital gains tax on real estate sales if the home is your primary residence or you are transferring title to your spouse or children.

For investment income, the same personal income tax rates outlined above apply. For property income, the tax rate is also 15%.

CHAPTER 17

CROATIA

Diocletian was on to something.

After more than two decades as emperor of Rome, during which time he'd put down all manner of threats to bring the Roman Empire back from the brink of collapse and create a lasting peace, he decided, in May 305, that he'd had enough.

Diocletian was worn out waging war and managing political squabbles and became the first Roman emperor to abdicate the position voluntarily.

He'd prepared for the day.

Diocletian built a 50,000-square-foot palace for himself on the glorious Dalmatian coast overlooking the Adriatic Sea. Here he lived out his days tending to his gardens and enjoying the views.

Diocletian's palace forms the core of the modern-day city of Split...

Making Croatia the world's first overseas retirement haven.

The region's history is one of its greatest appeals. You don't travel far in this part of the world without stumbling upon something ancient.

But I'd say that Croatia's biggest draw right now is its vision for its future.

On our most recent visit, Lief and I both had the same reaction...

This is a country on the up.

Croatia is tucked into southeastern Europe, bordering the Adriatic Sea, between Bosnia and Herzegovina and Slovenia. It has 3,700 miles of coastline and over 1,200 small islands, the majority of which are uninhabited.

This country is not only extraordinarily beautiful, charming, and historic. Its people are friendly. And its cities are safe. In many regards, it's an ideal choice for retirement living.

It's been 30 years since the Socialist Federal Republic of Yugoslavia was dissolved. Its six republics—Croatia, Bosnia and Herzegovina, Macedonia, Montenegro, Serbia, and Slovenia are all very much their own countries today.

Croatia has already been discovered by the outside world, in a lot of ways.

When the megahit TV show "Game of Thrones" used Dubrovnik as the location for King's Landing, that Croatian city and the country's entire Dalmatian Coast shot up on the tourist radar...

Croatia is a full member of the European Union and, on Jan. 1, 2023, became the latest nation to adopt the euro as its currency. On that day, it also joined the Schengen Area, Europe's 29-country, free-travel zone, which allows for movement across the continent without border checks...

Since joining the EU in 2013, Croatia has put the financial advantages of that status to good use, investing in highways, bridges, and tunnels through her mountains of white stone.

Everywhere is easier to get to... and now there's more to do when you arrive... more restaurants, more wineries, more art galleries...

It's a hidden gem on the Adriatic Sea that offers a luxurious Mediterranean lifestyle. And although prices are not as cheap as they used to be, you can still find some bargains.

Beach is one thing Croatia has in spades—this country's long Adriatic coastline is magnificent. What's more, Croatia enjoys more days of sunshine annually than any country in continental Europe.

In 2005, when we arrived in Croatia for the first time and set our eyes upon Istria, this delightful land of olive trees, grapevines, and sunflowers captured our hearts and our imaginations. We decided we wanted to stake a small claim in this place at a turning point in its history.

We placed a bet, way back then, on the future of Croatia, a country with an extraordinarily troubled and complicated past and an extremely open-minded, forward-looking population. Returning now, all these years later, we appreciate what this corner of our globe has to offer more than ever.

One rainy morning two decades ago, Lief and I found a 200-year-old white stone house that we liked in particular, perched as it was on a mountainside above a long valley of olive trees and grapevines. After that, we made an offer to the Istrian owner and agreed the terms with a handshake. The seller sealed the deal by making a gift to us of lavender oil his wife had bottled.

Then we returned to our lives and got distracted. At last, it's time to refocus.

That old farmhouse is being restored as you read this. We're hoping to enjoy our first family holiday in Istria next year.

In some parts of the world, nature outdoes herself. In others, that which man has built is impressive. In Croatia, nature and mankind have worked together over centuries, starting with the Romans, to create a land of delights you have to see to appreciate. Croatia offers one of the most appealing lifestyle options in Europe today.

Top Picks For A New Life In Croatia

Istria

Istria, in the westernmost region of Croatia, serves up some of the most delightful scenery on this planet... A peninsula surrounded by sea on three sides, it resembles a tiny heart-shaped emerald dangling into the intense blue of the Adriatic.

Istria covers 3,475 square kms (1,342 square miles)... It's tiny, and driving from north to south takes less than two hours. But delights are densely packed within its borders—part of the reason this region receives over a third of all Croatia's tourists.

Here, the land seems to rise up to embrace you. The landscape is a patchwork of meadows, vineyards, and olive groves... carefully tended gardens where trees are heavy with ripening cherries, figs, and olives. Everywhere you look, something nice is growing... Even the buildings seem to be of the earth, built of its white stone and red clay.

Like a fairy-tale illustration, pencil-thin bell towers rise above nests of terracotta-tiled roofs in the scattering of villages that make up the region. But while the interior of Istria can feel remote, few settlements are more than 30 miles from the coast.

Surrounding the peninsula are glittering expanses of the Adriatic. There's blue... and then there's the almost unearthly, crystal-clear blue that laps Istria's shores. Flotillas of white yachts tack their way across the horizon of this sailor's paradise.

The ancient Romans called this land *Tierra Magica*... the Magic Land. If you've any romance in your soul, we defy you not to fall in love with this part of the world.

Croatia has captured my imagination since my first visit. The entire family, in fact, was so taken with the beauty, the history, the culture, and the lifestyle of this country that, during that very first visit, we bought a tumbledown stone farmhouse on the side of a mountain on the Istrian Peninsula.

It was an impulse buy that we haven't regretted for an instant. I daydream often about spending time in this special spot overlooking an expanse of olive groves and vineyards with a view across the valley of a medieval village built entirely of the white stone the region is known for.

In Istria's larger seaside towns, street signs are labeled in Italian: *vias*, *piazzas*, and *lungomares*. Menus feature pizzas and smoke-dried hams, seafood risottos, and pasta sprinkled with white truffles. Locals are remarkably fashion-conscious...

It's no surprise that Istria's heritage is, in part, Italian. It has a tangled history of invasion and occupation. The Venetians bequeathed much of the architecture, and the Austro-Hungarian Empire left it with a taste for goulash, apple strudel, and other pastries.

Although traditional sea and sunshine vacations remain a huge attraction for many, they're not the only draw... Historical and cultural delights abound in Istria, with shifts in the ambiance depending on the season.

Fall and winter are quiet on the Istrian Peninsula. Towns are at their normal population levels, and many businesses close down for the season. Come spring, a buzz starts to develop as the first wave of tourists arrives. By summer, the buzz reaches a fever pitch, as the towns' populations swell, and the festival, fair, and events calendar are in full swing.

In summer, there's always something going on in Istria. In Pula, you can attend screenings at the annual film festival or a big-name classical music or rock concert. Classical music concerts also take place in Medulin, which also boasts a selection of 40-plus top-quality restaurants.

Porec offers jazz sessions, art festivals, and the gastronomic Istrafest, where you can try local delicacies for the equivalent of a couple of dollars. In Rabac, there's the annual Summer Festival, during which DJs play techno and house across multiple dance floors... a popular event among younger crowds.

In July, Motovun stages a film festival that attracts 20,000 people.

Svetvincenat's town square becomes the venue for a traditional summer festival of dance, and its Grimani Castle hosts the Umag-o Ethno Jazz and Blues Festival. The list of exciting cultural events is long...

Istria doesn't disappoint history buffs, either, with architecture, ruins, and vestiges of the ancient sprinkled throughout the region. Rovinj is perhaps the most picture-perfect small settlement along the entire Adriatic.

Snuggled down on a circular peninsula, its medieval quarter was once a separate island. However, 18th-century engineers added it to the mainland by filling in the narrow channel that lay between the two.

Above Rovinj's tightly packed red-tiled roofs soars Saint Euphemia's cathedral. Its bell tower is almost 200 feet high and visible from many miles away. Saint Euphemia was reputedly martyred by being thrown to the lions in Constantinople's Roman arena. Legend tells that the saint's body was miraculously washed ashore here in a stone sarcophagus.

In Porec, you can visit the ruins of the Roman forum. It's home to the Basilica of Euphrasius, a UNESCO World Heritage Site because of its dazzling Byzantine mosaics. Wafting out enticing scents of fresh seafood and smoked hams, appealing restaurants lie off the old town's pedestrianized and marble-paved main street.

Novigrad is another historic harbor settlement with a lovely old walled town on a peninsula. More cobbled lanes, Venetian-style houses, and ornate churches... Similar sights are on offer in Groznjan, a 14th-century Venetian fortified hill town, perched above the Mirna Valley.

More recently, Istria has started rebranding itself as a green, eco-friendly gastronomic paradise. Thanks to its white and black truffles, it's been described as "the Klondike of the culinary world."

The forests around Motovun are a lucrative truffle hunting ground... Every fall, hundreds of truffle hunters and their sniffing dogs trawl the woods for this buried treasure.

Must-try truffle dishes include *fritaja* (scrambled eggs) with truffles, scampi carpaccio, and octopus with truffles, hand-rolled pasta drizzled with truffle oil... You can even try truffle ice cream, although sheep's cheese with honey and truffles is a more traditional way to finish a meal.

With Croatia's long Adriatic coastline, it has no shortage of beaches. What's more, it enjoys more days of sunshine annually than almost any other country in Europe. When Europeans across the continent set out on their annual beach holidays, Istria is one of the destinations they target.

It's worth pointing out that sandy beaches aren't one of Istria's attractions. With the exception of a bit of sand at Medulin, beaches are pebbly, stony, or downright rocky. That applies to the whole of Croatia's coastline, too. If your definition of beach must involve sand, you may not be satisfied here.

One crowd that's a big fan of Istria's beaches, sandy or not, are nudists. Long before Yugoslavia's break-up, this region was attracting nudists from all over Europe. The majority are German, although the Dutch and Scandinavians aren't shy about stripping down either.

All kinds of ocean-based activities can be practiced in Istria. There is huge potential for yachting and nautical vacations. You can scuba dive offshore from Pula and in Brijuni National Park. Other leisure opportunities include boat trips, diving, and cycling. In Medulin, there are numerous sports facilities, including tennis, beach volleyball, and horse riding.

And if you ever grow tired of what immediately surrounds you in Istria, you can simply cross the border into one of Croatia's neighboring countries.

Tucked into southeastern Europe, Croatia borders the Adriatic Sea, Hungary, Serbia, Bosnia and Herzegovina, and Montenegro. It's near Vienna, Venice, and Budapest, as well as skiing in Austria and golf in Slovenia.

Some real estate agencies and vacation companies market it as "the new Tuscany," but we think it's even better. For one thing, Istria is a lot greener and less manicured. Its roads and villages aren't choked by tourist crowds...

A three-bedroom villa in Istria might cost $400,000. Renovation projects can start at less than $100,000. You won't find prices like this in Tuscany or along Europe's more famous Rivieras.

Where specifically in Istria should you be considering?

Along the coast, there's Pula, the closest thing Istria has to a big city, with around 57,000 inhabitants. It isn't Istria's prettiest settlement, but it has some impressive Roman remains and hosts a film festival and big-name classical music and rock concerts during summer.

Eight miles from Pula is Medulin, which boasts one of the region's only sandy beaches (the rest are rocky). A tiny town of about 1,800, it buzzes with activity come summer. Visitors are drawn to Medulinski Bay, which stretches for 26 miles and is indented with small coves, offering vistas of the nine tiny islets that lie offshore.

Rovinj, on the peninsula's west coast, has archways, stone stairways, Venetian-winged lions, and sea-view belvederes... a spider's web of cobbled alleys and hidden courtyards... a harbor with a pink clock tower, terraced cafés, and enticing fish restaurants. It's like a piece of Venice that somehow drifted south.

Inland in northern Istria, there's Motovun. Perched on a hill, with woods and vineyards below, this is the best-preserved of Istria's walled medieval towns. A 1,052-stair climb leads you to Motovun's Venetian town square, where you find more historical treasures: a Middle Age acropolis complete with towers, gateways, and palaces emblazoned with faded coats of arms.

Unspoiled, uncrowded, and with no over-building... If you're in the market for a vacation home or part-time living, Istria has much to tempt you with. And despite Croatia's complex residency rules that make full-time living here hard to achieve, Istria still has bundles of potential.

The cost of living in Croatia is higher than in many of its Eastern European neighbors... but compared with Western Europe and the United States, prices here are still affordable.

The average rent for a comfortable, two-bedroom apartment in Pula, one of the most expensive areas in Istria, is 850 euros. Typical monthly costs for running your accommodation are 55 euros for electricity (including heating and water), plus 25 euros to 42 euros for garbage collection, gas for cooking, and other maintenance fees.

Much depends on the lifestyle you expect... Eating out, paying for services, and local travel are affordable here. A two-course lunch costs about 17 euros if you stick to local restaurants. Half a liter of local wine will add another 6 euros. A seafood platter for two starts at about 38 euros.

Istria often gets compared to Tuscany, and with good reason. The geography and the history of these two regions have much in common. But the difference is that the average person can afford Istria, where a small, renovated cottage with lookouts over a valley and vineyards, perfect for regular visits, for rental, and for retirement, costs as little as 85,000 euros. Keep in mind that property taxes in Croatia are zero, too.

For groceries, expect to spend about 380 euros a month for two. A couple's basic monthly budget here should come to about 2,375 euros.

The nearest private hospital to Istria is Medico Polyclinic Hospital in Rijeka, about one hour away. More private hospitals and clinics are found in Zagreb (a three-hour drive away from central Istria) or Split (a five-hour drive away).

There are public hospitals and polyclinics in Istria's major towns and tourist centers. The largest general hospital is in Pula. Rovinj has an orthopedic hospital as well.

The Istrian Peninsula has a humid subtropical climate. Its protected position to the southeast of the Alps means that the weather is always pleasant. It doesn't get oppressively hot during the summer, and winters stay mild.

Using Pula to give an overview of temperatures for the entire region, the average high is 65°F (18°C) and the average low is 50°F (10°C), with humidity hovering around 71%. The height of summer is July and August, when it's usually 73°F (23°C); peak winter is January and February, when it's usually 43°F (6°C).

Winters are mild and pleasant—snowfall is rare here, but rain is common.

Sirocco winds from the south bring the rain during late summer. Pula gets about 34 inches of rain throughout the course of the year, with about 12 days of rain per month on average. Overall, the region gets an average of 2,400 annual sunshine hours per year.

The official language of Croatia is Croatian... a notoriously difficult language to learn. Even after years of practice, you still may not be able to achieve fluency.

Speaking and understanding a bit of Croatian will make your life infinitely easier in this country. If dealing with doctors or government officials, you should bring someone who can speak Croatian and English fluently with you. Finding an English-speaking staff member anywhere you go isn't a guarantee.

That said, the number of English speakers in Croatia is on the rise because English is a mandatory subject in schools. Most people under the age of 40 will speak some English. If you settle close to a tourist town in Istria, restaurant and store staff will likely speak a bit of English, too.

Istria is safe, and its people are friendly. In many regards, it's an ideal choice for retirement... but it has virtually no expat community.

Retiring here, you'd have no choice but to adopt a local lifestyle. This could be very appealing to you, depending on what type of person you are...

One of the most important choices you have to make as you think through your options for launching your new life overseas is whether you're more comfortable moving to an established expatriate community, a place where you'd have no trouble slipping into the local social scene and making friends with English-speakers who share your interests...

Or whether you want, instead, to go local, immersing yourself in the new culture completely.

If you prefer the former, Istria may not be the right choice for you...

There are a handful of ways to get to Istria: airplane, bus, car, train, and even ferry... but once you get here, your options are less diverse. There are really just two ways to get around Istria: car and bus.

Depending on where in Istria you settle, you might be able to rely on the bus as your only form of transportation. It connects the bigger coastal and interior towns... but it doesn't reach all the smaller villages.

To make the most of life in this region that's so dense with things to see and do, you should really have a car. A two-lane motorway connects Istria, with smaller, scenic roads linking major towns to smaller villages. Traffic is rarely a problem here, and roads are generally in great condition.

Pula Airport is the most important in Istria. It offers just one regular direct international flight to Russia... Seasonally, it offers direct flights to destinations across Europe, including the most convenient travel hubs (London, Paris, Amsterdam, etc.). If you're coming here from the States or Canada, it makes the most sense to connect to Pula through one of these hubs.

You could also fly to Venice's Marco Polo Airport in neighboring Italy, which has a much wider selection of international flights, including direct flights to the States and Canada (again, on a seasonal basis). From Venice to Istria, the drive is about three hours in a bus or car, or you can take the hydrofoil—a 90-minute journey across the Adriatic.

Istria is an extremely safe place to live. It's the type of place where you can leave your front door unlocked, allow your kid to play outside unattended, or walk down the street at any time of day without worrying. It's highly unlikely that you'd be a victim to any crime living here.

In some parts of the world, nature outdoes herself. In others, what humankind has built is impressive. In Istria, nature and humankind have worked together over centuries, starting with the Romans, to create a land of delights you have to see to appreciate.

Health Care In Croatia

Croatia's health care system is ranked #41 in the world by the Legatum Prosperity Index Health Rankings. Its public health facilities are improving year on year.

Long wait times can be a challenge, and certain drugs are in short supply... As an expat spending time in Croatia, you should invest in health insurance to avoid the issues of the public health care system. You'll need health insurance if you're seeking temporary residence in Croatia as a condition of your application anyway.

Some expats in Croatia who are eligible for public health care prefer to pay out of pocket when they need medical treatment to avoid the long wait times.

They estimate a budget of 70 euros per person per month for this.

Several English-speaking dentists across the country advertise their services through the internet. Prices vary considerably, so it pays to do some research before you need treatment. A tooth extraction, for example, can range from 40 euros to 55 euros or more.

Residency Requirements

As an American or Canadian, you can come to Croatia and stay for up to 90 days in any 180-day period without a visa. As of January 2024, Croatia is part of the Schengen Area.

Croatia does not make it easy for non-EU passport holders to stay for longer than 90 days... It doesn't score well for residency because the options are limited, although not impossible. For this reason, it's a good option as a top part-time go-overseas option rather than a full-time option.

Two potential paths to temporary residence permits in Croatia are purchasing property or prepaying for rent on a property where you plan to stay...

If you purchase residential property in Croatia, you can get a temporary residence permit that allows you to stay in the country for six months. After six months, you must leave for 90 days before you can reapply. You can't bring a spouse or dependent with this option unless they are listed as an owner of the property.

If you prepay for rent on a property where you plan to stay, you can get temporary residency in Croatia for up to one year. This permit is not renewable and requires you to leave the country for at least 90 days after the year is up. Neither this nor the former option is a path to permanent residency or citizenship in Croatia.

Croatia recently launched another option—a residence permit aimed at digital nomads and remote workers. You can qualify for this program if you're a non-EU citizen and work for a foreign company, have about 25,500 euros in a personal bank account, and have health insurance and a clean criminal record.

This gets you a residence permit that applies not only to Croatia but also to the entire EU. It offers a complete exemption on foreign-earned income, costs 85 euros to apply for, and can be issued in under two months. You can apply for it online or at a Croatian embassy in person.

That said, the digital nomad visa is limited: It's issued for a maximum period of one year. After that, you have to leave the country and wait for at least six months before you can apply for it again.

Real Estate Restrictions

To buy property in Croatia, foreigners must get permission from the Ministry of Justice.

Your country of nationality must have a reciprocity agreement in place with Croatia to be able to buy property here. Americans and Canadians can generally get permission to buy property in Croatia, although it can vary depending on which state or province you're from.

Taxes

Residents are taxed on worldwide income, while nonresidents are taxed only on Croatian-source income.

Croatia has a looser definition of a tax resident than most countries. You're considered a tax resident if you have your permanent residence or habitual abode in the country. Therefore, if you're only spending part of the year in Croatia and your permanent residence is still in the U.S., you won't be taxable on your U.S. income in Croatia.

If you move to Croatia, the tax consequences wouldn't be negative.

A tax treaty doesn't mean much for most individuals as it mostly just outlines which country gets to tax which income. Without a treaty, the U.S. is going to get first dibs on your U.S. income and any taxes paid in the U.S. can be taken as a credit against your income taxes in Croatia.

You should consult with a Croatian tax expert before making a move, but with lower tax rates than the U.S., the worst case you should have is that you pay as much as you're paying in the U.S. anyway.

Croatia is noteworthy for its property taxes, which are zero.

CHAPTER 18

NORTHERN CYPRUS

White-sand beaches... warm water... year-round sunshine... and one of the healthiest diets in the world... For sun and sand lovers, it's hard to beat the Mediterranean lifestyle.

The place where we see the biggest potential on the Med right now is Northern Cyprus, an area of the island of Cyprus. Because of its complicated political status, it's not on the radar of most would-be expats... but this former British colony has a lot to offer.

At 3,355 square kms (1,295 square miles), it comprises 36% of Cyprus's total land area. Its finger-shaped geography means that it's home to the longest stretch of coastline on the island... as well as the best beaches. It offers year-round good weather, with 340 sunny days a year. (That's more than the Spanish Costa del Sol's average of 320 days and the French Riviera's average of 300).

Northern Cyprus is also a safe, welcoming destination with developed tourism infrastructure, including clubs, casinos, and luxury hotels. The currency is the Turkish lira, meaning prices are 30% lower than in the eurozone.

It's possible to own an ocean-view condo with direct beach access for less than $100,000 at current exchange rates (real estate in Northern Cyprus trades in British pounds). It's also possible to buy with developer financing, meaning low capital requirements up-front.

But it's not just beach enthusiasts that flock here... Gambling was legalized in Northern Cyprus in the 1970s (it's only been legal in the Republic since 2018). Since the 1990s, a steady stream of high rollers has been hitting the region's casinos. It's even been dubbed the "Las

Vegas of the Mediterranean."

Medical tourism is another growing sector. First-class hospitals and health centers offer a range of procedures from hip replacement to dental implants at a fraction of the cost of the United States and the rest of Europe.

The origins of Northern Cyprus's complicated political status can be traced back across time. But in more recent history, the parliament of Northern Cyprus declared itself the Turkish Republic of Northern Cyprus (TRNC) in 1983, a claim that only one country in the international community has ever recognized: Turkey.

Today, the TRNC is a de facto state, though the Republic of Cyprus has de jure sovereignty of the entire island. Cyprus joined the European Union on May 1, 2004, but EU legislation is suspended in Northern Cyprus.

Talks of reunification have bubbled up and then fizzled out over the years... One sign of progress is that in 2003, restrictions on freedom of movement between north and south were eased, allowing Cypriots to travel freely across the island for the first time in 30 years.

Despite the political issues, business continues as usual on both sides of the border... though prices remain more affordable on the Turkish side.

Top Picks For A New Life In Northern Cyprus

Iskele, on the eastern coast, is known for having the nicest and longest stretch of beach on the island, as well as its seafood specialties...

Kyrenia is a small town on the northern coast of Northern Cyprus, sandwiched between the Kyrenia Mountains and the warm waters of the Med. It's home to seaside hotels, restaurants, and beach clubs but is most famous for its old harbor and castle.

Famagusta is a charming city of about 50,000 people, found on Northern Cyprus's southeast coast. It's a walled city, surrounded by roughly rectangular ramparts built by the Venetians in the 15th and

16th centuries.

Not after beach life? North Nicosia is Northern Cyprus's capital and biggest city with a population of 82,000. It's rich in architectural marvels and sites of cultural importance...

Regardless of where in Northern Cyprus you end up, retirement here would mean a life outside the more familiar comfort zones of Europe and the Americas.

If you're up for an adventure at this stage of your life while stretching your retirement budget to buy you a bona fide luxury standard of life on one of the world's most beautiful stretches of coastline, Northern Cyprus should be at the top of your list.

Northern Cyprus is far from being just a destination for beach bums... It also draws in history enthusiasts, with all sorts of testaments to its rich history to be discovered. The best place to start a historical tour of Northern Cyprus is its capital, North Nicosia...

Split between Northern Cyprus and the Republic of Cyprus, Nicosia is known as the "last divided capital in Europe." Inside North Nicosia are 672 buildings of recognized historical value and complete quarters that have retained the atmosphere of ancient times.

Ataturk Square, at the center of the walled city, is the cultural heart of Cyprus's Turkish community. It continues to be a hub of politics, a place where rallies are hosted and visiting Turkish prime ministers deliver speeches.

North Nicosia is culturally diverse because it's a base for several universities, which attract students from different backgrounds. It's also active in fine arts, with exhibitions and competitions held regularly. Multiple theaters and the Lefkosa Municipal Orchestra are headquartered here as well.

Kyrenia has seaside hotels, restaurants, and beach clubs but is most famous for its old harbor and castle. This imposing structure dates to the seventh century. It features four massive artillery towers that served the Byzantines, Crusaders, Venetians, Ottomans, and British throughout its history.

Famagusta is a walled city, surrounded by Venetian-built rectangular ramparts and full of interesting landmarks, like Lala Mustafa Pasha Mosque, a former Gothic cathedral turned mosque, and Othello's Tower, the setting for Shakespeare's "Othello."

For a more modern diversion, check out Northern Cyprus's casinos. More than 20 casinos attract gamblers from around the region, giving the area a reputation as the "Las Vegas of the Mediterranean." There are exclusive beach resorts, high-end restaurants, and nightclubs, yet despite this party reputation, it's still possible to enjoy a quiet, relaxing break here.

Another way to connect with Northern Cyprus's culture is through its cuisine. The Mediterranean diet is one of the healthiest in the world. In Northern Cyprus, dining on local food is very inexpensive, meaning you can indulge without hurting your wallet or your waistline.

Traditional dishes are often served as "mezzes"—tapas-style small plates. Typical mezzes include hummus, eggplant dip, yogurt with cucumber or carrots, feta, salad, and olives, particularly cracked green olives soaked in olive oil and coriander seeds called *chakistez*.

Halloumi (called *hellim* locally) is one of the island's claims to culinary fame. Halloumi is a local cheese made from goat and sheep's milk and often served grilled. Just like champagne, halloumi must be made in Cyprus to earn its name... otherwise it's a knockoff that should be labeled otherwise.

Northern Cyprus also features an active events calendar, with festivals that draw large crowds taking place throughout the year. One such festival is the Orange Festival, which takes place in the town of Morphou. This grand-scale event adds color to local culture and celebrates the yearly orange harvest with ceremonies, parades, concerts, folk dancing, and tournaments.

Northern Cyprus is more famous than its southern counterpoint for its unspoiled beaches. Despite being just one-third of Cyprus's total land area, it has more and better-quality beaches. It's shaped like a long finger that points out into the sea, providing a super-extended coastline.

The area consists of two bays—Morphou and Famagusta—and four capes: Apostolos Andreas, Kormakitis, Zeytin, and Kasa. There is a beach to suit every taste here, from low-key to luxury...

On the northern coast are golden-sand beaches, many of which feature oceanfront hotels and clubs. Two of the most well-known are Kaplica and Tatlisu—clean, peaceful beaches that offer a bit of luxury, with hotels, restaurants, and other amenities available nearby.

Along the Karpaz Peninsula, the elongated finger of land that points out towards the Turkish mainland, are a scattering of beaches. At the tip of the finger is Golden Beach—recognized as the most beautiful in the area.

Completely undeveloped, it boasts a long expanse of soft sand and brilliantly turquoise waters.

Along the eastern coast, there's Iskele, a town known for having one of the nicest and longest stretches of beach on the island. Its Long Beach is the "in" place to be, a place where you can enjoy cycling, surfing, skating, and more, attractive to any age group.

It offers fishing docks, sports fields, outdoor sports gear, picnic and lounging areas, food stalls, beach bars, and restaurants. It's famous for its seafood restaurants, where fish are delivered daily by local fishermen.

With all this waterfront available, so too are all kinds of water-based activities and watersports. You can scuba dive off of Kyrenia Harbor to see shipwrecks, coral reefs, and magnificent marine life. You can practice jet skiing, waterskiing, and windsurfing or organize boat or sailing trips.

Beyond its beaches, Northern Cyprus is a place to embrace the outdoors. Inland, it has mountains, hills, plains, and streams... The Kyrenia Mountains, with peaks of up to 3,360 feet (1,024 meters), offer opportunities for hiking, trekking, and even paragliding for the more adventurous types.

The area boasts the highly rated Korineum Golf & Beach Resort, and there are several gyms for those who enjoy working out.

Cyprus is one of the EU's most affordable places to live, especially considering this is a Mediterranean-island destination... But Northern Cyprus comes at an even greater discount because it's outside of the eurozone. The local currency is the Turkish lira, so whether you're coming here with euros or U.S. dollars, the currency exchange works in your favor.

Northern Cyprus holds a reputation as one of the most affordable places to buy property in the Mediterranean. Its property market is booming, but it's still a relatively new place of interest. You can still find investment opportunities at a fraction of the price of what you could in the southern part of Cyprus or other European countries. In fact, you can still get a beachfront property for $100,000 or less. Note that most property is priced in British pounds here.

If you're renting, budget $400 to $700 monthly for a two-bedroom apartment with a pool. Your utilities (electricity, gas, water, and internet) will cost you $50 a month.

For electricity, the specific amounts fluctuate depending on the seasons and how often you run your air conditioner in the summer months (and whether you run a heater during cooler months). In spring and autumn, electricity costs can be next to nothing.

Budget about $150 for monthly entertainment and $250 for groceries.

Northern Cyprus is fairly self-sufficient when it comes to agricultural production. Citrus fruits, vegetables, olive oil, and cheese are locally produced and priced. You can meet much of your shopping needs at roadside stalls and markets where prices are negotiable. As in any place in the world, imported goods are going to cost you more in Northern Cyprus.

Eating out is an inexpensive indulgence in Northern Cyprus. At local restaurants, you can eat traditional dishes (kebabs, hummus, salads, etc.) and pay the equivalent to a couple of dollars for a healthy and fulfilling Mediterranean meal. There are also fine-dining options available in five-star hotels and in tourist zones.

A couple's basic monthly budget here should come to about $1,400 to $2,000.

The climate here is characterized by dry, hot summers and mild winters.

It's popular with sun-seekers from all over the world because it gets so much sunshine annually. It gets between 2,700 and 3,500 hours of sun per year.

Compare that to London, which receives 1,461 hours of sunshine per year, and it becomes obvious why Northern Cyprus is so popular with people from the U.K. and other parts of Northern Europe.

Temperatures range between an average high of 75°F (24°C) and an average low of 57°F (14°C), with humidity hovering between 60% and 80%. The warm season lasts eight months, April to November. During this time, the sun shines for upwards of 11 hours a day, and temperatures average 72°F (22°C). The height of summer is June to August when temperatures regularly reach 95°F (35°C).

During the cool season, December to March, temperatures are mild, with a daily mean of 55°F (13°C). These are also Northern Cyprus's rainiest months, when 60% of the yearly precipitation comes down. But precipitation isn't significant in Northern Cyprus. It gets about 14 inches a year.

The official language of Northern Cyprus is Turkish, although the spoken language is Cypriot Turkish—a dialect that's fairly different to standard Turkish.

In the Republic of Cyprus (south Cyprus), both Greek and Turkish hold official language status, but most people speak Cypriot Greek (which is also a dialect that's fairly different to standard Greek).

Across the entire island, English is widely spoken and used in advertisements, street signs, public notices, and so on. Picking up a few words of Cypriot Turkish would ingratiate you to the locals, but it's not necessary to live well in Northern Cyprus.

Northern Cyprus may be an off-the-radar choice for North Americans, but that doesn't mean it's an unheard-of retire-overseas destination. A strong expat community already calls the area home, with some 16% of the population made up of people from outside the area.

The majority of this group are from the U.K., although there are also people from other parts of Europe. The community is active, offering social events and gatherings, interest-based clubs, and recreation opportunities.

Golf, bowling leagues, badminton, and darts competitions are a few of the ways Northern Cyprus expats spend their time.

It's easy to slip into the local social scene in Northern Cyprus, as locals are friendly and English-speaking, and the expat community is big and active.

One downside of living here is that public transport is lacking.

Buses connect the main cities (Nicosia, Kyrenia, and Famagusta) until 6 p.m. every day. There are bus terminals within each of these cities that provide onward connections to more rural areas, but generally speaking, the bus isn't an efficient way to get around.

The area is well-serviced by taxis, but they are expensive. A more budget-friendly travel option are *dolmus* or *kombos*, which are shared taxis that pick up multiple passengers and therefore multiple fares as they make their journeys.

The most effective way of getting around Northern Cyprus is driving your own car. Renovation works have upgraded the highways to 21st-century standards over the past several decades. These works are ongoing; two-thirds of Northern Cyprus's 7,000 kms of roads are paved. If you own a car, expect to pay about $34 monthly to run it.

The best way to get to Northern Cyprus from the States or Canada is to fly to Larnaca International Airport in the Republic of Cyprus and then cross the land border into Northern Cyprus. There are no direct flights from North America to Larnaca. You'll have to connect in one of the major European or Middle Eastern hubs.

To get from Larnaca to Northern Cyprus, you can take a taxi or pre-arrange for a transfer for about $60. If you rent a car and plan on driving onwards to Northern Cyprus, make sure your insurance will cover you on both sides of the border.

Another way to get to Northern Cyprus is to fly directly into its international airport, Ercan International Airport, located near North Nicosia. Note that because of economic sanctions, your flight would have to make a stop in Istanbul, Turkey, first, before continuing onwards to Northern Cyprus.

You'll feel extremely safe living here. It's highly unlikely that you'd fall victim to any crime. Expats report feeling more at ease in Northern Cyprus than in their home countries. Crime rates are statistically lower in Northern Cyprus than they are in the Republic of Cyprus.

Northern Cyprus is a welcoming destination with developed tourism infrastructure, great beaches, and friendly locals and expats. This is the best of the Mediterranean at a fraction of the cost of living the Med life elsewhere.

Health Care In Northern Cyprus

Visitors from around the world are traveling to Northern Cyprus to take advantage of its affordable and high-quality medical care. They take the opportunity to combine low-cost medical treatment with a Mediterranean beach holiday.

Several hospitals in Northern Cyprus offer world-class treatments. Some medical tourists also come for the low cost of MRIs, CT scans, and other complex investigations as well as inexpensive dental care. Costs are so low that many pay out of pocket. The average price to see a specialist medical practitioner with a same-day appointment is about $45.

For residents of Northern Cyprus, both private and public medical care options are available. Standards are excellent, and medical professionals are English-speaking and well-qualified.

In all of Northern Cyprus's cities, you'll find private and state-run clinics and hospitals as well as surgeries, emergency medical facilities, dentists, opticians, and even alternative health care options. Near East University Hospital has the best reputation in Northern Cyprus, noteworthy for its state-of-the-art equipment and diagnostic imaging center.

To get public health care, residents must apply for state health insurance in the capital. A requirement of applying for residency, however, is that you have private insurance, which would mean that you already have coverage in place.

Emergency care is provided to everyone in Northern Cyprus, regardless of whether they have the financial means to pay for it. The 112 TRNC Ambulance Service is staffed by trained paramedics and offers rapid response times.

Pharmacies are found across Northern Cyprus and operate almost like clinics. Their staff is English-speaking and can recommend treatments for minor ailments. A range of medications are available, and pharmacists can dispense a wider variety of drugs than in the States, Canada, or the U.K.

Northern Cyprus dentists are excellent and often trained abroad in Europe, Turkey, or the States. Prices can be as low as one-third the cost of equivalent care in the States, making up for the travel expense in getting to Northern Cyprus to have treatments done.

Residency Requirements

Tourists can come to Northern Cyprus for between 30 and 90 days. The standard tourist allowance is 30 days, but if you present proof of paid accommodation, up to 90 days can be given. Note that you can't stay for longer than 90 days within any 180-day period without a residence permit.

Most expats qualify for residence permits for Northern Cyprus through the purchase of immovable property. This gets you a one-year renewable residence permit for the first three years; after this, you can get a two-year renewable permit (assuming you have the title deeds registered to your name).

There are a few requirements you must meet to qualify. You must own a property that's suitable for residence and be using it for that purpose. If the property is purchased by multiple shareholders, only one residence permit will be granted for the dwelling.

You'll need to have paid at least one-third of the sales price to qualify for a residence permit, and you must have received permission from the Council of Ministers when buying your property. You'll also need to prove income equal to one monthly minimum wage ($985). This is on top of any monthly amounts you need to pay if you're paying for your property in instalments.

There are other ways to get a residence permit in Northern Cyprus... Expats can qualify for short-term residence permits (maximum one year) by showing that they meet certain income requirements. You must receive a monthly income equal to three times the monthly minimum wage or the annual equivalent of this amount.

The approval and duration of residence permits depend on the discretion of the judicial and administrative authorities. It varies depending on the applicant's reason for requesting a residence permit.

Real Estate Restrictions

Foreigners are restricted in property ownership in Northern Cyprus.

Non-citizens can buy one detached house or one apartment per person, or up to 1 donum of land or 3.5 donums if it's land with a home already on it. (One donum equals 1,338 square meters.)

Setting up a company in Northern Cyprus or using a trustee can allow you to make bigger acquisitions.

Permission from the TRNC Council of Ministers must also be granted before title deeds to property can be registered in your name.

Taxes

Residents are taxed on worldwide income. Non-residents are taxed only on locally earned income.

CHAPTER 19

ALBANIA

Albania has long been a popular low-cost beach escape for European vacationers. Now, it's showing up on the radars of U.S. travelers—and it's easy to understand the appeal.

With a population of around 2.4 million, Albania is situated in southeast Europe. It borders Montenegro to the northwest, Kosovo to the northeast, North Macedonia to the east, and Greece to the south.

It boasts a lively capital city (Tirana), rugged mountain scenery, and a stunning coastline along the Adriatic and Ionian Seas of the Mediterranean.

Albania has already gone viral on TikTok, and since that's not going anywhere, there's sure to be a steady stream of influencers making content about this misunderstood Balkan nation.

For a nation that lived in the shadows of Nazi Germany and the Soviet Union for the better part of a century, the sun is finally starting to shine on Albania—for some 300 days a year in parts of the country. Even in the winter months, you can enjoy warmer temperatures and some sunshine.

During his tenure, George W. Bush became the first sitting U.S. president to visit Albania in 2007. The Albanians were excited for this historic occasion and we've been told by locals just how much Albanians love the U.S. and how happy they are to have Americans booking tours with them to come visit their country.

Albania's quest to join the EU has been going on since 2009, when it first applied for membership. Five years later, it was granted candidate status.

Progress was delayed as Albania's bid was linked to that of North Macedonia, but the two nations were decoupled a few years ago, and Albania can now move forward in an independent bid.

The biggest hurdle in Albania's rise to the EU continues to be the nation's rather large problem with corruption. A few years ago, the mayor of Tirana was arrested and accused of corruption and money laundering to the tune of 1 million euros.

Such a scandal is an obvious roadblock to the nation's ambitious goal of full EU membership by 2030. On the bright side, it was just the mayor of the country's biggest city and not their president…

That would be Bajram Begaj, who took office in July of 2022 after three decades of military service. The first part of his five-year term focused on developing the country's international relations and advancing democratic reforms, including the implementation of voting rights for Albanians abroad in elections.

Tirana County is home to nearly a third of Albania's population, with over 750,000 residents. Coming in a distant second is Durrës County with just under 300,000. For those used to big cities like New York and Toronto, even Albania's biggest cities will feel more like towns.

The country recognizes nine ethnic minorities—Aromanians, Balkan Egyptians, Greeks, Bulgarians, Bosniaks, Macedonians, Montenegrins, Serbs, and Roma.

More and more expats have been finding their way here as well from all corners of the world—the U.S., Turkey, China, and beyond. Even some digital nomads are giving Albania a try these days.

There's definitely a north-south split in Albania, as there are two different dialects on either side of the Shkumbin River. Everyone speaks Albanian (Shqip), but Gheg is spoken in the north, while Tosk is spoken down south.

English is not very widely spoken in Albania, so have patience with the locals, many of whom are happy to chat and practice with you.

Americans can stay in Albania for one year visa-free. That's not a typo. You can stay there for 365 days just because you have an American passport. That gives you plenty of time to bounce around and check out a few different places to see if you like it and find the best fit for you.

Albania's currency is called the lek, and you'll get used to seeing the bills and coins since cash is still widely used here, so it's best to keep cash on you for transactions in shops, restaurants, taxis, buses, etc.

As well as vying for full EU membership, Albania is a NATO member, and development is underway, including infrastructure improvements and a growing tourism sector.

If you're looking for an easy way to spend quality time in Europe, Albania is a great option. The generous one-year tourist visa is tough to beat, and traveling to neighboring countries like Montenegro, North Macedonia, Kosovo, and Serbia doesn't count towards your Schengen Zone days.

Italy and Greece are easily accessible by ferry, and you can catch cheap flights all over Europe from Tirana, so it's a solid choice for a home base in the region. There's also plenty to see and do in Albania, with beaches, mountains, national parks, historical towns, and much more.

Top Picks For A New Life In Albania

Vlorë

One of the most popular destinations in Albania is Vlorë, a coastal town along the Albanian Riviera with rich history and gorgeous beaches. Here, it's possible to buy property for $100,000 or perhaps much less. And rent is low cost, too. For a place right on the coast in Vlorë, you can get a one-bedroom apartment with a balcony overlooking the sea for about $750 per month.

This is an up-and-coming destination so now may be the time to check it out while it's still somewhat off the radar, because this place is going to attract the crowds sooner than later.

It's a tourist beach town, and it's also the former capital and the country's third-largest city...and offers all the amenities you'd need for year-round living.

In the shoulder season, Vlorë is quiet. In these winter months you can enjoy long walks on the coast or relax on the beach or in a restaurant or café.

In the busier summer months, there are beach clubs and all sorts of water activities to keep you entertained, including boat trips, snorkeling, and kayaking. The beaches along this riviera are stunning, with turquoise waters and white sand. You can explore caves and coves or hike in the nearby Ceraunian mountains.

As Vlorë has a rich history, there is plenty to do for culture with museums, monuments, and Ottoman architecture all around.

Or visit the ancient city of Apollonia (33 kms from Vlorë), where you'll see Greek and Roman ruins. Entrance tickets cost $6.40 per person to visit the ruins and a small museum on-site. It's interesting to see from a historical point of view, as Apollonia was once a thriving city where Augustus (first emperor of Rome) studied.

All within driving distance of Vlorë, you can visit natural mountain springs, castles, and national parks. All stunning and worth the trip.

Although cash is king in Albania, cards are accepted at most supermarkets and restaurants.

There are plenty of options for grocery shopping in Vlorë and you'll get the essentials you need for about $25 to $40. That includes coffee, milk, juice, yogurt, granola, some snacks, pasta, pesto, and shrimp.

For less than $5 you can pick up a big bag of fresh produce from a roadside stand.

The bigger, nicer supermarkets are located in the central part of town, like the Italian store Conad, which can be a little pricier than the local stores.

Your monthly grocery bill will come to about $350. Budget about $70 a month for utilities—electricity, water, heating, and cooling.

Albanians love their espresso, and if you do too, the good news is that it only costs a couple bucks. For lunch, coffee and a grilled cheese sandwich will cost $3 to $4 per person.

For a mid-range dinner, you'll be paying about $10 to $15. That would get you a kebab or grilled chicken, including a draft beer.

For a more upmarket restaurant, expect to pay about $25 for a nice dinner with a few drinks. Even in a traditional Albanian restaurant where you can get fresh seafood and a generous pour of wine, it will cost just under $50 for two.

A couple can live very well in Vlorë on $1,500 to $1,700 a month.

For transport, a cab won't cost more than $10, and the local bus will only set you back 42 cents. To get out and explore the area, you can rent a motorbike, which costs $25 a day.

The roads on the coast are quite steep and winding, but they are well paved. You just need to be careful on hair-pin bends. Drive slowly. The good news is that the roads are relatively quiet.

There are no direct flights to the U.S. at the moment. You can make a connection through various different European hubs like Paris, Istanbul, Amsterdam, London, Frankfurt, or Munich. Flights arrive into Tirana, and Vlorë is another three hours away by car.

You can fly to Tirana from Toronto nonstop with Air Transat during the high season.

A new international airport in Vlorë is opening this summer. Currently, there are no plans for flights from the U.S. or Canada, but low-cost European airlines have shown an interest in connecting flights from Europe. The airport is located only 10 miles from Vlorë city center.

If and when it operates direct options to the U.S., this could be a boon for the tourism industry in Albania. Without the need for the three- to four-hour ride from Tirana, the Albanian coast could see an influx of American visitors.

It's also possible to travel to Albania by ferry from Corfu, Greece, which is just a short trip from Vlorë. You'll arrive in Sarande, and from there, the journey is 50 miles.

You can travel to Albania by ferry from Italy as well—from Bari to

Vlorë or Durres, from Ancona to Durres, and from Brindisi to Vlorë. There are overnight options for these longer trips that take seven to nine hours.

Uber does not operate in Albania, but there are local rideshare apps that you can download, such as MerrTaxi.

Vlorë enjoys a Mediterranean climate. Summers are hot and dry with temperatures ranging from 82 to 90°F, but the sea breeze keeps things cool for the most part. Winters are a little cooler with temperatures ranging from 46 to 77°F. November is typically the wettest month, and it rarely snows.

The public hospital in Vlorë (Vlorë Regional Hospital) has recently undergone major renovations and equipment upgrades. It caters for emergency care, surgery, pediatrics, diagnostics, internal medicine, and outpatient services.

There is also a growing network of private clinics with English-speaking doctors. The Primus Medical Center offers specialty practices such as cardiology, dental, and physiotherapy.

For anything more serious, expats tend to travel to Tirana's private hospitals.

Vlorë is generally safe for expats. Albanians are friendly and hospitable, and petty crime is rare. Though not a common occurrence, you should watch out for things like phone theft and taxi drivers overcharging. The risk of violent crime is low.

Albania is still somewhat unknown, and it hasn't been overrun with tourists... yet. That could change as infrastructure improves and the stunning beaches of the Albanian Riviera become more accessible.

For now, Albania flies under the radar and still has that hidden gem feel to it.

Health Care In Albania

The public health care system in Albania is improving year on year, and all residents receive free primary care. Doctors are well trained and have often studied abroad. All major cities have a public hospital, and the main hospital in the country—University Hospital Center "Mother Teresa"—is in Tirana.

Expats usually opt for private care, as there are usually long wait times for non-urgent cases in the public sector.

In the private sector, you'll find more English-speaking doctors and better facilities. Private insurance is cheap—about $40 to $110 a month, depending on your coverage. A visit to a GP will cost you $30 to $65, and a specialist is $45 to $110.

Most of the private hospitals are based in Tirana, but you'll find private clinics throughout the country.

Residency Requirements

If you're American and are hoping to spend some quality time in Albania, there's great news—you can stay for up to a year visa-free. There's no paperwork or cost involved whatsoever, either. Albania will let you stay for 365 days just because.

Compared to the policy of the Schengen Zone (which Albania isn't part of)—where you can spend 90 days in a 180-day period across the 29 member states—this is a much easier way to relocate to Europe.

Albania has also followed in the footsteps of many nations by offering a "Unique Permit" that's being referred to by many as a digital nomad visa. You can apply for it online, and it's valid for up to one year, which you can then renew annually for up to five years. At that point, it's possible to apply for permanent residency.

The fine print says a requirement is that you have "sufficient income to afford accommodation and living in Albania," but there's no specific figure given. After digging around, we found that $10,000 is good enough.

Who knows, though... With a shrinking population, it's possible that Albania is swinging the doors wide open for foreigners looking to relocate there, especially those who already have employment that they can do remotely.

The application is conducted online through the official e-Albania portal. Applicants need to provide documentation such as proof of employment or freelance contracts, evidence of income, a valid passport, proof of accommodation in Albania, a clean criminal record, and health insurance coverage valid in Albania.

If you feel like one year isn't enough and you know you want to stay longer than that, you can apply for temporary residency upon arrival in Albania. This needs to be done within 30 days of arrival and can be done through the e-Albania online portal.

After five years of extending your temporary residency, you can apply to become a permanent resident of Albania. While the process to gain permanent residency in Albania is clearly defined, it requires careful adherence to application timelines and documentation requirements. Seeking assistance from legal experts familiar with Albanian immigration laws can facilitate a smoother experience.

Real Estate Restrictions

Foreigners are permitted to buy residential and commercial property in Albania but there are restrictions on agricultural land and coastal land within 200 meters of the shoreline.

Taxes

Personal income tax runs on a progressive rate from 0% to 23%. There's a capital gains tax of 15%, which is applied on rental income and the same in the case of resale properties. If you live in Albania for more than 183 days over a period of 365 days, you are considered a resident for tax purposes.

VII

SOUTHEAST ASIA

For those with an eye on both the bottom line and big adventure, Asia can be a great choice.

Not only does it offer some of the world's most cost-friendly expat havens, but it's also a land of rich culture, stunning natural beauty, and friendly locals who respect older folks.

Southeast Asia is a remarkably diverse land that over the past decades has become much more welcoming to Westerners. In several countries in this region, you no longer need to make visa runs in order to stay long-term.

Nor is it necessary to invest great sums of cash in order to buy residency through investment visas. Today, even while living on a modest pension or savings, you have the opportunity to live full-time in several welcoming, tropical paradises.

Although there are many advantages to living in this part of the world, the low cost of living is the one factor that probably attracts the most people. With the exception of Singapore, your money goes much further in Southeast Asia than it would in the United States or any other Western country. This doesn't mean that the standard of living is less; it only means that things cost less here.

You will also get better value for health care. Doctor visits cost less than $20 throughout most of Southeast Asia, and the care that you receive will likely exceed your expectations. Highly skilled, English-speaking doctors are the norm here. They work in hygienic offices with modern equipment, and may be affiliated with state-of-the-art, internationally accredited hospitals. Both Thailand and Malaysia are considered among the top five countries in the world for medical tourism.

There are practical financial reasons for living in Southeast Asia. Several countries will gladly waive any minimum monthly income requirements for long-term or permanent residency if you invest in a fixed deposit account at a local bank. In countries where a monthly pension is required, the qualifying amount is often surprisingly low and your monthly social security would more than cover your costs.

One thing you should factor into your yearly budget is the cost of flying to and from North America. Southeast Asia is great for the low cost of living it allows, but it's far from the States and Canada, and long-distance international flights can quickly add up.

English is widely understood throughout this region. It is an official language of the Philippines and parts of Malaysia.

This rapidly developing part of the world is practically bursting with opportunity. Whether you're interested in exploring, retiring, or investing in this region, you'll have your pick of places to consider. With unspoiled tropical islands and beaches, thoroughly cosmopolitan cities, lush jungles and mountains, sunny weather, friendly locals, and welcoming immigration laws, there is something for everybody in Southeast Asia.

CHAPTER 20

THAILAND

Thailand became a big draw for expats over 30 years ago. Expats arrived for the extremely low cost of living and warm weather all year. The food is great, there's a range of living options—on the beach, amongst the mountains, and for the brave, the jungle... Thailand has modern cities, with opportunities for entrepreneurs and slow-paced historic cities for a more relaxed life... there's somewhere in Thailand to suit everyone.

The capital, Bangkok, is where most expats choose to live and has the best facilities. If you have children, Bangkok offers a number of quality international schools for you to choose from. Depending on which country you come from, you can find a school that will teach your native curriculum.

Thailand has plenty of expat-owned businesses and expat communities are not hard to find. Much of the social life revolves around bars and restaurants, but you can also find expat clubs who organize things like trips to the beach, scuba diving, football leagues, and trekking. Yoga classes and rooftop bars also act as a magnet for expats.

Thailand is a safe place to live and the cities are well policed. Many expats report that they feel safer in Thailand than they did at home.

The language is difficult to learn and most foreigners fail to learn more than a few basic phrases. Fortunately, most locals speak some English, so it's possible to get by on English alone.

Real estate in Thailand covers all price ranges. You can live in a small studio apartment, suitable for Western tastes, in some spots for $500. It is possible to find cheaper, but they are likely to be too cramped and without air conditioning. There is also an array of luxury properties on offer. In an apples-to-apples comparison, these are cheap compared to luxury properties in other countries.

Thailand boasts a world-class culinary scene and eating out is a major perk when you live here. Expats have plenty of historic sites to visit and you are unlikely to run out of things to do or see. Taxis, the best way of getting around Thailand, are affordable.

Expat communities are a vital resource for many on an overseas adventure. They can help you with everything from finding a good plumber to buying a car or setting up a broadband provider. Many expats have social activities and are involved helping in the local community, giving you different ways to make use of your time.

Moving to an area with other expats provides you with a safety net and a social network. Not only that, they are the walking, talking proof that "It can be done."

If you're having doubts about succeeding overseas, you only need to look at your fellow expats to see that it is possible.

Top Picks For A New Life In Thailand

Hua Hin

For most retirees, Hua Hin fits the bill of the ideal retirement haven. This charming seaside town is nestled along the Gulf of Thailand and offers miles of soft, sandy beaches.

It enjoys warm, sunny weather year-round, which means residents can take full advantage of the excellent recreation opportunities available. Hiking, taking strolls on the beach, water sports, and playing rounds at world-class golf courses are just a few of the highlights of Hua Hin's active lifestyle.

Hua Hin stands out for its elegant, relaxed atmosphere. It's been the preferred retreat for the Thai royal family since the 1920s, and this heritage adds a layer of charm to the city. It also means that Hua Hin is calmer, cleaner, and safer than other places in Thailand, like Pattaya and Phuket, which have reputations as party destinations.

Today's Hua Hin blends traditional Thai charm with modern convenience. The town is steeped in history and culture, which is reflected in its unique architecture, parks, and festivals.

It's well-appointed with solid infrastructure and all kinds of urban amenities—countless restaurants, shopping centers, internationally accredited medical care, and more. For everything that you can't find in Hua Hin, Bangkok, Thailand's bustling capital city, is only a three-hour drive away.

Its vast open-air markets are hives of activity. You can shop, enjoy tasty, affordable food at market stalls, or just take in the lively ambiance. Hua Hin also has modern, air-conditioned malls if you prefer a more Western-style shopping experience.

There's an abundance of restaurants here, from seafood restaurants along the waterfront to steakhouses to Indian restaurants to traditional Thai dishes. Eating out is an affordable indulgence.

As the former summer home of the Thai royal family, there are some historically significant buildings in Hua Hin. Some examples are the Railway Station, which features the Royal Waiting Room, and Buddhist temples, such as Khao Takiab, built for King Rama VII in the 1920s.

Hua Hin hosts an annual jazz festival on the beach, attracting musicians from around the world. There's also an artist village that features art galleries, antiques, artist studios, rare collections, and more.

The main beach is a three-mile stretch of soft, clean sand punctuated by rocky outcrops. The waves are calm and the waters are shallow, making them safe for swimming.

Water sports (especially kiteboarding) are popular here. You can swim, take kite or sailboarding lessons, jet ski, sail, windsurf, parasail, kayak, snorkel, and scuba dive. Game fishing and boat trips are also available.

The Royal Hua Hin 18-hole golf course is just five minutes from the town center. In the city's radius, there are a further 14 courses, all top of the line, with high-end amenities and beautiful views, yet affordable.

Hua Hin also has plenty of other recreation opportunities, including gyms, Muay Thai boxing, paths for cycling and walking, and several national parks nearby.

True of most Southeast Asian destinations, Hua Hin is an affordable place to live. The cost of living is significantly lower than that of the United States or Canada. On average, a couple's basic monthly budget here will range from $1,400 to $2,000. Generally speaking, it's around 70% cheaper than the cost of living in the United States.

Spend a bit more and you can enjoy a bona fide luxury standard of living, with high-end accommodation and household staff.

Whether you're dining at a seafront restaurant, playing a round of golf, or indulging in wellness activities like yoga or spa treatments, opportunities for indulgence are abundant and budget-friendly.

You can save on the cost of rent (the typical range is $300 to $800 per month), eating out, and groceries. Groceries are cheap as well, especially if you shop for local products. As always, imported items cost a premium.

You can buy studio condos here for under $50,000. One-bedroom condos start around $70,000 and houses from around $85,000.

One area where you can easily afford to indulge in Hua Hin is eating out. Thai food is world-renowned for its flavors and healthy ingredients and as expats will tell you, eating out is usually cheaper (and better!) than cooking for yourself.

A couple can dine out for as little as $10. Opt for more upscale restaurants and you'll pay around $25 for two. Include a bottle of wine and a table in a sea-view restaurant and dinner still won't set you back more than $50, including tax and tip.

Coffees run from $1 to $2, a beer is around $2, and a glass of wine around $5.

For groceries, you'll find Western-style supermarkets including Lotus's, Tops, and Big C. It's also worth a trip to the local market or other street vendors for fresh produce which will be cheaper than in the big stores. You'll also find plenty of 7-Eleven stores handy for snacks and drinks.

Little luxuries like massages can also be a part of your weekly routine here with an hour-long massage costing as little as $10. A visit to a national park is around $8, a pass for the nearby water park is $35, a one-day cookery class is $55, and a kite-surfing lesson is around $100.

For golfers, 18 holes will set you back anywhere from $45 to $120 depending on your pick of the nearby courses.

Hua Hin is very walkable, keeping transport costs low. A *songthaew* (local shared minibus) or tuk-tuk trip across town won't cost more than a couple bucks. A round-trip train ticket to Bangkok starts at just $20.

Hua Hin has one of the most agreeable climates in Thailand. Unlike the rest of the country, it doesn't get heavy rain. It's naturally drier. There are two seasons: rainy and dry. Rainy season is from June to October, when you get daily but short-lived showers. Dry season is from November to April, when conditions are dry and sunny.

Hua Hin is perfect for lovers of warm weather, but you'll want air conditioning at home to live comfortably.

Health care is high-quality and so affordable that many expats pay out of pocket. A GP visit will cost around $30.

In Thailand, you'll find a mix of public hospitals and high-quality private hospitals. Many of the private facilities are internationally accredited and have English-speaking staff, state-of-the-art equipment, and spotless facilities.

One such hospital is located in Hua Hin. It's called Bangkok Hospital Hua Hin, and it's JCI-accredited because of its excellent standards of care. You should feel confident having your health care needs taken care of here...

A 24-hour stay in a standard room (which has A/C, a TV, bathroom, intercom, a sofa for relatives, and WiFi) is $233—which includes meals and a nursing fee. Opt for the executive suite and you'll pay

$359. For stays of less than 12 hours, the rate will be reduced by 50%.

Plus, as part of the BDMS network, patients at Bangkok Hospital Hua Hin have access to a broad range of specialists across Thailand. The hospital has English-speaking staff, an online appointment booking service, and appointments with a consultant start from around $25.

Hua Hin is also home to a second private hospital, San Paulo Hospital, which offers a range of services, including 24/7 emergency care, and specialized care in areas including cardiology, orthopedics, and internal medicine. They also offer a "Silver Age Health Screening" for patients aged 55 and over which costs around $300 for men and $430 for women. General consultations start from just $15.

San Paulo Hospital has English speaking staff and extensive experience in working with patients making use of a range of overseas health and travel insurance policies.

Hua Hin Hospital is a public facility which is even more affordable but wait times will be longer. Thailand's public health care system is known as the Universal Coverage Scheme (UCS) and is used by both locals and expats.

Hua Hin is also home to a number of excellent multi-purpose clinics offering convenient walk-in services, English-speaking staff, labs, pharmacies, and treatment options ranging from physiotherapy to acupuncture. Prices start from $15.

Dental services here are professional, reliable, and affordable. Nana Dental Clinic is a popular choice for expats. A cleaning costs from $25 to $46, fillings from $25 to $125, root canals run from $215 to $340, and implants start from $1,400.

Because Thailand receives so many tourists, many locals speak English fairly well... enough for you to order food at restaurants, buy groceries successfully, and achieve day-to-day tasks.

English is a required class for all Thai school children as well as anyone attending university, so, as is often the case, the younger generation is more fluent than the older.

Locals may speak English with an accent that's hard for newcomers to understand. It's not a requirement, but picking up the basics of Thai is recommended.

Of Hua Hin's 85,000 people, roughly 20% are expats. The community is vibrant and active, organizing clubs and events—from book clubs to wine tastings to golf groups—so that, on any given day, there's something to do in Hua Hin.

Hua Hin's expat community is fairly large and diverse, made up of people of different age demographics—retirees, families with children, workers, and digital nomads from around the world.

Something social is almost always going on, from soccer leagues to pool tournaments, darts leagues to running groups, volunteering, language classes, and more.

Resources like Hua Hin Expats and Expats in Hua Hin on Facebook, plus websites like Hua Hin Forum and Hua Hin Today, are available for newcomers.

Public transportation options are quirky but functional. They consist of *songthaews*, which are pickup trucks converted into shared taxis, as well as tuk-tuks, buses, and trains. You won't need a car here.

To get to Hua Hin from overseas, you'll need to take long-haul flights with layovers en route. Southeast Asia is about as far as you can go from North America, and there's no international airport in town.

You'll likely fly to Suvarnabhumi International Airport in Bangkok, connecting through another city in Asia or Europe, and then drive from Bangkok to Hua Hin (about three hours).

From Montreal you can fly to Bangkok via Paris, Istanbul, or Dubai and total travel time is around 21 hours.

From Philadelphia you can fly to Bangkok via Paris, Milan, or Amsterdam and total travel time is around 22 hours.

From Hawaii you can fly to Bangkok via Tokyo, Manila, or Seoul and total travel time is around 18 hours.

From Bangkok, getting to Hua Hin is straightforward: you can book a private transfer or taxi, catch the direct airport bus, or take a train on the Southern Line.

Thailand is generally a safe country. It ranks at #86 on the Global Peace Index. Violent crime is relatively low. Petty crime, particularly tourist scams and low-level theft, can be a concern.

Thailand receives a huge number of tourists, many of whom come here to party and lose all inhibitions, making them easy targets. Hua Hin does not have a party town reputation, so this is less of risk here. It's considered one of Thailand's safest towns, although you should always be mindful of pickpocketing and bag-snatching.

Hua Hin could be your ideal retirement haven if you're looking for a low-key Thai city with a tranquil ambiance and royal heritage, plus beautiful beaches, plenty of opportunities to golf, and excellent cuisine.

Phuket

With gorgeous beaches, a low cost of living, and excellent health care, Phuket offers a lifestyle so appealing that it has attracted an expat community of more than 115,000.

The reason for its popularity? Beautiful beaches, first and foremost.

Phuket is the biggest island in Thailand, floating off the west coast of the mainland. It's ringed by pearly white sands, hemmed in by limestone cliffs, and lapped by the warm waters of the Andaman Sea.

Natural beauty in general helps explain Phuket's popularity. On land, there are sprawling national parks that are dense with jungle, spliced by rivers and waterfalls, and pocked with caves.

All of this gives way to plenty of outdoor recreation opportunities. Everything from snorkeling and island-hopping to hiking and golfing at world-renowned courses is available from your doorstep in Phuket.

Cultural entertainment begins with the cuisine. Thai food is world-famous for being healthy, affordable, and extremely tasty.

Phuket has regional dishes that you can sample for a dollar or two per plate. You'll also find international fare. Dining options range from market stalls to Michelin-starred experiences...

The local culture is predominantly Buddhist, with dozens of temples scattered around the island. Old Phuket Town is an eclectic historical hub, famed for its colorful Sino-Portuguese architecture as well as funky cafés, restaurants, bars, and boutiques.

Wellness is a big trend in Phuket, particularly massage and yoga, but also breathing, meditation, and mindfulness. You can indulge in high-quality spa treatments for a fraction of what you'd pay back home—about $10 for an hour-long massage.

Phuket is also a dream destination for outdoor recreation lovers.

The beaches are the biggest draw. They range in size and style from luxury set-ups inside exquisite resorts to laid-back, little-known stretches where you can sprawl out directly on the sand.

Most offer activities like surfing, snorkeling, swimming, and diving. Yachting, jet-skiing, parasailing, kite surfing, and deep sea fishing are also popular activities.

In southeastern Phuket, you can catch boats to small islands, like the Phi Phi Islands, famous for their turquoise waters, white-sand beaches, and jagged limestone cliffs.

On land, you can chase waterfalls and explore sprawling national parks, full of unique wildlife species.

Golf is a beloved pastime here, with nine courses in the vicinity. There are also gyms across the island where you can exercise or pick up the national sport, Muay Thai.

Southeast Asia is famous for its affordability, and while Phuket's popularity with tourists and expats has driven up prices, it's still budget-friendly by most people's standards. The average monthly cost of living for two is about $1,702.

Rent ranges from $500 to $800. Your utilities, including air conditioning, will be about $92 per month. Eating out twice a week, going for drinks twice a week, and going to the movies twice a month will cost you and yours about $370 and a grocery shop will be about $450 to $500 a month.

That said, budgets can swing in both directions: if you shop and eat local, you'll save greatly; if you indulge in the luxury amenities available, you can also spend big.

Phuket has a tropical monsoon climate, with significant rains during its wet season (April to November). Dry season is from December to March.

It's close to the equator, so it has hot to warm weather throughout the year. Average highs are 90°F (32°C); average lows are 75°F (24°C); and humidity is 77%.

There are two private hospitals in Phuket: Bangkok Phuket Hospital and Phuket International Hospital. They treat thousands of foreigners and locals every year, offering superb quality care and English-speaking staff.

There are also four government hospitals and plenty of medical centers, dental offices, and pharmacies across Phuket.

Medical fees vary, but you can expect to pay about $30 for a regular visit at a private hospital. The same visit at a public hospital costs about $10.

Because Phuket attracts people from all over the world, the locals have become handy with English, to the point where you can have casual conversations with them. Plenty of expats get by without ever learning Thai, although learning the basics is always a good idea.

Phuket's expat community is big and well-established. Social groups organize around diverse interests. There are sports leagues, volunteer opportunities, get-togethers at bars, trivia nights, charity events, networking events, and more, making it easy to build connections here.

Public transportation options include taxis, ride-sharing apps, tuk-tuks, *songthaews* (converted pickup trucks), and buses, but you will be more comfortable with a car.

To get here from abroad, you'll likely need to make a stopover at a bigger Asian travel hub before making an onward connection to Phuket. The trip is long and can be expensive...

In Phuket, serious crime rates are low, and it's generally a safe place to live and visit... But the abundance of tourists, especially those attracted by the island's party reputation, has given rise to scams and a seedy underbelly in Phuket.

Foreigners are seen as easy targets for scams, gringo-pricing, and pickpocketing in touristy areas. ATM skimming is an issue. Crime is something you have to think about day-to-day here, although keeping safe is relatively easy.

Phuket offers a large, well-established expat community with many English-speakers, gorgeous beaches and golfing opportunities, plus a low cost of living for a high quality of life, including top-notch health care.

Chiang Mai

Located in northern Thailand, about 435 miles (700 km) north of Bangkok in the mountainous Thai highlands, Chiang Mai isn't just Thailand's second city... it's the country's favorite city.

Chiang Mai is probably the most livable city in Southeast Asia for foreigners. Good infrastructure, a thriving expat community, and friendly native hosts ensure it will hold that distinction for years to come.

With a population of just over 1.2 million, Chiang Mai is not a big city by Southeast Asian standards. Big sister Bangkok boasts 12 million inhabitants, a figure considered an understatement by folks who live there.

Chiang Mai only has a few buildings that could be considered high rise, and even those are less than 30 floors. Chinese-style shophouse architecture is what you'll see here, with some modern developments mixed in.

The city viewed from a higher elevation looks like a collection of neighborhoods that grew into each other to fill in the river valley. Chiang Mai is pretty busy, but it's by no means Bangkok busy.

Rather than suffer island-style isolation, residents enjoy total connection to the rest of the world. Internet connections are high-speed and reliable, great roads lead in every direction, and an ever-expanding international airport is at your disposal. The overnight train to Bangkok is a trip everyone should take at least once.

Because Chiang Mai is a relatively compact city, drive times are minimal. Small cars, motorbikes, scooters, and even bicycles make up the majority of personal transportation. Folks who desire a more suburban or rural setting definitely need their own transportation.

Many people new to Chiang Mai start out in the Old City before moving on to a different part of town. This is the historical center of Chiang Mai and a great place to live if you like being surrounded by temples, monuments, and monks— making for a great starting point.

The moat and surrounding park are immaculately maintained and this is a pleasant neighborhood to discover on foot or bicycle. The area is awash in restaurants, bars, and cafés of all descriptions: Thai-style markets and street vendors are also found everywhere.

Residents who live inside the Old City, surrounded by the moat in the center of Chiang Mai, have the most vehicular freedom. A wide variety of public transport is available.

Thailand's Northern capital retains all the charms of past lives while graciously embracing the present. Among more than 300 ancient temples and monuments you'll find museums and seven universities.

There are 10 national parks, 12 golf courses, more than a dozen waterfalls, and an international airport that handles 130 flights per day. Chiang Mai is a complex little metropolis with many layers to unfold.

Eating and drinking is a favorite pastime here. Restaurants from virtually every corner of the world thrive all around the city. Markets of every description supply farm-fresh fish, meat, fruits, and vegetables for those who cook at home. Northern Thai cuisine is some of the best eats in Asia.

The big market near the Chiang Mai Gate in the Old City is a good place to shop for *kanom* (Thai desserts). If you've never tried Thai desserts, put it on your list. They are colorful and packed with unexpected flavors.

From antique shops to mega malls, Chiang Mai has everything you need to get your shopping fix. Malls and shopping centers serve many purposes. Some people go to buy things they need… others go to be entertained or enjoy a good meal… many families make a trip to the mall a big event.

The Ping River (sometimes called Mae Ping) runs through Chiang Mai and offers some of the city's more spectacular views. Most of the taller apartments, condo buildings, and nice hotels make good use of the river view. Residents of Riverside neighborhoods enjoy a connection to nature and the convenience of living near the city. Transportation in this area can be solved with tuk-tuks, baht buses, bicycles, and pedicabs.

Riverside is also walking distance to the Night Bazaar, which is a fun attraction. It's great for people watching and home to some funky local music joints.

If hip and trendy is what you crave, head to Nimmanhaemin Road… aka Nimman. You could probably drink coffee in a different café every day and never visit the same place twice.

One of the best features of Chiang Mai is how quickly you can be out of the city and into the countryside. Several further flung suburbs have attracted expats who desire an easy-going, stay-at-home lifestyle. With the natural backdrop of misty mountains, it's easy to just sit in your garden or on your balcony and soak it in.

House rentals located in the winding back streets cover a wide range of prices. For $350 you could get a two-bedroom bungalow with a garden, for $750 you could rent a three-bedroom villa with a private swimming pool. The best way to find an individual house for rent is to get on a bicycle and ride around looking for signs.

Many serviced apartments are located in the Old City. For $482 you can get a spacious one- or two-bedroom flat with hot water, air conditioning, nice furnishings, and good WiFi (utilities and basic cable are normally included). Serviced apartments offer the best deals for renting month-to-month without a long-term lease.

The rental market in Nimmanhaemin is split between brand-new buildings and those several years old. Shop carefully and you can find some real bargains.

No matter what your budget might be, you'll never go hungry in Chiang Mai... Local Thai markets are usually open-air establishments either in a static location or recurring at a set place and time weekly. Most offer a wide variety of fruits, vegetables, herbs, spices, and anything else related to cooking. Shopping at the market will cost you approximately 30% less than shopping at the supermarket.

You can live a comfortable life for $1,500. Retirees with a $2,000 monthly budget could live a great life in Chiang Mai.

Utilities will come in around $140 a month, which include electricity, heating and cooling, water, internet and cable. Your monthly grocery bill will be about $300 a month. Budget another $300 a month for entertainment—that includes eating out twice a week, going to the movies, or enjoying drinks at a local watering hole.

The health care options in Chiang Mai are second only to big sister Bangkok. Several private international hospitals are at your service, including Chiang Ram Hospital; Sri Pat Medical Center And Maharaj Nakorn Hospital; Lanna Hospital; Rajavej Hospital; McCormick Hospital; and Bangkok Hospital Chiang Mai.

All have state of the art facilities and English-speaking staff.

Dozens of other clinics, smaller hospitals, and specialty treatment centers are scattered around Chiang Mai. Those that serve foreigners make that fact apparent. Government hospitals in Thailand are generally for Thai people participating in their national health plan.

Pharmacies are found all over Chiang Mai but not all dispense medicine. Sometimes a pharmacy sign is on the door, but a shampoo and whitening cream store is what's inside.

Many Thai-owned and run pharmacies are legitimate, but until you find one you can depend on, go with a trusted name: Use international-brand pharmacies like Boots or Watsons.

With a range of 68 to 86°F (20 to 30°C), Chiang Mai enjoys the mildest climate in the country, its average temperatures are rather like the Southeastern United States. The season for heavy rain is short (July through September) and November through February is perfect.

In Chiang Mai, foreigners live all over town, they experience many different lifestyles, and they connect to Thai culture in a more meaningful way. Chiang Mai is not a "tourists-who-stayed" kind of town.

The depth and quality of the expat community in a retirement location can be the most important variable in the whole equation. An idyllic backdrop and affordable housing do not a paradise make.

In fact, your little slice of heaven can turn into a palm-tree-lined prison if you don't have someone to share a beer with. Isolation is the dark side of being an expat that nobody talks about.

Fortunately, you won't have that problem in Chiang Mai—conservative estimates say there are 30,000 foreigners living here. Of course, not all 30,000 are here full-time, some are snowbirds—they come when it gets cold wherever they are from and stay until springtime.

There is a recognizable group of retired American servicemen and State Department types that were bitten by the Chiang Mai bug and returned to retire here. The U.S. government has a consulate in Chiang Mai that also makes this a favorite locale for Americans.

With 30,000 expats in Chiang Mai, you can bet there are plenty of clubs and organizations a new arrival can get into. The Chiang Mai Expat Club (CEC) is easily the turnkey operation to contact. This is a good hub to make connections to other organizations.

It is entirely possible that Chiang Mai could be the safest place you've ever lived—it's the most peaceful and least violent of any major metropolitan area in Thailand. What late night party scene there is in Chiang Mai is pretty tame. Bars and clubs are told to close at a certain time, and they do. Tourists come to Chiang Mai to see the temples and spot elephants... there's just not that much trouble to get into.

Even petty crime is uncommon in Chiang Mai. If you come from a place that is desensitized to large amounts of criminal activity, Chiang Mai will seem like Mayberry.

The police in Chiang Mai are polite and helpful. While some police departments in other cities have tarnished reputations for being corrupt and opportunistic, Chiang Mai police are respectful and respected.

Chiang Mai, Thailand's "Rose of the North," is hugely popular with expats for a reason. Here, you'll enjoy great health care, safety, lots of things to do and people to see, and to top it off, you'll have a comfortable standard of living on a very low monthly budget.

Health Care In Thailand

The quality and availability of health care in major Thai cities is often superior to the States. Patients are flown from all over Asia for life-saving and one-of-a-kind procedures that could only be performed in Bangkok. Bumrungrad International Hospital hosts a million medical tourists per year. Professional athletes from the States come to Pivavate Hospital for orthopedic surgery critical to their careers.

Stories about how affordable health care in Thailand can be are true. A routine visit to the dentist that includes cleaning and minor filling costs less than $30. An annual head-to-toe physical examination, including blood work, chest X-rays, EKG, and CT scan is around $500. Most surgery costs 30% to 40% less than in the West.

Many major insurance companies offer health care plans that cover expats in Asia. If you are from the United States or Canada, be prepared—the best rates are achieved by choosing to be covered anywhere in the world excluding the States and Canada.

Moving to Thailand to simply be close to the medical care is a key driver for some expats. It's a good idea to maintain private insurance in order to access private facilities. Some popular private health insurers in Thailand are Thai Health Insurance, AIA Thailand, and Bangkok Insurance.

Medical procedures in Thailand cost anywhere from 20% to 80% less than they do in the States.

Residency Requirements

Thailand offers several paths to residency, although for retirees, the most straightforward is the Non-Immigrant O-A Visa. The basic requirement is that you are at least 50 years old and meet one of the following requirements:

- Make a security deposit of 800,000 baht (about $23,750) into a Thai bank two months before applying;
- Show monthly income of 65,000 baht (about $1,930);
- A combination of the security deposit and annual income that equals 800,000 baht.
- Other requirements include a medical certificate, criminal record check, and health insurance (minimum coverage: 400,000 THB inpatient (around $12,000), 40,000 THB outpatient (around $1,200).

The visa is granted for one year and can be renewed annually, provided you continue to meet the financial and insurance conditions.

Real Estate Restrictions

Like many Southeast Asian countries, Thailand has some restrictions for foreigners when it comes to buying property.

Foreigners can't own land unless there's a treaty or exemption in place. The only option is to lease land on a long-term (usually 30-year) renewable basis.

Ownership of a condo apartment is allowed, but only 49% of the units in any condo building can be foreign-owned.

Taxes

Thailand's income tax rates range from 5% to 35%. Capital gains are generally taxed as income (except in a handful of specific cases).

Thailand does not impose a wealth tax, but it imposes an inheritance tax of 10% on legacies valued at over 100 million baht (about $2.9 million). In the case of heirs, the rate is 5%.

CHAPTER 21

THE PHILIPPINES

With its low-key lifestyle, exotic culture, and natural beauty, it's easy to see why the Philippines is a popular retirement destination for many.

Retirees on a budget also benefit from the low cost of living you can enjoy there. In fact, a couple could live comfortably in the Philippines from as little as $1,500 a month. For $2,300 per month, you could enjoy a lux lifestyle.

Plus, if you don't want the hassle of learning a new language, the Philippines truly is a great option—English is widely spoken (more than half the country's population of 120 million people speak it), making daily life easy to navigate.

The Filipino culture is social and family oriented. If you're looking to be well-received among a community that is warm, welcoming, and respectful, the Philippines fits the bill.

In terms of residency, the Philippines offers specific, easy to attain programs to incentivize expats to move. One such option is the Special Resident Retiree's Visa (SRRV), a non-immigrant visa that allows multiple-entry and indefinite stay in the Philippines.

The SRRV offers other special benefits, which allows you to work, study, or invest in the country, and also grants you discounts from the Philippine Retirement Authority partners.

The government has also introduced a new digital nomad visa for non-immigrant foreigners who want to stay in the country for a temporary maximum period of one year, and holders may renew the visa for an additional year.

The Philippines offers a wide variety of lifestyle options—from laid-back coastal towns to buzzing city centers. With over 7,500 islands, otherworldly landscapes with tropical beaches and crystal-clear waters, and a very low cost of living, the Philippines is undeniably enticing as an overseas retirement haven.

Top Picks For A New Life In The Philippines

Dumaguete

Dumaguete, a city of 135,000 on the island of Negros, is known as "The City of Gentle People." This university city is popular with expats for its affordable lifestyle, attractive harbor-front promenade, and convenient location that allows for easy getaways.

Silliman University, founded in 1901, is the province's largest school and a commanding presence in central Dumaguete. The college campus covers over 610,000 square meters, mainly in the downtown area.

Dumaguete has been featured among Forbes' top picks of international retirement destinations and targeted by the Philippine Retirement Agency for development as a retiree-friendly town.

It's found in the southwest of Negros Island, which sits in a central location in the Philippines, naturally shielded from the bad weather (like typhoons) that can affect these parts.

Dumaguete is close to attractions like Apo Island, a marine paradise, and Siquijor, famous for its waterfalls and white-sand beaches... it's the perfect base for island-hopping, scuba and snorkel adventures, and jungle excursions.

While downtown Dumaguete can be crowded and chaotic, down by the harbor you'll find upscale restaurants, bars, and food stalls along a promenade backed by sea views...

Explore the local markets and get chatting to the vendors. There are markets held every week and it's a great opportunity to get to know people and also support the local community.

There are many festivals and events celebrated throughout the year. It's a great way to experience the culture of the city and meet lots of new people...locals and expats alike.

The local tourism office describes Dumaguete (pronounced "Doo-ma-GET-tee") as "bustling yet charming," and this really does describe the city well. When you first arrive, you may be put off by the cacophony of loud motorbikes and a cityscape that looks a bit "well used," but as you linger, the town will grow on you.

The low cost of living is a major draw: a couple can live comfortably here for about $1,500 to $1,800 per month.

Housing is good value in Dumaguete and the surrounding area. You will have no difficulty finding a modern and comfortable home to rent for $400 to $500 a month.

Dining out is a very popular and affordable pastime here. Two people can enjoy a fine Western meal at one of the better restaurants in town, complete with drinks, for about $20. If you want to go out for local food, you can expect to pay less than half that. Your monthly utilities will cost around $90 and your grocery bill will be $300.

The transition to life in the Philippines is easy (much easier than in other Southeast Asian nations) because English is an official language and over 90% of the population speaks it fluently.

There is a large expat community here with about 5,000 expats who organize social events and activities regularly.

Expat pockets are found across the Philippine islands, including a huge number of U.S. veterans. Veterans who live in the Philippines are entitled to the same VA benefits as those living stateside.

Safety can be an issue across the Philippines, but Dumaguete is considered safe. Still, you'll want to take basic precautions and ideally live in a building that has a security guard.

Health care options in Dumaguete are only decent—fine for basic procedures. There are a handful of hospitals and medical centers nearby, the top one being Silliman University Medical Center.

Prices are low enough that you can pay out of pocket for many procedures, but taking out local insurance is always a better idea.

Dumaguete has a tropical-dry climate, with slightly cooler temperatures than much of the rest of the Philippines. The average high is 88°F (31°C), and the average low is 77°F (25°C).

Dumaguete's infrastructure is still in the process of development. Electricity supply (and therefore internet availability) isn't reliable, and brownouts are fairly common...

This is the reality of living in a remote area in any part of the world—not just the Philippines—and the trade-off for the low cost of living. You can skirt the brownout issue by installing a generator in your home.

To get here, you'll likely fly to Manila, which offers limited direct flights to North America (by way of Los Angeles, New York, San Francisco, Toronto, and Vancouver), and catch an onward connection to Dumaguete.

All in all, Dumaguete can make a great choice for retirement if what you're after is a low cost of living, access to natural beauty, and a low-key lifestyle in a friendly, culturally exciting environment.

Health Care In The Philippines

The Philippines private health care sector is booming, fueling a fast-growing medical tourism industry.

The hospitals that are considered "first rate" in the Philippines might be considered average in the United States. Although throughout the country there are some excellent hospitals.

It's important to note that in the Philippines, the actual medical care provided by doctors and nurses is similar but the day-to-day care of the patient is left to family members.

It is expected that patients will have family members stay with them throughout their whole hospital stay. It is the family's responsibility to change the bed linens, get water, and even to help the patient bathe, get to the bathroom, and eat.

The second point is that a hospital can refuse you care if you do not have the cash to pay for it. And be warned, you will often need to pay in advance for treatment.

There is a charge for your room, for your doctor, and you pay for all medications as you go. The hospital does not keep medications in a centralized pharmacy. Your doctor will write prescriptions for what you need, and a family member is expected to go to a local pharmacy to get these for you.

Public facilities in this country likely would not be of a standard you'd find acceptable. Medical and dental care are good, with new hospitals under construction and international-standard health care is available in the major cities.

The Philippine government has a national health service available to all citizens. This is known as PhilHealth and most of the population are enrolled.

PhilHealth is available to expats. You will need to go to a health insurance office and complete a registration form. Once you have been accepted you will get an ID card and number in the PhilHealth system. You will need to pay a monthly contribution.

You will need health insurance if you are planning to relocate to the Philippines. Make sure you check your policy thoroughly for any exclusions. Some health insurance providers will not cover expats over the age of 65.

If you are looking for surgery or specialist treatment, it can be a good idea to speak with other expats or search online forums for reviews. The standard of health care in the Philippines varies widely and so finding someone with good references is essential.

The Philippines shines when it comes to alternative health care. Medical doctors here are trained in "Western Medicine," but they are also very open to using alternative healing methods, especially herbal medicines.

Residency Requirements

The Philippines offers the Special Resident Retiree's Visa (SRRV), a type of independent means visa.

To qualify for the "SRRV Classic" subset of this visa, you must be at least 50 years old. You must also make a bank deposit that you will use towards the purchase of a condominium or long-term lease of a house and lot. If you don't have a pension, the deposit must be at least $20,000. If you do have a pension, the deposit must be at least $10,000, plus you must show proof of income of at least $800 per month.

On top of these requirements, you must provide a medical certificate from a facility or physician in the Philippines. You must also provide a criminal background check from your country of origin or residence.

The SRRV is a renewable temporary resident visa that gives you the right to live in the Philippines indefinitely.

The Philippines also has a new digital nomad visa, allowing remote workers to stay for up to two years. The visa is available to qualifying non-immigrant foreigners for an initial period of one year, with the option to renew for a second year.

To qualify for the visa, applicants must be at least 18 years old, be able to show they work remotely using digital technology, demonstrate proof of sufficient income earned outside the Philippines, have a clean criminal record, and hold valid health insurance for the duration of their stay in the country.

Additionally, applicants are not permitted to be employed within the Philippines and must not pose a security threat.

Real Estate Restrictions

The Philippines restricts foreign ownership of land. You can lease land from Filipino landowners on a long-term basis (50 years for the initial lease, renewable for up to 25 years).

You can, however, own condominiums. In a single project, foreigners can't make up more than 40% of the total ownership of units.

Taxes

Income taxes in the Philippines are moderate, ranging from 0% to 35%. Capital gains on the sale of property is fixed at 6% of the sales price, and there is no inheritance tax.

The Philippines has tax treaties with the United States and Canada, reducing the risk of double taxation.

CHAPTER 22

MALAYSIA

Located just north of the equator, Malaysia enjoys a tropical climate year-round. The country is divided into two parts, Peninsular Malaysia and Malaysian Borneo.

Most people live near the west coast of Peninsular Malaysia, an attractive and ecologically diverse strip of land that borders Thailand to the north and Singapore to the south.

Vibrant towns and cities, separated by long stretches of sandy beaches, make up the coastline on either side of the peninsula, while the rugged and less populated interior consists of cool jungle highlands, coffee and tea plantations, mountains, rivers, and caves.

Of all the countries in Southeast Asia, Malaysia is probably the most culturally diverse. Fifty percent of the population belongs to the ethnic group called Malay.

Malay are technically Muslim and practice a moderate form of Islam, but Malay women are liberated by Islamic standards. They drive cars, hold jobs, and enjoy equal rights with their male counterparts. Modern Malaysia prides itself on moderation and tolerance.

Malaysia is a regional and a global hub—for trade, for business, and for cultures. As a result, expats invariably find Malaysia to be an extraordinary place to partake in a diversity of traditions, foods, and festivals.

English is spoken and understood by almost everyone. Modern divided highways serve the length of the Malaysian mainland, and almost all roads in Peninsular Malaysia are paved.

Malaysians are friendly and gracious, the cost of living is some of the cheapest in the world, the health care is world-class (and affordable), and, to boot, Malaysia is a world-renowned foodie haven.

Top Picks For A New Life In Malaysia

Malacca

Malacca City (also spelled "Melaka") is the capital of the state of Malacca, which is found in southwestern Malaysia, with a coast along the Strait of Malacca—a channel between the Indian and Pacific Oceans.

The city is a small but vibrant metropolis, offering an exciting blend of history, culture, and modern convenience.

It has a population of about 1 million people that come from a wide variety of ethnic backgrounds—Malays, Chinese, Indians, Baba Nyonya, Kristang, Chitty, Temuan, and Eurasians, to name a few.

This UNESCO-listed city is a tapestry of races, ethnicities, languages, and cultures, and diversity is everywhere you look in Malacca City...

From the hawker stands serving up sizzling satay and freshly baked Portuguese egg tarts... to the intricately decorated temples and mosques standing side by side... to the architectural fusion of Malay kampung houses, colonial-era Dutch buildings, and modern high-rises.

Malacca City is located in the southern region of the Malay Peninsula, facing the Strait of Malacca—one of the world's most important maritime routes.

Its strategic location made it a cultural crossroads for centuries, shaped by trades, settlers, and colonizers. From the Portuguese to the Dutch, British, and even a brief period under Japanese rule, Malacca's history is a narrative of global influence.

Today, Malacca City is a mash-up of influences. It's all colorful sights, enticing scents, and exciting sounds. Every day, you can take in the scent of fresh *kopi* (coffee) as you stroll along the river past colorful colonial buildings...

By afternoon, you can navigate the bustling streets lined with vendors selling everything from handcrafted jewelry to steaming bowls of *laksa* (spicy noodle soup).

In the evening, you can follow the crowds to bustling public markets like Jonker Street to shop for trinkets or listen to live music.

For expats, Malacca offers a compelling mix of affordability, accessibility, and adventure...

Whether you're looking for an exciting location with a lower cost of living, you want to immerse yourself in a unique cultural melting pot, or you're an adventurer searching for something new, Malacca has something to offer.

Tourism is the driving force behind the city's economy, and the city is the economic center of Malacca state. It also hosts international conferences, congresses, and trade fairs.

Malacca City mixes history and culture, with well-known attractions like Jonker Street and A Famosa. Beyond the tourist spots, locals enjoy a deeper and more authentic side of the city.

Malacca's culinary scene is incredibly diverse, and this reflects its multicultural heritage. Locals enjoy authentic flavors at hawker centers, which are open-air food markets. You can sample everything from biryani to dim sum to *laksa* to steak and potatoes, often in a single location.

Malacca City's UNESCO-recognized historic center is a living museum, with well-preserved architecture influenced by Peranakan, Portuguese, Dutch, and British styles. Key sites include Stadthuys, a Dutch administrative building that dates to 1650; Christ Church, an 18th century Anglican church; and Tokong Street, home to Taoist, Confucian, and Buddhist temples.

The city has a lively theater and performing arts scene. It's home to a high-tech theater, the only one of its kind in Asia, called Encore Melaka. It features 5D elements, including a stage that rotates 360 degrees. Traditional performances of *Dondang Sayang*, a form of Malay-Portuguese poetry and song, can be enjoyed. You can also catch live music—jazz, indie, and acoustic—at bars and informal venues around the city.

Festivals are held throughout the year here. *Chap Goh Meh* is celebrated by the Chinese community with processions; *Hari Raya* open houses are enjoyed by Malays; the San Pedro Festival is held by the Portuguese-Eurasian community with parades and feasts.

You can cycle along the Malacca River, passing traditional wooden homes, stopping at hidden cafés, and taking in other interesting sites.

Malacca State has a long coastline along the Strait of Malacca. You can enjoy the beach at Pantai Klebang, which is famous for its sand dunes and sea breezes, or fish or enjoy seafood feasts at Umbai and Kuala Linggi.

Life in Malacca City is extremely affordable for North American retirees. This is a place where you can live a comfortable life on a Social Security check alone.

The biggest expense for most expats is accommodation. To rent a two-bedroom apartment, you'll pay anywhere from $500 to $800 per month. Utilities are an additional $115 per month, depending on how often you run your air conditioner.

Groceries are affordable, although your total spend will be impacted by how many imported goods you buy, as these always cost a premium. Expect to spend about $100 to $180 monthly.

A meal at an inexpensive restaurant or hawker stand can cost as little as $2.50. At a mid-range restaurant, the average meal costs about $18.

Alcohol, spirits especially, can increase your spending on a night out. The average draft beer costs about $4 per pint, while a cocktail costs about $6.

An expat couple's overall budget in Malacca should come out to $1,500 to $2,000 per month.

Because it's on the coast, Malacca is hot and muggy. You'll need to use air conditioning all day, every day. It has an equatorial climate with a significant rainy season from September to November. The mean daily maximum is 90°F (32°C), and the mean daily minimum is 75°F (24°C). It gets 79 inches of precipitation per year.

Malacca City is fairly easy to reach by plane, boat, or car. It's home to Malacca Airport, which offers direct flights to Singapore. A two-hour drive away is Kuala Lumpur International Airport, which serves dozens of cities around the world with direct flights.

It does not, however, offer any direct flights to North America. You'll have to connect in another hub en route to Kuala Lumpur.

A range of transportation options are available to you in Malacca City... although if you lived here you may want your own car to be able to travel comfortably and explore the surrounding areas. Be warned though... Everyone in Malacca complains about the traffic. The streets are busy, whether you're going for a walk or driving from point A to point B.

Melaka Sentral is the main bus and taxi terminal that connects the city with the rest of Malaysia and beyond. There's also a railway service as well as the Melaka Monorail, which runs along the Malacca River.

Elaborately decorated rickshaws are available to take you around town. There are also plenty of taxis in Malacca City as well as ride-hailing services like Grab and EzCab.

The historic city, which unravels on both sides of the river, is also a fantastic place for walking. You can follow paths along the river and stop off for a cool drink or snack at the many cafés and restaurants. There are also pedestrianized areas of the city, like Jonker Walk in Chinatown.

Malaysia is a multicultural, multiethnic, and multilingual society. It's home to 137 living languages. The official language is Malaysian Malay, although, interestingly, most of the population learns a vernacular Malay dialect or another native language first.

English remains an active second language used for some official purposes. Manglish, a mix of English, Malay, Chinese, and Tamil influences, is also widely used. As an expat in Malacca, you can get by on English alone.

Malaysia has long been a popular retirement destination thanks to its use of English and friendly residency policies. As many as 250,000 expats live here, and the most popular destinations are Kuala Lumpur, Penang, and Johor Baru.

Malacca is an up-and-comer in this context. It has a more laidback, community feel than Malaysia's more popular expat havens, but its expat community is much smaller. U.S. and Canadian retirees who relocate here will have to be trailblazers and make more of an effort to socialize than they'd need to in a more established expat haven.

To meet other expats, the best place to start is often social media. Start with a Facebook group dedicated to expats in Malaysia, and then narrow it down from there. You can also use social media to find local events, clubs, and activities in Malacca.

Malacca is a safe place to live and is community-minded.

If you have mobility issues, you may struggle here. The historical center was built hundreds of years ago. It has a convoluted layout, uneven paving, and multi-tiered homes with steep staircases.

If you're wheelchair-bound or mobility impaired, you could live in a newer-built property outside of the historic center, although it's a significantly less charming area.

Malaysia is known for its high health care standards. People from surrounding countries and beyond travel here for access to its high-quality health facilities. It's a top global medical tourism destination.

In Malacca specifically, the primary public hospital is Malacca General Hospital, with over 350 hospital beds.

Also available are Mahkota Medical Centre (a facility with 305 beds that services tens of thousands of international patients annually), Putra Specialist Hospital (a facility with over 240 beds in the heart of Malacca City), and Pantai Hospital Ayer Keroh (accredited by the Malaysian Society for Quality in Health).

If you're a foodie, you should add Malacca to your retirement wish list. The culinary scene is truly outstanding. But the city also offers plenty if you're a fan of history and architecture. Add all this to a low cost of living and excellent health care...and English-speaking Malacca could be for you.

Penang

Just west of mainland Malaysia lies the tropical island of Penang. This safe, stable little island offers excellent medical care, a melting pot of cultures, and diverse lifestyle, entertainment, and recreational options.

As a former British colony, English is widely spoken.

And, with jungle trails and deserted beaches co-existing with modern infrastructure and luxury, water-front condos, it's understandable why this island is home to such a large expat population.

The street food here is world-class, meaning you can dine out for just a few dollars or take your pick from a host of fine dining options if you prefer.

Penang has a thriving arts scene, hosting festivals in music and film throughout the year.

It also has a popular country club where you'll find grass tennis courts, a swimming pool, a library, bars, and restaurants. The island's members-only Swimming Club offers an impressive sailing program and facilities, including squash, tennis, and badminton courts, as well as an outdoor pool overlooking the glittering waters of the Straits of Malacca.

Retired here, you could while away the hours wandering around historic George Town (the capital), kick back at the beach, explore stunning mountains and waterfalls, shop 'til you drop, or partake in some of the world's finest and most affordable cuisine.

Also known as the "Pearl of the Orient," Penang Island is an exceptionally beautiful location, and with a population of just 740,000, George Town, the island's capital, is small enough that it's easy to make friends and meet your neighbors.

One of the many charms of George Town is the feeling it gives you of stepping back in time. Even beyond the city's UNESCO-designated World Heritage Site heart, this city is a cornucopia of Chinese shop houses, pagodas, temples, churches, mosques, British-colonial buildings and landscaped parks.

Wholesalers, import and export businesses, and shipping companies dominate the southern section of Beach Street, as they have since the 1880s, and the docks of Weld Quay, which was established more than 120 years ago, are little changed today.

Impressive British-colonial buildings serve the same functions as they did more than a century ago, while many of the dilapidated Chinese shop houses have been scrubbed, painted, and renovated into attractive hotels, community centers, cafes, galleries and private homes.

In George Town, you'd never run out of things to do, from outdoor fun and historical exploration to dining adventures, nightlife, or an evening at the symphony.

The costs are a draw, too. Penang isn't cheap in the context of Southeast Asia, but the value for money you'll find here is outstanding. On a monthly budget of $2,200, a couple could live in luxury, renting a large condo in a unit with a gym, pool, balcony, and 24-hour security.

You'll pay between $800 to $1,000 for rent. Your utilities will cost about $120. Budget about $335 for entertainment for two and another $360 for your monthly groceries. Transportation costs will be about $80 a month.

The thing that expats living in Penang are most grateful for is the health care, which is among the world's best—and cheapest. Hospitals and clinics have excellent medical staff. There's a reason planeloads of medical tourists land in Penang every day. There are several hospitals here, including Gleneagles Penang, KPJ Penang Specialist Hospital, and Penang Adventist Hospital.

Malaysia has an equatorial climate which is dominated by the monsoon season. The temperature in Penang typically ranges between 70°F and 90°F throughout the year. Average annual humidity is around 80%.

There are a significant number of retirees in Penang and the expat community is diverse and welcoming. Because it's English-speaking, a lot of multinational companies have set up offices here. You won't have any trouble meeting other expats.

Malaysia is a peaceful country and living in Penang is safe with violent crime almost unheard of.

Year-round sunny, warm weather, First World infrastructure, easy permanent residency, and English-speaking locals make living in Penang easy. Here, you could soak up the rich local culture in the morning, make the most of the great sports facilities in the afternoon...and finish the day with delicious, cheap food at a street-side stall or top-notch restaurant by night.

Health Care In Malaysia

Malaysia promotes itself as a medical tourism destination, and the major cities (especially Kuala Lumpur) offer state-of-the-art medical care at a fraction the cost you'd expect to pay for comparable care and procedures in other parts of the world, especially in the United States.

A visit to an English-speaking general practitioner costs about $10, while an English-speaking, Europe- or U.S.-educated specialist will charge you about $30, including free follow-up visits. A complete dental examination is about $30; a crown is less than $300.

You can have your health care needs taken care of comfortably at many hospitals and clinics throughout the country, or you can travel to Kuala Lumpur, which boasts extensive health care facilities, for any complex health issues.

Hospital Kuala Lumpur has some 2,300 beds; Gleneagles Kuala Lumpur is a private hospital with a wide range of medical services; Prince Court Medical Centre is another private facility with state-of-the-art tech and patient-centered services.

The health infrastructure in the capital is extremely well-developed and affordable, even paying out of pocket. An overnight stay in a hospital can cost around $45 per night.

You can also get private health insurance in Malaysia for an affordable cost—$400 to $600 per year, depending on your age and health status.

Most medications prescribed by Western physicians can be found in Malaysia, often at much lower prices. Many drugs, including most antibiotics, can be purchased over the counter. Some routine medications, though—mostly painkillers such as ibuprofen—require a prescription. Authorities are strict on this rule, so you must pay close attention to the classification on the package. "NP" is noted on packages for non-scheduled or over-the-counter products. All other classifications (from A to D and P2) are subject to certain restrictions.

Residency Requirements

U.S. and Canadian travelers can come to Malaysia visa-free as tourists and stay for 90 days. To stay longer than that, you'll need a residency visa. Malaysia has relatively friendly visa policies...

It offers the Malaysia My Second Home (MM2H) visa, an invest-for-residency program with different tiers (and different requirements and time allowances). Here's an overview of the MM2H's four main categories:

- **Silver** – This is valid for five years and has the lowest requirements and fewest allowances. You need to make a fixed deposit of $150,000 (in a Malaysian financial institution), pay a "participating fee" of $225, and buy a home worth at least $135,000.
- **Gold** – This is valid for 15 years and has moderate requirements and allowances. You need to make a fixed deposit of $500,000, pay a participating fee of $675, and buy a home worth at least $225,000.

- **Platinum** – This is valid for 20 years and has high requirements but generous allowances. You need to make a fixed deposit of $1,000,000, pay a participating fee of $45,000, and buy a home worth at least $450,000.
- **Special Economic Zone** – This is valid for 10 years. You need to make a fixed deposit of $32,000 (for those 50 and above), pay a participating fee of $225, and buy a home sold by developers (not real estate agents or existing owners), meeting the minimum price according to your state.

Note that investment amounts are originally quoted in Malaysian ringgit, so exact amounts are subject to currency fluctuations. In all cases, you're required to stay in Malaysia for 90 days per year to maintain your residency status.

The MM2H has been changed many times across the years, and it has very specific rules. Make sure to read the fine print of any tier you select.

Malaysia's digital nomad visa launched in 2022. Known as the DE Rantau Nomad Pass or the Professional Visit Pass, the visa allows location-independent workers in the digital sphere to stay in Malaysia for up to 12 months, with the possibility of renewing for a further year.

Under the terms of the visa, you can work as an employee, business owner, or freelancer for companies or clients outside of Malaysia.

Real Estate Restrictions

As a foreigner, you can own property in Malaysia with some restrictions. You can't own low- and medium-cost affordable units, developments on Malay reserved lands, or properties allocated to Bumiputera groups.

The property value thresholds that you have to meet vary from state to state in Malaysia. In Malacca, if you buy a landed property, it must be worth at least $250,000; if you buy a high-rise or strata title, it must be worth at least $112,300.

Taxes

Malaysia can be tax-friendly for retirees who apply for the MM2H program...

The MM2H makes you eligible for tax exemptions on most forms of overseas income (investment-related income, retirement income, periodic payments, property and intellectual property income, and other gains and profits). The cash that you import to meet the MM2H fixed deposit requirement is also tax-exempt.

Income generated from employment (including overseas income) is subject to taxation in Malaysia if you're considered a tax resident—in other words, if you spend 182 days or more in the country. Employment income tax rates range from 1% to 30%.

Malaysia does not levy net wealth or worth taxes, nor does it levy inheritance, estate, or gift taxes. It has a tax treaty in place with Canada but not the U.S.

CHAPTER 23

VIETNAM

Vietnam is one of the world's most affordable places to live. It's difficult to find a place where you can enjoy such a high standard of living at such a low cost.

The downsides to Vietnam are its restrictive policies toward foreigners when it comes to property ownership and its limited residency options.

Vietnamese food is some of the healthiest in the world because of its heavy emphasis on fresh herbs and vegetables and avoidance of oil and dairy. Out of necessity, Vietnamese people have learned to do a lot with a little. Dishes are made from simple, inexpensive ingredients but masterfully prepared.

Vietnam is arguably one of the cheapest places on earth to live well. This is a land of beautiful, world-class beaches, cool mountain retreats, and cities seething with vitality.

Many Westerners who end up living in Vietnam love it. Others complain about the hustle, the noise, and the lack of Western influence, particularly in the northern part of the country (Hanoi).

The population is youthful, and an energy permeates everything. So, the Vietnam that existed in the 1960s and early 1970s exists only in memories.

The country has moved on toward a much brighter future.

Top Picks For A New Life In Vietnam

Da Lat

In 1893, Dr. Alexandre Yersin, famed French physician and bacteriologist, was sent into Vietnam's Central Highlands to find a place of rest and relaxation for Indochina's French population... It was the heyday of French colonialism in Vietnam, and the Governor General wanted to establish a hill station for the colonists, an escape from the heat, grime, and tropical malady of life in Saigon (now Ho Chi Minh City)...

What he came upon was Da Lat, a cool-weather town perched at 1,500 meters (4,921 feet) in the Lang Bian Plateau. Surrounded by natural beauty, including pine forest and misty peaks, game-hunting and abundant freshwater, the town had an almost Alpine-like quality... At first, only hunters and adventure-seekers would brave the treacherous road from Saigon to Da Lat... Tigers, elephants, and wild boars were said to roam the area and kept more prudent visitors at bay.

In 1922, The Palace, a luxury hotel, was established to help change Da Lat's image. It attracted affluent clientele—members of royal families, artists, politicians—and put Da Lat on the map. Urban planning was carried out by Ernest Hébrard (a renowned French architect), and Da Lat was endowed with all the trappings of a proper resort town: a health complex, schools, a golf course, several parks and manmade lakes, villas, and boulevards...

Architectural and cultural remnants from that era remain today, casting a historic and otherworldly charm over the place. Today, it's a domestic tourism destination and the honeymoon capital of Vietnam. You'll see young lovers strolling hand in hand or newlyweds taking wedding photos against kitschy backdrops.

Da Lat has a far-reaching reputation for natural beauty, surrounded by verdant countryside dotted with strawberry fields, forests, rivers, waterfalls, and lakes.

The best way to discover all this beauty is to rent a motorbike—the undisputed king of transport in Southeast Asia—and get lost among the backroads with the scent of pine forest and fresh air on your face. You can also hike, cycle, go for strolls, and take a canoe out on the rivers or lakes.

This is Asia's City of Eternal Spring. Its temperate mountainous climate is pretty much perfect—never too hot or cold, the temperature perpetually hovering at about 65°F (18°C)—a far cry from the rest of South Vietnam's steamy conditions. The climate doesn't just make Da Lat an enjoyable place to spend time outdoors; it also makes it the City of Flowers, garden bed of Vietnam...

From January to March, the coldest months of the year at around 62°F (17°C), cherry blossoms are in bloom. They hold huge significance in East Asian cultures, and people from around the region flock to Da Lat to see its blossoms. April to June, things heat up to about 66°F (19°C), and lavender, hydrangea, and purple phoenix paint the city a different set of hues.

July to September is the height of rainy season (Da Lat gets about 70 inches of rain a year), so it's a good time to hunker down in one of the city's cozy cafés and enjoy some of Vietnam's world-renowned coffee. October to December, temperatures drop back down to about 62°F (17°C), and the town becomes truly colorful.

Also because of the highland climate, you can get fruits and veggies that aren't possible to grow in other parts of the country: coffee, strawberries, cabbage, cauliflower... Da Lat even has its own wine industry. It's famous for having some of the best food in Vietnam (a country famous for delicious cuisine). A lot of the herbs and vegetables that are essential in Vietnamese dishes are at their freshest in Da Lat.

You can sample them at the central market—the hub of all cultural activity in Da Lat where you can buy anything from cheap sunglasses to fresh asparagus and tomatoes, winter coats to succulents and potted orchids. At sundown, the market percolates with activity, expanding even larger with the addition of food stalls that sell Dalatese street snacks.

Natural beauty is what made Da Lat popular among the French in the 1900s, who came here in search of an Alpine-like chalet town. The town continues to impress with its natural beauty. The cool weather, pine forest, abundance of fresh water, and vibrant blue skies give way to a huge number of outdoor recreation opportunities.

Da Lat is not a coastal town, but it has several lakes nearby. Xuan Huong Lake (formerly known as *Grand Lac*) in the center of town was created by the French. There's a walking trail or you can rent a paddleboat for an afternoon on the lake—paddle boating is popular on almost all of Da Lat's lakes...

Just four miles outside Da Lat, Da Thien Lake is in the aptly named Valley of Love, also known as the Niagara Falls of Vietnam because its frequented by honeymooners. The romantic spot features benches around the lake, flower gardens, and views of the Lang Biang peaks. Da Lat has plenty of streams, rivers, and waterfalls, too.

Da Lat has three golf courses. Da Lat Palace Golf Club, five minutes from Da Lat, dates to the 1920s and is frequently rated the best course in Vietnam and one of the best in Asia.

SAM Tuyen Lam Golf Club, 20 minutes from the town center, flanks Tuyen Lam Lake and, situated in a valley, features many slopes. The Da Lat at 1200 Country Club is about an hour from Da Lat. As its name suggests, the course sits at an elevation of between 1,000 and 1,500 meters (3,280 and 4,921 feet) above sea level.

Da Lat isn't a bustling metropolis with multifaceted entertainment options on tap, but that doesn't mean it's not a culturally interesting place to be. It's religiously diverse, home to Buddhist pagodas and Christian churches, Cao Dai temples and cathedrals and abbeys.

It makes sense that so many religious institutions would establish themselves here... The cool weather and gorgeous scenery lend themselves to a tranquil, contemplative atmosphere. This is what Da Lat's small but tight-knit expat community enjoys about the town. It offers a chance at peace and tranquility, a stunning natural environment, and temperate climate... all at an impossibly low cost to expats.

Your cost of living in Da Lat will vary depending on your lifestyle but it will be lower here than it is in the States, no question. A couple can live comfortably on about $1,800 a month or even less.

This number changes depending on where you live (rent is higher in central areas), the size and modernity of your rental, what you eat (eating at expat restaurants and buying imported groceries add to your budget), and your habits (how often you shop, your indulgences, travel expenses, etc.).

Most importantly, if you eat and shop like a local, you'll save greatly. You can enjoy a meal for two at a local Vietnamese restaurant for about $6.50. A grocery trip to a local market is about $22. This is one place in the world where eating out can save you money.

The same isn't true of the expat restaurants, where an average meal for two costs about $25. Likewise, if you shop for imported goods at stores, you'll spend much more on groceries.

Rent can be as low as $200 a month for a studio apartment on the edge of town. For a more central apartment, expect to pay between $450 to $700 monthly. Air conditioning isn't needed here, so electricity bills are always low, and utilities are usually included in the cost of rent. The average pension goes a lot further in Vietnam than it does nearly anywhere else in thc world.

The town experiences just two seasons: rainy and dry. Rainy season lasts from May to October, when you might get upwards of 20 days of rain in a month. About 70 inches of precipitation falls here annually. Dry season hits in November and lasts until June. It corresponds with the coolest temperatures of the year.

Temperatures range between an average low of 57°F and an average high of 73°F (14°C to 23°C) with humidity hovering around 85%. Temperature fluctuates little in Da Lat, with the daily mean hovering at 64°F (18°C) annually.

Landslides and flooding can happen in Da Lat, but it's unlikely that a tropical storm would affect the town because of its inland, up-mountain position.

Da Lat is home to a handful of public and private hospitals... Expats use the private hospitals, like Lam Dong General and Hoan My Hospital, where the standards of care are sufficient for basic procedures.

Hoan My Hospital is the more highly recommended of the two because it's clean, modern, and part of the Hoan My Medical Group, the largest private hospital and clinic group in the country. Several expats visit this hospital to see Dr. Ho Thi Delin, who is professional and speaks English.

Also, the cost of private care is low enough that most expats can afford to pay out of pocket... But there are a few options for local health insurance providers, such as HSBC Vietnam, Baoviet Health Insurance, and Pacific Cross Vietnam.

The Pasteur Institute is also recommended for vaccines, injuries, and illnesses. An infectious-disease research center, it's mainly responsible for vaccine production and administration but since 2014 has also operated a free-standing clinic to serve the local population's general health needs.

For more serious medical needs, you should make your way to Ho Chi Minh City where you can access an excellent standard of care. The French-Vietnamese Hospital earned Joint Commission International accreditation in 2016, and Vinmec International Central Park Hospital received it in 2017, ensuring better quality health care and patient safety.

If you can't find an English-speaking doctor in Da Lat, expats tend to ask a Vietnamese friend who can translate to accompany them to appointments. That, or the Google Translate app on your cell phone, are your best options.

Vietnam's big cities, like HCMC and Hanoi, are where you'll find the most English speakers... but even then, their numbers aren't high, and their English ability isn't great. Da Lat is small and its tourism industry is geared towards Vietnamese people... There hasn't been much impetus to learn English here.

That said, getting by is not as difficult as you might imagine. For day-to-day activities like ordering food in a restaurant, getting gas, or asking for directions, simple gesturing works surprisingly well. If you're traveling by bus or taxi, it helps to show the driver the destination name in written form.

Learning Vietnamese will be a challenge. This Austroasiatic language has five different dialects, and it's a tonal language, so word meaning is determined by pronunciation... Picking up even a little bit of Vietnamese is good practice, though, even if it's just "hello", "goodbye", and "thank you". The best way to do that in Da Lat is to hire a local tutor, which is inexpensive.

Da Lat is home to a small, close-knit expat community (between 300 and 500 expats live here). Retirees from Canada, Australia, the States, the U.K., Russia, Spain, Japan, and Italy have permanently settled here or live in Da Lat on a part-time basis. Some run small business or work as digital nomads, taking advantage of the very-low cost of living for a couple of months a year before going back home or on to their next destination.

There are organized groups, like the Expats in Da Lat and What's On Da Lat Facebook groups, that are dedicated to bringing people together for different activities and events. You can find groups based on your specific interests, like language-exchanges, vegan foodie groups, women's forums, volunteer opportunities, and so on...

There are one or two expat haunts where you're bound to bump into other expats in Da Lat. One More Café, owned by an Australian expat, is one of them, serving lattes and baked goods. Escape Bar, a live-music bar that plays the classics and has 1970s décor, and Botea Bistro, a French restaurant with a backwall library full of books, are other expat-favorites.

You can get around much of Da Lat on foot. It's relatively small at just under 400 square kms (154 square miles). Walking around is a nice activity as it's not too hot, sidewalks are abundant, and the main thoroughfares are embellished with flowering plants... Just be careful when crossing the street—crosswalks aren't easy to come by and aren't always respected by drivers.

Taxis are cheap and useful for going longer distances. Mai Linh is the taxi company preferred by locals... They stand out because their cars are bright green.

The best option for getting around Da Lat is on a motorbike. Most trips you'll take in and around town are slightly too far to walk but too close to warrant a taxi. Motorbikes are the happy medium. They afford flexibility and are cheap to buy, rent, and fill up with gas.

Da Lat is served by a small international airport, which is found 30 minutes outside of the town center. Though technically an international airport, Lien Khuong only serves four countries outside of Vietnam: China, Korea, Malaysia, and Thailand.

Your best option for getting to Da Lat is to fly into one of the country's major hubs—Hanoi or Ho Chi Minh City—and then arrange onward travel on a low-cost domestic airline to Da Lat. You can also fly into Ho Chi Minh City and take a bus to Da Lat, which is an eight-hour journey.

Da Lat is extremely safe, whether you're male, female, single, or accompanied. One thing to watch out for is motorbike theft. Always park your bike in a well-lit parking lot, preferably one where there is an attendant, to avoid having it snatched.

Da Lat is a peaceful, scenic place that inspires tranquility. The pace of life is slow, entertainment options are simple and low-key, and with its near-perfect weather you'll want to spend as much time outdoors as possible, which leads to an active, healthier lifestyle full of walking, hiking, and more.

Hanoi

Located in the north, Hanoi is the cultural and spiritual heart of Vietnam. It's a vibrant city of more than 3 million people. Less influenced by the West than Ho Chi Minh City to the south, this modern city has retained its traditional roots, with small, family-owned businesses instead of fast-food chains, mega-supermarkets, and international department stores.

With its bustling streets, constant traffic, quick-moving scooters, vibrant markets, and street hawkers, Hanoi has a buzz about it. It pulls people in and keeps them constantly entertained.

Its chief attraction is its Old Quarter, a labyrinth of a neighborhood that features a mix of architectural styles, from French mansions to Chinese temples to Buddhist pagodas. It's a dense neighborhood that's full of landmarks, restaurants, and cafés and is best explored on foot.

Street food tours are a great way to sample the best of Hanoian cuisine and can also be a way to give back, as they're often hosted by local university students who are eager to practice their English skills.

The best way to experience Hanoi is to walk through the many micro-neighborhoods in the Old Quarter (the Hoan Kiem District). You'll hear the tin street before you get there, as a block full of tinsmiths hammer from dawn until dusk manufacturing the goods of their trade.

Nearby is Hang Ma, where bright lanterns, elaborate gift baskets, stacks of paper offerings, cards, lights, and holiday decorations erupt in a carnival of color.

Hang Bac, where you can shop for every sort or silver imaginable, is near Lan Ong, where the tantalizing smells of Chinese herbs and teas drift over the sidewalks.

There are linen streets, candy streets, fish streets, toy streets, art streets, audio streets, baby clothes streets, silk streets, cellphone streets...

The Turtle Tower, an ancient pagoda that sits in the middle of Hoan Kiem Lake, was built in the 15th century, and is worth a visit.

The Tran Quoc Pagoda, which overlooks pretty West Lake and is within walking distance of the Old Quarter, was built more than 1,400 years ago. In the city's Old Quarter, it's easy to imagine life as it was a millennium ago.

There is an abundance of street vendors and restaurants to try out in the city. The Hanoi diet revolves around noodles and potatoes, pork and chicken, oranges and plums. It's hard to find the classic northern dishes of *bun cha* (a pork and noodle Hanoi specialty), *bun bo nam bo* (a rice-noodle and beef dish) *or cha ca* (grilled fish, Hanoi-style) outside of Hanoi.

Part of what makes Hanoi so unique is the exuberant and incredibly energetic nature of its people. They are intoxicated with the enthusiasm and hope that come from improving living conditions and expanded freedoms. The laughter of children and the honest curiosity of the people are welcoming. The arousing atmosphere of ordered chaos, seasoned with a hint of luck and fortune, sharpens the senses.

Vietnam was consumed by struggle for decades. It has emerged victorious. Its population, most born after the wars ended, are irrepressible idealists. They see their world developing and evolving and are determined to be successful participants.

Vietnam is arguably one of the cheapest places in the world to live well. The government has taken every step necessary to make this an extremely foreigner-friendly country.

In Hanoi (and the country's other major cities), prices will be a bit higher but still very affordable. Rent in Hanoi will likely take up a good chunk from your budget, but it'll still be cheaper than in many other cities around the world. A couple could live well in Hanoi for as little as $1,400 a month.

You can rent a two-bedroom property for $700; utilities will be about $140 a month; transportation (motorbike rental and gas) will cost $50; budget about $140 a month for entertainment costs; and groceries will set you back about $200.

The Vietnamese are some of the friendliest and most welcoming people that you'll find anywhere in the world. Hanoi has large numbers of expats and foreigners, and it's easy to make friends with Westerners and locals.

Hanoi offers a wide range of amenities for Westerners who don't want to "go native," with fine dining, cultural shows, spas, and other activities that will appeal to everyone. If you're thinking of Vietnam, it's worth checking out your options in Hanoi.

Health care has improved in Vietnam over the past few years, and all but the most serious or complicated conditions can be treated without having to leave the country.

Physicians will likely be very educated and will make accurate diagnoses and treatment plans. There are a large number of private and public hospitals in Hanoi and for the most part they are clean and equipped with top-notch medical facilities.

Winters in Hanoi can be cool and summers are much hotter than they are in the south of the country. The climate is humid. The rainiest period is from June to September. The average temperature is 69.8°F in January and 91.5°F in September.

Vietnam is a friendly, safe place to visit and live. *Lonely Planet* even called Vietnam an "extremely safe place to travel." While no place in the world is perfect, with a little common sense and literal street sense you should have a wonderful experience in Hanoi.

Violent crime is almost non-existent in Vietnam. The most common crimes in the larger cities like Hanoi are petty theft, pickpocketing, and random bag snatching.

Sneaky thieves target large crowds where people are distracted and grab unprotected valuables. Also, beware of unscrupulous motorcyclists who try to snatch your belongings as they zoom past.

Be sure to keep all valuables close to your body, preferably in a money belt or other secure location, and don't wear your bag on the street-side of your body. Always be aware of your surroundings and don't carry more money than you need. Also, just like in every other large city in the world, don't flash wealth, jewelry, large sums of money, or expensive equipment like phones or cameras that could make you a target.

Since tourism improves the local economy and the country's overall reputation, the Vietnamese are working hard to make their homeland a safe and welcoming place where foreigners will be eager to visit and live. So far, they are doing a great job.

Hanoi has a character rarely seen in modern Asian cities. It boasts beautiful examples of French colonial architecture, trees on every street, and busy cafés and shops spilling onto the sidewalks.

Health Care In Vietnam

In Vietnam, medical care is practiced almost entirely in public, government-run hospitals. As a foreigner, there are two choices: You can pay to go to one of the private, English- or French-speaking hospitals, or, if you have a Vietnamese interpreter, you can go with them to a government hospital and receive inexpensive tests and treatments.

Many foreigners living in Vietnam say that the care that they have received at these facilities has been excellent. Any medical condition can be treated at the French Hospitals, including trauma.

There are also SOS clinics in Ho Chi Minh City and Hanoi, which specialize in providing high-quality (but expensive) care to foreigners.

The doctors in big cities like Hanoi and Ho Chi Minh City are highly skilled regardless of the hospital you attend, and the government hospitals have modern equipment and competent technicians.

Prescriptions are rarely required for medication. However, many medications available in North America have not yet made it to this corner of the world. If you require regular medication, be sure that you have both the generic and chemical name for it.

The local pharmacy may either carry that exact medication or may be able to find a suitable substitute. Otherwise, you may wish to consider ordering your usual medication online and having it shipped to Vietnam.

In general, medications here cost a fraction of what they cost in the West, and chances are good that they will be authentic. When in doubt about authenticity, though, get your medications at the hospital or at one of the larger pharmacies.

Residency Requirements

Visas must be arranged before entering the country and can be for one- or three-month's duration. When the visa nears expiration, an agent can get you one or two extensions. Each extension is valid for the same length of time as your original visa, so if you entered Vietnam with a one-month visa, you could stay in the country for a total of three months; if you entered with a three-month visa, you could stay in Vietnam for a total of nine months. After the visa has been extended twice, you must leave the country to renew it.

If you are visiting Vietnam with a Vietnamese travel agency operating in your country of origin, you can apply for visa-on-arrival approval, which is a written statement of permission to obtain your visa in Vietnam.

To stay past the maximum tourist visa length, you have to be working, have a Vietnamese spouse, or own and operate a business in the country. If you have a work permit, business visas are typically issued for one year and can be extended. On occasion, it may be possible to get a two- or even three-year business visa.

At this time, if you do not have a work permit, the maximum duration of a standard business visa is three months.

Vietnamese visa laws are in a constant state of flux. Although the rules for qualifying remain roughly the same, the length of stay that is granted changes frequently. If the laws change during the tenure of your visa, the original terms are still honored. It is occasionally possible to get a six- or even 12-month business visa even if you don't have a work permit—you just have to keep checking.

Investment for residency is a way to receive a DT category visa. This type of residency is valid for five years.

You are required to invest (provide capital or purchase equity) at least $12,000 in a Vietnamese-owned company and have your name registered as a co-owner of that business. In other cases, this type of visa is granted to workers at the office of a foreign company operating in Vietnam.

Five years of continuous permanent residency makes it possible for foreign nationals to apply for citizenship. Vietnam grants citizenship if the applicant meets these guidelines:

- Living in accord with Vietnamese laws, practices, and customs
- Demonstrating proficiency with the Vietnamese language
- Proof of the ability to support their household

We recommend following up with the Vietnamese Consulate in your home country about any other specific inquiries you may have regarding citizenship.

Real Estate Restrictions

Vietnam is an interesting case... As a communist country, all the land in the country is owned collectively by the Vietnamese people and administrated through the government. No one can own land here; Vietnamese people can only lease it indefinitely and foreigners can only lease it for 50 years, potentially renewable one time.

In 2015, significant changes were made to Vietnam's property laws, allowing foreigners to own property in Vietnam with restrictions... So long as you enter the country legally, you're eligible to buy residential property. So, too, are foreign entities like investment funds, banks, Vietnamese branches and representative offices of companies established in Vietnam.

You can buy property in all residential sectors, including apartments and landed properties (like townhouses and villas). Your restrictions as a foreigner are that you can own a maximum of 30% of the units in a condominium complex or 250 landed properties per administrative unit. Your property can be sold, sub-leased, inherited, and collateralized.

Taxes

You become a tax resident of Vietnam if you spend 183 days or more in a calendar year in the country. You can also be considered a tax resident if you have a permanent residence in Vietnam.

As a tax resident of Vietnam, you owe tax on your worldwide income. As a non-resident, you owe income tax at a flat rate of 20% on your Vietnam-sourced income.

Employment income is taxed at progressive rates between 5% and 35%. For non-employment income, tax rates vary:

- Business income: 0.5% to 5%
- Investment income: 5%
- Sale of shares: 0.1%
- Capital assignment: 20%
- Sale of real estate: 2%
- Income from franchising/royalties: 5%
- Inheritance, gifts, winnings: 10%

Pension income may be exempt from income taxes, as pensions paid under Vietnam's social insurance law or its foreign equivalent are non-taxable. This is worth checking with a professional tax advisor.

Vietnam does not impose a net wealth or worth tax. It has tax treaties in place with both Canada and the United States.

VIII

TAKING THAT EXCITING NEXT STEP

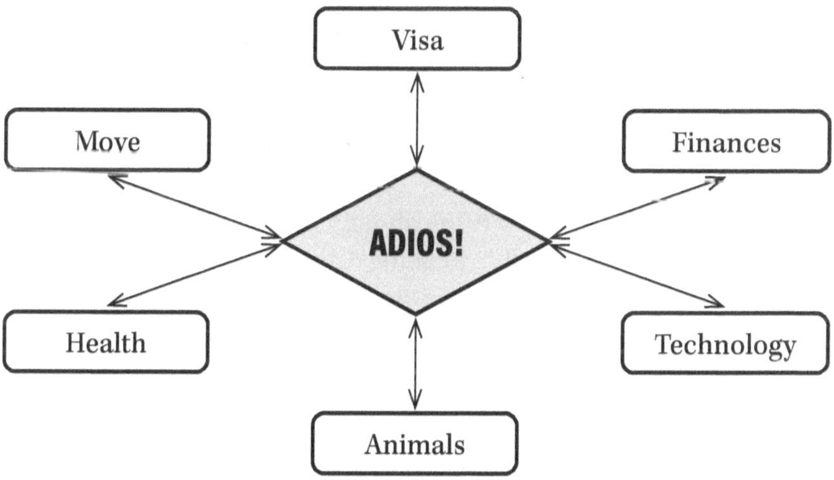

With a new culture, perhaps a new language, a new climate... choosing what's right for you is an exhilarating experience. When you begin researching all the possibilities, it's all this newness that excites and intrigues you. Falling in love with a new place is the first step. But, as in any relationship, before you make a long-term commitment, you need to know how well the two of you can live together day-to-day.

There's so much choice out there. At the end of the day, you may wonder: where do I go from here? How do I narrow this down?

Moving overseas can be an opportunity to reinvent yourself—leave behind the stresses and worries of where you're currently living and launch a new life in an exciting location with new scenery, new faces, new adventures, and more.

It's understandable why this idea is taking off in the United States, with more people than ever considering settling in another country. Moving abroad can be an opportunity to add more fun and adventure to your life.

But moving to a new country involves a major life change, and as such, it also requires a great deal of introspection, planning, and work to pull it off.

Before jumping on a plane, define your priorities, agendas, and preferences. Determine what you're willing to give up from your current lifestyle and what you're not. If you're moving with your significant other, you need to have a mutual understanding of the journey you're embarking on.

Do you care what people think about your decision to move overseas? If so, you're susceptible to being dissuaded by your friends and family. If moving abroad is your goal, you must learn to continue with your plans despite this.

The first thing you need to do is to choose the lifestyle you want. Ask yourself: What do you enjoy doing in the evening? What do you want to see when you look out the window in the morning? Do you like to go to cultural events, or would you be happy sitting in your back yard at sundown with a drink? Would you prefer to wake up to a sea view...or overlooking a lush valley?

You need to determine first what your ideal lifestyle overseas looks like. Is it an expat enclave where all your neighbors are from the U.S. and Canada, speak English, and talk about the same things people talked about back home? Or a setting that's more authentic to the country you're living in, where your neighbors are locals, and where you'll likely grapple with a language barrier?

Both options exist, as well as half-measures between them. There is no right or wrong choice when it comes to lifestyle; there's only the choice that works best for you.

It sounds simple, but it's the most important step to take. Ask yourself those questions before going further.

You can eliminate many places just by deciding what you *don't* want to see—like high-rises—or what you *do* want—like the ocean. Or perhaps you don't want to be too far from home...or have to learn a new language...or be in a climate that's too hot or too cold.

Then you need to decide if you want to live abroad part-time or full-time? This doesn't have to be all or nothing. You take a cue from snowbirds, who "fly south" for winter, spending a handful of months in a warmer climate before returning home for the spring and summer. You can try living overseas on for size and live in a new country for a month or two per year until you feel comfortable enough to extend your stay. Or you can take the plunge and relocate, settling into your new home full-time.

And this brings us to the residency issue. Just about every country in the world makes it easy to visit as a tourist and support the local economy with your money—as long as you leave again within a specific time frame (typically 30 to 90 days).

But each country has its own rules about who qualifies, and how to remain within its borders as a long-term resident. The countries that we at Live And Invest Overseas recommend, and the ones you just read about in this book, all offer residency visas with reasonable requirements.

Still, the requirements vary considerably, and most countries offer more than one option.

Some places are better for full-time living, others for vacation homes. Some countries make it harder to get residency, like Croatia for example, so part-time living would be a better option here.

Your financial situation and age are critical considerations and have a lot to do with determining which options are available to you and which make the most sense. So before you spend lots of time and money in plans for a new life overseas, you want to take a close look at the options for establishing residency in every country on your list.

To apply for residency, you'll have to meet certain requirements (such as providing a background check, proof that you have health insurance, evidence of funds that you can use to sustain yourself in your new country, etc.). Working with a residency lawyer who speaks both the local language and English is usually the easiest way to obtain residency.

Decide whether to rent or buy. That alone could be a full discussion, but it will guide your next steps.

If you're buying a property as a pure investment, your priorities will differ from choosing a home for yourself. If it's an investment, focus on high-return areas. If it's a home, focus on comfort and lifestyle.

Arrange an exploratory visit. Try different places and see what daily life feels like.

When going overseas to investigate your options and to determine if it's a place you'd see yourself spending time in, don't evaluate that exploratory trip like a vacation—look at it as a resident. Check stores, noise levels, and convenience to all the amenities you might need.

Then settle on a place—or at least a starting point. Don't let perfection stop you from taking action.

Even if you change your mind later, you won't lose time by getting started.

Renting first is always a recommended strategy. Even if you're sure you like the country that you're planning on moving to and you've scoped out which city you'll choose, you may not yet know which neighborhood in that city suits you best.

Renting allows you to try out several different neighborhoods before committing to a property purchase, if that's on your agenda. While property is a solid investment class, you may decide that renting indefinitely is better for you.

Renting allows for a more mobile and flexible lifestyle, and overseas, it can be affordable—as inexpensive as a couple hundred dollars per month. You avoid the carrying costs of property ownership, as well as the administrative processes of making a purchase and estate planning.

Plus, if you don't have the cash, you might have no choice but to rent. In many countries, cash purchases of homes are the norm, and financing for foreigners (even resident ones) is not an option. In countries where you can get financing, you'll find high interest rates and strict requirements.

In countries like Belize and rural Italy, the best way to find a rental is through word of mouth. Many countries lack central databases of available listings, so it's best to put boots on the ground and deal with local agents directly. By searching on the internet (in English), you'll find only the most expensive rentals that are aimed at tourists.

Having said that, there are advantages of buying right away—it simply allows you to "take the plunge." That is, it helps you to move your life forward, unequivocally, embracing the new adventure.

Many who rent before they buy do so to be able to maintain a property back home, "just in case." While this is conservative and can be sensible, it's also an anchor... a drag. It divides your attention and keeps you looking backward instead of ahead to your new life. Keeping one foot on the pier and the other on the departing boat is stressful. You may remain only partially committed, which will be a handicap.

Real estate is a long-term investment, so look beyond a year or two into the future. And don't let past appreciation keep you from making a solid buy decision today.

Health is one of life's most important considerations, and it only becomes more important as we get older.

If you have a serious health condition that requires regular medical attention or special medication, this can limit your range of options abroad. But this is not always a deal-breaker. Researching what's available locally is crucial, but rest assured that many excellent options for affordable, quality medical care exist internationally.

Even if you're perfectly healthy, you'll have to decide what type of health insurance to use in your new life abroad. You have a couple of options: local health insurance, international health insurance, travel health insurance, or no insurance at all.

Going without health coverage might be unfathomable to you, but in certain destinations, it can be a reasonable approach. In some countries, medical care is so affordable that it makes more sense to pay out of pocket for regular health needs, putting what you would've paid for health insurance into an interest-yielding savings account.

An international or travel health insurance plan makes the most sense if you plan on traveling a lot once you move. If you're staying put in one country, a local insurance policy is likely the best option.

You should start thinking about health early in the relocation process. Many policies only accept new clients up to certain ages. If you enter into a policy before the cut-off, you can usually stay in it past that age, but if you wait too long, you could age yourself out of some good health insurance options.

The next step is to get up to speed with your finances.

Instead of asking how much money you need to move overseas, ask yourself how much you currently have.

The minimum you'll need to secure a comfortable life in select low-cost havens is $1,400 per month. With that budget, your selection of international havens to move to is more limited, although there are still some good options out there. With a budget of $2,000 to $4,000 per month, your selection expands exponentially.

But here's the real point: You owe it to yourself to go find out for yourself just how affordable and, more important, just how fun and adventure-filled a new life in a new country can be.

The truth is, you can't afford not to do this.

The best way to determine how much you have is to prepare a spreadsheet. Document your assets and liabilities to determine your net worth. After figuring out your nest egg, you can turn that into your budget for your new life abroad.

The good news is that many goods and services start out at a lower price overseas, which can allow you to reduce how much you spend on basic necessities (creating more budget for discretionary spending). You may be able to cut out expensive items like a car, depending on where you're moving.

If you are up for learning a new language, you'll enjoy the widest selection of havens to move to.

If not, you can relocate to a country where English is an official language (Belize, Malta, Ireland, the Philippines, etc.) or where the locals speak English to a standard that's high enough that you can get by. Lisbon, Portugal and Panama City, Panama, are a few examples of places where you don't necessarily need to speak the local language to live well.

That said, you will be doing yourself a disservice by not picking up at least the basics ("Thank you," "Goodbye," "Please," and so on). It will be more difficult to form connections with locals, which can be one of the best aspects of moving abroad.

Learning the basics is almost always appreciated. The more effort you make, the easier it will be to become a part of your new community. Watching and listening to media (TV shows, movies, podcasts, etc.) in the language you're trying to learn and striking up conversations are good ways to practice. Taking language classes can also be a fun way to meet new people.

The best way of settling in to your new life overseas is to get involved in your community—volunteer or learn new skills. Stay socially engaged, even if it takes effort. Have a purpose—something to motivate you daily.

To fit in and enjoy your new adventure, you need to appreciate what your new country does well. Don't constantly compare your new country to your old one. Otherwise, you risk dissatisfaction.

The final step is to take action sooner rather than later. We hear it time and time again—most expats wish they had moved earlier. So plan on going when you're able to—not when everything feels perfect. Waiting for perfect conditions can delay you indefinitely.

You can plan to reinvent your life in retirement overseas... or you can launch a new life overseas and then make some plans. In the nearly 40 years I've been covering this beat, I've never known anyone who regretted making a move... but I've met hundreds of folks living dream lives in Shangri-las across the globe who regret they didn't make their move sooner.

Seek happiness, not perfection. You can always move again later if needed. If a country feels right, go for it. If not, keep exploring.

There's a place out there for everyone.

Now, some practical things you need to do before you move which involve some logistics.

You'll need a visa, financial documents, notarized paperwork, and possibly marriage certificates. Get everything from the consulate and prepare translations as required.

International moving can be complex—plan ahead and organize inventory. Decide on a contract mover. Prepare your inventory. Have a yard sale to sell off anything you're not bringing with you. Sell your vehicles. Follow import rules to bring household items duty-free.

Get a health check. You should get a physical exam, a dental check-up, prescriptions you'll need, and health insurance before moving. Don't arrive needing urgent medical refills.

For your finances you might need to close bank accounts, open bank accounts in your new country, update your brokerage accounts and assets, and get your credit cards in order.

From a technical standpoint, use email that travels with you (like Gmail), not ISP-based email. Set up a mailing address in your home country if needed. Telecommunications are easier now, but still plan ahead to stay connected. Update software before moving to avoid regional restrictions.

If you're traveling with pets, check airline requirements and health documentation early. Look into this at least three months before your departure date. Also check if your pet can get the medication they need in your new country if required.

After all this, you're ready to go and on your way to an exciting next chapter in your new life abroad.

www.ingramcontent.com/pod-product-compliance
Lightning Source LLC
LaVergne TN
LVHW090301210926
848480LV00001B/95